# NUREMBERG'S VOICE of DOOM

## THE AUTOBIOGRAPHY OF
## THE CHIEF INTERPRETER
## AT HISTORY'S GREATEST TRIALS

*DEDICATED TO THE MEMORY OF WOLFE FRANK*

# NUREMBERG'S VOICE of DOOM

## THE AUTOBIOGRAPHY OF
## THE CHIEF INTERPRETER
## AT HISTORY'S GREATEST TRIALS

Wolfe Frank

**Edited by Paul Hooley**

Frontline Books

# NUREMBERG'S VOICE OF DOOM
## The Autobiography of the Chief Interpreter at History's Greatest Trials

First published in Great Britain in 2018 by Frontline Books,
an imprint of Pen & Sword Books Ltd, Yorkshire - Philadelphia

Also by Paul Hooley
From Lockington to Gillingham
One Foot In The Grave

Typeset in 10.5/12.5 Palatino and Gill Sans Light
Printed and bound in Great Britain by TJ International Ltd

Pen & Sword Books Ltd incorporates the imprints of Pen & Sword Archaeology,
Atlas, Aviation, Battleground, Discovery, Family History, History, Maritime,
Military, Naval, Politics, Social History, Transport, True Crime, Claymore Press,
Frontline Books, Praetorian Press, Seaforth Publishing and White Owl

For a complete list of Pen & Sword titles please contact:

PEN & SWORD BOOKS LTD
47 Church Street, Barnsley, South Yorkshire, S70 2AS, UK.
E-mail: enquiries@pen-and-sword.co.uk
Website: www.pen-and-sword.co.uk

Or

PEN AND SWORD BOOKS,
1950 Lawrence Roadd, Havertown, PA 19083, USA
E-mail: Uspen-and-sword@casematepublishers.com
Website: www.penandswordbooks.com

# CONTENTS

# INTRODUCTION

In 2015 retired panel beater and paint sprayer Mike Dilliway was about to move home. During the course of clearing out his property he came across some six to eight cardboard boxes, a number of files and two briefcases crammed full of assorted papers – mostly in English but some in German – that he had not thought about for many years.

Mike had inherited this cache of documents from a gentleman he had befriended in the Wiltshire village of Mere – where his business had been based – and, not knowing quite what to do with them, had placed them in his loft for safe keeping. Mike recalled that his friend had often mentioned he had been involved as a translator and an interpreter at the trials of the Nazi war criminals in Nuremberg, and that he had also once been a successful businessman. Illness and some unfortunate involvements in both his professional and personal life had however reduced him to a low ebb – physically and financially – and this had led him to take his own life in 1988.

So impoverished had Mike's friend become during the period leading up to his death that he had been forced to approach his local authority for accommodation, furniture and financial support. He was also overdrawn at the bank and a utility supplier was threatening to take him to court over an unpaid debt. There was nothing of value amongst the chattels of the deceased and there was no money left within his estate. Rather than see his friend suffer the indignity of a pauper's burial Mike Dilliway settled his affairs, paid the funeral expenses, distributed what little furniture there was to local charities and consigned the aforementioned documents to his attic where they laid undisturbed for over a quarter of a century.

Needing to make a decision on what to do with the collection and not knowing quite what he had – Mike asked me (as a writer he knew who had an interest in historical and military matters) if I would take a look at the material to see if there was anything there that might be of importance.

I inwardly shuddered when I took delivery of the consignment, not just because of the sheer volume of paperwork involved but because it was in no particular order. I was at a loss as to know where to start.

# INTRODUCTION

Start I did however and twelve months later – after having sorted, resorted, catalogued, assessed, researched and checked several thousand sheets of data – I had a complete picture of the life of Wolfe Frank, Chief Interpreter at the Nuremberg Trials. Whilst my heart may have initially sunk at the thought of the task ahead of me, my pulse quickened with almost every piece of paper I investigated and by the end of my researches that same heart had soared with excitement at the realisation of the important discoveries I had made and the knowledge I had acquired – knowledge I felt compelled to share with a wider audience.

This book therefore is the result of those discoveries. It consists of a posthumous autobiography of the first half of Wolfe Frank's astonishing life – that stands up to the closest scrutiny – plus a potted biography of his later days (based on his memoirs) and further added information that chronicles the life, times and involvements of a brave, dedicated and gifted man whose exploits and achievements should not be allowed to fade into obscurity.

Frank's participation throughout the trials at Nuremberg places him in the quite unique position of having been totally immersed in the proceedings from the very first day of the war crimes investigations – he was asked to translate the then only known piece of evidence. He then became one of the most active players in the forensic and interrogations processes and the setting up and pioneering of the world's first ever system of simultaneous interpretation (a triumph in itself). Once the International Military Tribunal (IMT) started, Frank became a central figure in all stages of the trials. He interpreted the Tribunal's opening remarks, was used more than any other interpreter during the ten month duration of the IMT, and then finally brought proceedings to a close by informing the defendants of their fate – a duty, simultaneously listened to by an estimated radio audience of four hundred million.

It is true to say therefore that the first and last words the defendants heard in their own language at Nuremberg were uttered by Wolfe Frank, a man they – like the Tribunal, the prosecutors and their own counsels – trusted implicitly and for whom they had the highest possible regard and respect.

These memoirs add substantially to what is already known about the trials and include further important insights about what went on behind the scenes. They include details of personal encounters with defendants Goering, Ribbentrop, Keital, Kaltenbrunner, Speer, et al. as seen through the eyes of one (perhaps the only one) who was involved at every stage of what has been described as having been 'the greatest trial in history'[1].

Within his manuscript Wolfe states: 'I had been involved in the writing of a chapter of human history that would be read, talked about and remembered forever. I had been more totally and decisively immersed in recording the horrors of the war than most of the millions who had fought in it.'

By the time I had concluded my investigations I knew it was my duty to ensure that Frank's involvements at, and remembrances of, the Nuremberg Trials were more properly documented. It was also very clear to me that he hoped his insights of the events, as part of his life's story, would be published posthumously to complete the record he refers to in his comment above.

Frank's contributions were considered to be major factors in seeing that justice was fairly and meticulously interpreted and translated to all parties in a way that, it is said, shortened proceedings by an estimated three years, and by the end of the trials he was considered to be the finest interpreter in the world – as these few, of many, typical observations attest:

'The Office of Chief Counsel for War Crimes acknowledged their debt to him [Frank] "for superlative scholarship and administrative assistance … and intellectual integrity … satisfactory alike to the bench, the defence, and the prosecution".' – *New York Herald Tribune.*

'Wolfe Frank … star of the language division. Given the English he spoke, Frank could have passed himself off as a lord … Frank spoke English with an upper-class accent … and could move flawlessly back and forth between English and German.' Joseph E. Persico, *Nuremberg: Infamy on Trial.*

'Wolfe Frank was by unanimous judgement the best interpreter of the Trial.' – Francesca Gaiba, *The Origins of Simultaneous Interpretation: The Nuremberg Trial.*

'His [Frank's] use of German and English was noticeably better than that of most native speakers. His voice and manner, the nuances of his vocabulary, the ability to convey the character of the person for whom he was translating were all outstanding.' – R.W. Cooper, *The Nuremberg Trial.*

'In the courtroom, however, we encountered only hostile faces, icy dogmas. The only exception was the interpreters' booth. From there I might expect a friendly nod.' – Albert Speer, Minister of Armament and War Production in Nazi Germany who, during the trial, requested and was granted a private audience with Wolfe Frank – *Inside the Third Reich: Memoirs by Albert Speer.*

'A standout among the interpreters was Wolfe Frank, a handsome young Bavarian who had fled to England before the war and mastered English so perfectly that, unlike the others, he was used to render English into German and vice versa.' – Brigadier General Telford Taylor, USA Chief of Counsel for War Crimes, *The Anatomy of the Nuremberg Trials.*

Quite apart from what Wolfe Frank has written about Nuremberg there is so much more included in his memoirs about the exploits and achievements of a man who must surely be numbered amongst the most extraordinary, courageous, flamboyant, charismatic, and romantic figures of the twentieth century; including details of his five marriages and countless love affairs, many of which, I feel obliged to warn readers, he describes intimately and graphically.

Of great importance too were documents – touched upon herein but fully recorded in a separate book to be entitled: *The Undercover Nazi Hunter: Unmasking Evil in Post-war Germany*[2] – which cover Frank's post war covert investigations in both East and West Germany on behalf of the *New York Herald Tribune*. During this period, he single-handedly tracked down the 'fourth' ranked SS officer on the Allies most wanted list before personally taking the Nazi's confession and handing him over to the authorities.

The Wolfe Frank story, which pulls no punches and holds nothing back from a licentious and hedonistic private life, chronicles the astonishing adventures of a privileged Bavarian playboy of Jewish descent, who became actively involved in smuggling Jews and money out of Nazi Germany. On the point of arrest and incarceration in a concentration camp, and having been branded 'an enemy of Germany to be shot on sight', he was forced to flee his homeland (after just six days of marriage to a Baroness – whom he did not see again for nine years) and eventually arrived in England, penniless and unable to speak the language. Following a rapid integration that saw him rise to become CEO of several companies he was interned at the outbreak of war as 'an enemy alien'. After a relentless and successful campaign, he was eventually released and allowed to join the British Army; where, through sheer hard work and ability, he rose to the rank of captain.

Throughout his army career, and even at Nuremberg, Frank often sailed close to the wind – for which many less capable men would have been suspended, court-martialled, or even dismissed. His value to the cause however cannot be overstated and this, it seems, made him almost indispensable – a position that he never exploited or took advantage of. Consequently, he remained popular at all levels within the army, at Nuremberg and in civilian life and, in spite of his licentious and cavalier private persona, he was also a brave, capable, highly intelligent, honourable, committed man of great integrity and ability who one would most definitely want on one's side in a crisis.

By the end of the war Frank was so fluent in written and spoken English he was said to speak the language with the depth, clarity, expression, accent and diction of a highly educated British aristocrat. This set him apart from all others and brought him to the notice of General Eisenhower's personal interpreter and Head of Translations, Colonel Leon Dostert, who personally interviewed and immediately seconded Frank on to the USA interpreting team. This in turn led to his eventual appointment as Chief Interpreter.

**The vast majority of this book is the Wolfe Frank Story as Wolfe Frank would have wanted to see it published and all Frank's text is printed in what is known as a serif typeface (Palatino) – as this paragraph.**

However, there are passages, interspersed within the text, together with this Introduction, the Epilogue and the Notes at the end of each chapter, that I have added to clarify matters, explain situations and to add further and better particulars to what Frank has written. To clearly show a distinction from the words of Wolfe Frank, mine are printed in an alternative typeface (Gill Sans Light) – as used for this paragraph and indeed the whole of the rest of this Introduction.

My words are not intended to detract from Frank's writing or to in any way alter the content or direction of his thoughts and/or story. Rather they are included to assist the reader to better understand certain situations Frank describes, or that he takes for granted, were more widely known at the time he committed them to paper (sometime prior to 1984).

I believe that historians, students, linguists and those interested in military matters will find *Nuremberg's Voice of Doom* to be a further valuable record. I feel this book will also appeal to a much wider audience that is not so well versed in the trials and/or the terminology used. If I seem therefore at times to be 'teaching grandmothers to suck eggs' it is only to assist those who may be less familiar with some of the historical references and jargon used, or to more clearly explain what Frank is saying and/or to expand upon the context or situations he is describing.

Likewise, I have included seven pages of plates (Plates 10 to 16) that I believe will greatly assist all readers. These pages show: a plan of the courtroom at the Palace of Justice in Nuremberg; the names and positions of all the principals involved; brief details and a photographic image of each of the defendants at the IMT; who sat where; and a short-form chart recording the counts, verdicts and sentences of the court.

*Nuremberg's Voice of Doom* is a record of two interwoven themes – one of love, adventure and excitement, the other of a former German citizen's fight for the right to become a British soldier and his extraordinary commitment to service, duty and justice. This was seen to be scrupulously fair to the prosecution, defence and the prisoners throughout what many consider to have been the greatest and most important trial the world has ever seen.

There are also some remarkable coincidences. Prior to the war Joachim von Ribbentrop (the first of the war criminals to be hanged) helped Frank regain his first wife's passport. It was ironic therefore that it should be Frank who interpreted for him, interrogated him and then announced to him that his sentence was to be 'Death by the rope'.

It was also ironic that it should be the man who had been present at the very moment of Hitler's Machtergreifung (seizure of power), and who immediately afterwards witnessed what was probably the first act of aggression against a Jew under the Third Reich[3] – the same man who for over three years took refreshment in the presence of the Fuehrer without once giving him the Nazi salute – who should be chosen to, as one witness so aptly recorded, 'Utter the words that set the seal on Hitler's little day!'[4]

xi

All this, and so very much more, is narrated for the first time in this fascinating tale and important military record.

*Paul Hooley,*
*Dorset, 2018.*

## NOTES:

1. Sir Norman Birkett, the Alternate British Member of the International Military Tribunal (IMT) at Nuremberg.

2. *The Undercover Nazi Hunter: Unmasking Evil in Post-war Germany* is to be published by *Frontline Books* during 2019.

3. The Third Reich (Realm) is the name given to that period of German history under the dictatorship of Adolf Hitler through the Nazi Party (1933–1945). The First Reich was the period known as the Holy Roman Empire (962–1806) and the Second Reich the German Empire (1871–1918).

4. R.W. Cooper, *The Nuremberg Trial.*

# ABBREVIATIONS AND GLOSSARY

| | |
|---|---|
| AMPC | Auxiliary Military Pioneer Corps |
| Ariernachweis | Proof of being of pure Aryan Race |
| Ausgebuergert | De-citizenized |
| AWOL | Absent without leave |
| BBC | British Broadcasting Corporation |
| Blockleiter | A lower political rank within the Nazi Party |
| BWCE | British War Crimes Executive |
| CAT | Civilian Actress Technician |
| CEO | Chief Executive Officer |
| CIC | Counter Intelligence Corps |
| CO | Commanding Officer |
| DDL | Deputy Director of Labour |
| EEC | European Economic Community |
| Einsatzgruppen | SS Task Force |
| EU | European Union |
| Fuehrer | (or Führer) Leader |
| Gestapo | Gehelme Staatspolizei (Secret State Police) |
| HM | His Majesty |
| Holocaust | Second World War genocide that saw the Nazis kill some six million Jews and other persecuted peoples |
| IBM | International Business Machines |
| IMT | International Military Tribunal |
| IOS | Investors Overseas Services |
| IRA | Irish Republican Army |
| IS | Infantry Support |
| Justizpalast | Palace of Justice |
| Luftwaffe | German Air Force |
| Machtergreifung | Seizure of power |
| *Mein Kampf* | *My Fight* |

| | |
|---|---|
| MFI | Mutual Fund Industry |
| MI | Military Intelligence |
| MO | Medical Officer |
| MPC | Military Pioneer Corps |
| MTO | Military Testing Officer |
| *Nacht und Nebel* | *Night and Fog* |
| Nazi Party | Nationalsozialistische Deutsche Arbeiter-partei (National Socialist German Workers' Party) |
| NBC | National Broadcasting Company |
| NCO | Non-Commissioned Officer |
| Nicht-arisch | Non-Aryan |
| NMT | Trials of War Criminals Before the Nuremberg Military Tribunals |
| NSDAP | Nationalsozialistische Deutsche Arbeiter-partei (National Socialist German Workers' Party) – the Nazi Party |
| *NYHT* | *New York Herald Tribune* |
| Obergefreiter | Senior Lance Corporal |
| Obergruppenfuehrer | General |
| OCCWC | Office of Chief of Counsel for War Crimes |
| OCTU | Officer Cadet Training Unit |
| OKW | Oberkommando der Wehrmacht – High Command of the Armed Forces |
| OR | Other Rank – personnel who are not commissioned officers |
| OSS | Office of Strategic Services |
| PC | Pioneer Corps |
| Plenipotentiary | Having full power to action on behalf of a Government |
| PoW | Prisoner of War |
| PR | Public Relations |
| Prima facie | Accepted as being correct until proved otherwise |
| PT | Physical Training |
| PX | Post Exchange – a shop on an American Army Base |
| RAC | Royal Armoured Corps or Royal Automobile Club |
| RAF | Royal Air Force |
| RASC | Royal Army Service Corps |
| Rassenschande | Racial shame |

| | |
|---|---|
| Reich | Realm |
| Reichsfuehrer | Commander |
| Reichsjaegermeister | A person who goes to the cinema |
| Reichsmarschall | Marshal of the Reich – the highest rank in the Wehrmacht of Nazi Germany |
| RMC | Royal Military College |
| RPM | Revolutions Per Minute |
| RSHA | Reichssicherheitshauptamt (The Reich Main Security Office) |
| RuSHA | Rasse und Siedlungshauptamt (the Race and Settlement Main Office) |
| SA | Sturmabteilung (Storm Detachment) |
| Saujuden | Jewish swine |
| Schwarze | The Black Curse |
| Schmach, die Seigneur | A dignified or aristocratic man |
| SI | Simultaneous Interpretation |
| SP or ST | Subsequent Proceedings or Subsequent Trials (formally The Trials of War Criminals Before the Nuremberg Military Tribunals) |
| Sperrmarks | Blocked marks |
| SS | Schutzstaffel (Protection Squadron) |
| Strafkompagnie | Punitive Unit (penal work) |
| Trifurcate | Divide into three branches or forks |
| UK | United Kingdom |
| UN | United Nations |
| UNESCO | United Nations Educational, Scientific and Cultural Organization |
| Ungezieferbekampfung | Pest control/removal |
| US/USA | United States/United States of America |
| VE | Victory in Europe |
| WC | Water Closet (toilet) |
| Waffen-SS | The armed wing of the SS |
| Wehrmacht | Defence Force – the unified armed forces of Nazi Germany |
| WOSB | War Office Selection Board |
| ZI | Zone of the Interior (being sent home) |
| Zyklon B | (Cyclone B), A cyanide-based pesticide |

# LIST OF ILLUSTRATIONS

IMAGE CREDITS

Henry and Peter Goyert: Plates 3, 4, 6, 7, 8.
Nuremberg City Archives: Plate 17.
United States National Archives: Plates 9, 16 (top), 18 (top).
United States Library of Congress: Plate 12.
United Artists: Plate 19 (bottom).

# PROLOGUE

'AN EXCELLENT JURIST, THIS MAN ASCHENAUER,' Judge Michael Musmanno[1] pronounced after the session of the Einsatzgruppen Military Tribunal[2] on that grey November day in 1947 in Nuremberg; 'a pity, his motion will cost us weeks in time.'

'And, you know as well as I do, Mr Frank, a late verdict means a mild verdict for my client,' said German defence counsel Dr Aschenauer[3] to me during a brief conversation in the corridors of the Palace of Justice five minutes later.

We had reached a late stage in the so-called 'Subsequent Proceedings'[4] instituted by the United States of America against Nazi war criminals, a phase during which political considerations were beginning to influence the attitude of the Allies towards the German people and, consequently, the meting-out of justice at Nuremberg. We had meted it out with a golden ladle during the International Military Trial (IMT) of Goering et al.[5] at which a lot of people had been condemned to death, and hanged, for crimes which were now drawing prison sentences – soon to be shortened, or even remitted, in the wake of the Western World's awakening to the true Russia and the resulting warming of feelings towards the fast-developing new Germany.

That was the moment I decided it was time for me to quit. I had been one of the main interpreters during the 'big trial' and then Chief Interpreter at the Subsequent Proceedings (SP) for thirteen more months – I had heard enough about atrocities, mass murder, war crimes, extermination camps and genocide.

I was also thinking of a passage covering the sentencing at Nuremberg in R.W. Cooper's book *The Nuremberg Trial*: 'Tod durch den Strang! – Death by the Rope! – The words came to them in German through the headphones as each prisoner was brought up alone into the vast emptiness of the dock – the identical words pronounced by the Nazi People's Court upon the perpetrators of the July plot[6]. They were uttered in translation by Captain Wolfe Frank, himself of German origin, who before departing from his country had watched the torchlight procession in Munich that hailed Hitler's coming to power. A strange turn of the wheel that he was now to utter the words that set the seal on Hitler's little day'.

I was remembering too a meeting I had had with Lord Mount Temple[7], the pre-war Chairman of the Anglo/German Fellowship, who I went see at his castle near Winchester just four years after that torchlight procession of January 1933. I had gone there to ask his help in getting my first wife's passport restored to her. It had been confiscated to stop her from joining me in England. His Lordship didn't trust my account of the events which had gone before, but he promised to help – and did so by interceding with his friend Joachim von Ribbentrop[8], the then German Ambassador in London. The passport was returned. It was not valid for journeys abroad.

'Silly of you to get into trouble over there in Germany,' said Lord Mount Temple. 'Hitler's a great man, he'll change the world for the better.'

I disagreed, rather heatedly. 'He'll change the world alright,' I said, 'he's preparing for war, anybody can see that. I could while I still lived there until just a few months ago. And the concentration camps …'

I was firmly interrupted, 'I think it is best for you to leave now,' said his Lordship. 'I will see what I can do for your wife. Good-bye!'

Some two and-a-half-years later I was walking past one of the clubs in London's Pall Mall when I was hailed by the same Lord Mount Temple. 'I say, young man,' said the Lord from the top of the club's steps.

I walked up to him. 'You came to see me some time ago,' he said sternly, 'we, err, had a bit of an argument. I don't like having to admit this to a young whippersnapper like you – I was wrong – good day!'

He, and many people with him, had been wrong then. They could be wrong again, I reflected, as I walked away from Dr Aschenauer on that November day in 1947 – as Judge Musmanno had been in his assessment of Aschenauer's motives. There was clearly nothing I could do.

*Wolfe Frank.*

**NOTES:**

1. Rear Admiral Michael Angelo Musmanno (1897-1968) was the Presiding Judge at the Einsatzgruppen Trial (see Plate 2). He had served in the military

justice system of the US Navy during the Second World War and then as a governor of an occupied district of Italy before becoming a trial judge at Nuremberg. In the judgement of the Einsatzgruppen Trial, Judge Musmanno wrote: 'One reads and reads these accounts of which here we can give only a few excerpts and yet there remains the instinct to disbelieve, to question, to doubt. There is less of a mental barrier in accepting the weirdest stories of supernatural phenomena, as for instance, water running up hill and trees with roots reaching toward the sky, than in taking at face value these narratives which go beyond the frontiers of human cruelty and savagery. Only the fact that the reports from which we have quoted came from the pens of men within the accused organizations can the human mind be assured that all this actually happened. The reports and the statements of the defendants themselves verify what otherwise would be dismissed as the product of a disordered imagination.'

2. The Einsatzgruppen Trial (officially, The United States of America v Otto Ohlendorf, et al.) was the ninth of the twelve SP trials. The Einsatzgruppen (task forces) were Schutzstaffel (SS) paramilitary death squads of the Nazis. They were responsible for the murder of much of the intelligentsia, including members of the priesthood, and they played an integral role in the implementation of the so-called 'Final Solution to the Jewish Question'. In the opening statement of the trial the prosecution stated: 'The judgement of the IMT declared 2 million Jews were murdered by the Einsatzgruppen and other units of the Security Police. The defendants in the dock were the cruel executioners, whose terror wrote the blackest page in human history. Death was their tool and life their toy. If these men be immune, then law has lost its meaning and man must live in fear.'

3. Rudolf Aschenauer (1913-1983) was a German lawyer who became known as a 'criminal defendant in war crimes and Nazi trials'. Aschenauer represented hundreds of accused war criminals, including Otto Ohlendorf in the Einsatzgruppen Trial. The address to which Judge Musmanno was referring (in note 4 above) and which caused Wolfe Frank to consider and then resign his position as Chief Interpreter was no doubt Aschenauer's opening statement on behalf of Otto Ohlendorf (the defendant whose boasts and admissions under his interrogation Frank had found to be perhaps the most harrowing of all he heard and translated at the Nuremberg Trials). 'Mr President! High Tribunal!' Aschenauer had begun, 'after submission of the documents on the part of the prosecution in the Case of the United States versus Ohlendorf et al. it will be the task of the defence to make their comments concerning the documents themselves. The defence will be able to point out errors, to make clear to the Tribunal points which are contradictions in themselves, thus

destroying in some cases the value the documents possess as evidence, as well as reducing the value of the entire evidence brought forth by the prosecution'. Aschenauer's plea may have delayed proceedings, however in the end it made no difference in Ohlendorf's case, he was convicted of crimes against humanity and war crimes committed during the Second World War. He was sentenced to death and hanged at the Landsberg Prison in Bavaria on 7 June 1951.

4.  The 'Subsequent Trials' (ST) or more commonly 'Subsequent Proceedings' (SP) – formally the Trials of War Criminals before the Nuremberg Military Tribunals – were a series of twelve US military tribunals for war crimes against members of the leadership of Nazi Germany other than those tried by the IMT (Note 5). The SP, like the IMT, were also held in the Palace of Justice.

5.  The Nuremberg Trials were the military tribunals held by the Allied forces after the Second World War. The trials were the prosecution of prominent members of the political, military, judicial and economic leadership of Nazi Germany, who planned, carried out, or otherwise participated in the Holocaust and other war crimes. They were held within the Palace of Justice in Nuremberg, Germany. The first and most high profile of the trials were those of the major war criminals (Goering and other leading Nazis). Held before the International Military Tribunal (IMT), they were described as being 'the greatest trial in history' by Norman Birkett, one of the British judges who presided over them. Held between 20 November 1945 and 1 October 1946 the IMT tried twenty-four of the most important political and military leaders of the Third Reich.

6.  On 20 July 1944, a plot by senior German military officials to murder Adolf Hitler and take control of his government failed when a bomb planted in a briefcase went off but did not kill the Nazi leader. Hundreds of people thought to be involved in the conspiracy were arrested and brought before the Nazi People's Court – around 200 were executed.

7.  Lord Mount Temple was Chairman of The Anglo-German Fellowship, an organisation which existed from 1935 to 1939, and which aimed to build up friendship between the United Kingdom and Germany. Having publicly stated that membership of the Society did not assume support for Nazism or anti-Semitism, Lord Mount Temple resigned in November 1938 because of the Nazis treatment of German Jews.

8.  Ulrich Friedrich Wilhelm Joachim von Ribbentrop (1893–1946), more commonly known as Joachim von Ribbentrop, was Foreign Minister of Nazi

Germany from 1938 until 1945, having served as German Ambassador to the United Kingdom from 1936. Ribbentrop was tried at Nuremberg and convicted for his role in starting the Second World War and enabling the Holocaust. Ironically, after having assisted Wolfe Frank to get his wife's passport back, it was Frank who interrogated him, interpreted at his trial and announced to him the sentence of the court. On 16 October 1946 Joachim von Ribbentrop became the first of the Nazi war criminals to be hanged.

# EARLY LIFE AND FORMATIVE YEARS

THERE IS, IN THIS OPENING CHAPTER, a considerable lack of the kind of details usually reported at the beginning of a biographical tale.

I never had the slightest interest in ancestry and family trees, but it seems clear, on the strength of sketchy documentation, that my grandfather[1] was a Jew and his wife was not.

I knew my father[2] only as an atheist who paid taxes to the local church and had dual British/German nationality. No evidence now exists of either, and my attempts to trace his British citizenship ended in failure – I only have his word for it. He was, at one time, a wealthy industrialist but he died, a suicide, without leaving any assets worth mentioning.

Mother[3] was totally angelic, very beautiful in her younger days and very superstitious. Consequently, she apparently managed to persuade the local registrar to record my birth[4] in 1913 as being in the early morning of Saturday, 14 February when, in reality, I had appeared during the closing hours of Friday 13th! I cannot, of course, judge whether my mother's white lie brought me luck, but it certainly brought me many Valentine's cards!

My school years[5] did not produce any remarkable achievements or events. They were lived at Villa Frank in the small village of Beierfeld, Saxony, where I was born, and later in Berlin and they were, generally, happy years.

Sex, in those days, was a closed book of mysterious, hidden things that we could not imagine.

When one of my playmates, who was two years older than the rest of my group, had his first brush with sex he claimed that, 'It is nowhere near as nice as you imagine when you masturbate', we were, all of us, very disappointed and we decided to put things off until the distant future.

1

I had a shattering clash with reality, however, when I was about fifteen years old. A voluptuous soprano, in her mid-thirties, of the Munich Opera, kidnapped me to her apartment and performed fellatio upon me as I was standing before an upright piano playing airs. I was terribly shocked and enjoyed none of it, simply because I had no clue as to what it was all about.

A little later, my father became involved in a serious affair with his secretary (which lasted until his death in 1933). I remember going to a musical revue in Berlin during that period – it must have been around 1929, so I would have been sixteen. My best school friend and I had heard that there were girls dancing topless. They were indeed, but we found the sight uninteresting.

That night however we spotted my father in the front row, holding hands with a blonde – who was not his mistress. I felt fairly confused because he had already inflicted much suffering on my mother when he took up with his secretary. Now here he was clearly working on yet another alternative. Father was home when I returned, and he began to berate me for being out late without his permission. 'I was at the Admiralspalast,' I said. He never assaulted me again with disciplinary action, but he still managed to make some most uncomfortable contributions to my upbringing. He refused to let me study engineering when I left school, but sent me to a large factory for 'practical technical training'. For nine months I had to rise at 04.30 hours, travel for an hour and-a-half and return at 18.00 hours. My 'technical training' was later continued in a municipal training workshop[6] – but it was never finished, because I ran away from home when I was18-years-old.

I had one last terrible clash with father over his mistress whom I hated passionately, mostly out of love for my mother. In a fit of rage, I stuffed all her belongings – she was living with us by then – into suitcases and cardboard boxes and threw them into the street. Father decreed, 'Commitment to a home for wayward boys' but I didn't wait around. I hurriedly left Berlin for Munich and went 'underground' as an apprentice in the BMW Motor Works where love came into my life for the first time. However, the lady was snatched away by my best and much older friend and this resulted in an unsuccessful suicide attempt.

I had had no contact with my father after I left Berlin, but he promised an uncle of mine that he would leave me in peace and 'Un-committed to any penal institution'. The road was clear and, having got suicide and such out of my youthful and immature system, I started to enjoy life.

I was fired by BMW for 'Improper conduct towards a superior'. My 'technical' training included an unreasonable amount of workshop sweeping and I had suggested my 'superior' should sweep away some of his own shit. This led to my sacking and then my appointment, aged nineteen, as a car sales trainee at the Munich showrooms of the (now defunct) Adler Works. I also borrowed some money and bought and sold cars on my own account.

One such vehicle provided me with the opportunity to meet my father for what was to be the last time. The car was a 2.4 litre Bugatti – white and blue and beautiful. I had sold it to a firm of dealers in Berlin who wanted a rapid delivery. Before leaving, and on the spur of the moment, I phoned my father and suggested we meet at the *Cafe Kranzler* on *Kurfürstendamm*, to which he agreed. The car broke down on the way and, although I drove like a madman, I was forty minutes late. As I approached Kranzler I was truly apprehensive. Father was a fanatic regarding punctuality. My reconciliation attempt seemed doomed to failure. However, when I arrived he was still there, immaculately and severely dressed in elegant black jacket, striped trousers, grey vest and wing-collar. He was radiating censorious displeasure. Then, he saw the car and, as I extricated myself from it, he came over to me. 'Leave the keys' he said, as an opener. Then he got into the Bugatti and roared off up the *Kurfürstendamm*.

He loved fast cars and was gone for over forty minutes, having driven one complete circuit of the Berlin Avus Racetrack, which is normally open to traffic. His hands trembled slightly when he got out of the car – he was sixty-six-years-old, after all. We chatted, amiably and impersonally, for half an hour then he left. There was no dinner invitation, no further meetings, and there was no reproach for my having been late. On balance, a very positive result I thought. A few months later, in January 1933, he invited his eighteen-year-old girlfriend to his flat, having sent his mistress off somewhere for the evening. A candlelit dinner was served to them by his manservant, then the young lady was driven home. When his mistress arrived home later that evening he was dead. She found him with his head in the gas oven, still dressed in his dinner jacket.

No explanation was ever found as to why he killed himself, however being of the same ilk, I can venture a guess. Father had lived tremendously well and had never denied himself any pleasure, but his funds had diminished, as had his income. His fun was also dwindling as he was aging. Now the Nazis were at his door and he, who had a Jewish father, had no wish to learn what that might mean[7]. So – he exited. What a wise decision that turned out to be in the light of what was to come!

There was one very typical sequel to these events. Father left a letter with his last will, decreeing that none of his family were to attend his cremation (we all went, except my poor mother). The reason he wished us to be excluded soon became apparent – he had written a speech for whoever officiated. In it, he was described as a loving father, family man and husband who had God-fearingly toiled for all those who depended upon him. We, the loved ones, hadn't noticed. We were highly amused and his oldest brother, my Munich uncle, kept chuckling audibly whilst I got very drunk and returned to Munich feeling adventurously adult.

## NOTES:

1. Albert Frank (1835–1894), Wolfe's grandfather, was an industrialist and head of the metal-ware company of the same name. The company was well known for the manufacture of parts for automobiles and bicycles and a wide range of lanterns that bore the company's well-known 'Muncher Kindl' (Munich Child-Angel) logo.

2. Wolfe's father, Ferdinand Frank (1866–1933), was the son of Albert Frank and his wife Bertha (née Pappenheimer). He took over as head of the family business following his father's death and floated it on the Berlin Stock Exchange in 1914 under the name Frankonia AG on the expectation of large military orders (see photographs of Frank family and the Frankonia factory at Plates 3–5). The company had factories in Beierfeld, Berlin-Adleshof and Elbing. Prior to his marriage to Wolfe's mother (Ida) Ferdinand had been married to, and divorced from, Alice Frank (née Rosenbaum) who later died in a concentration camp. The couple had two children Maria, who also died in a concentration camp, and Olly. Busts of these two children were carved in the home that Ferdinand had designed – possibly by the famous German architect Erich Mendelsohn – and built in Beierfeld (see Plate 6).

3. Wolfe's mother, Ida Therese Frank (née Hennig), was born in 1879 in Leipzig. She was the daughter of a retired Gas Inspector. Ferdinand and Ida were married at the Register Office, Hackney, London, on 9 April 1908. At the time of the marriage Ferdinand was residing at the Cecil Hotel in the Strand and Ida at 10 Portland Road, Finsbury Park. A fortnight later, on 24 April, the couple were also married in Munich.

4. Wolfe was originally named Johann Wolfgang Frank, and then Hans Wolfgang Frank. He later became Hugh Wolfe Frank – the name under which he was granted British passports and, in 1948, British citizenship – however he preferred to be known as Wolfe Hugh Frank or just plain Wolfe Frank.

5.  Wolfe attended an elementary school in Beierfeld and Grunewald Gymnasium in Berlin, a grammar and boarding school for boys, until 'Mittlere Reife' (pre-college examination).

6.  Berlin Institute for Practical Mechanics.

7.  Documents have been discovered that show Ferdinand was himself a member of the Jewish faith whilst his wife Ida and Wolfe were both Protestants.

# AN INTRODUCTION TO SEX
# AND COOKING

MY MOTHER MOVED TO MUNICH at the end of 1932 and I was living with her in a pleasant flat that was part of a converted villa, complete with swimming pool, in the suburb of Pasing.

I took an early morning train to work each day, and an early morning train back home the following morning. I had made friends, within what may be said to be the fore-runner of today's playboy set, all of whom made valuable contributions to my post-graduate education and they saw to it that I lost my virginity. The lady they chose was a member of the oldest profession in the world and her beat was the sidewalk of the Theatinerstrasse; certainly the most elegant location for such activities. Her name was Hansi and she was utterly charming in a gamine-sort-of-way. After the first round – to which I was treated by my playmates, all of who had far more money than me, Hansi and I became friends – and then lovers. She had an attic apartment in the suburb of Schwabing where I spent my evenings waiting for her to return with her target sum of the day. A year or so later she became one of the few ladies of pleasure to actually buy the little shop of which they all dream, but which so few of them ever acquire.

I have had a very soft spot for those ladies ever since. Anyone would, I think, who owes so much know-how in the field of sex to one of them, particularly when taught as gently and as understandingly as I was by Hansi – and there is more to it than that. 'The prostitute in her private life' we read in the *Encyclopaedia Britannica* 'is as responsive as, or perhaps more so than the average housewife … the prostitute is prone to be starved of love. This deficiency is remedied by a lover who is frequently also a procurer, or pimp.' Frequently, but not always, as my case would seem to prove, since the merchandise I continued to sell was cars, not Hansi!

Another passion came into my life soon after Hansi had departed for parts and a shop unknown – cooking! However, the damsel who was at the bottom of it all displayed far less understanding than Hansi.

Now aged twenty, I had fallen in love with a very elegant member of Munich's bridge-playing and ballroom dancing set. Her name was Margarete Busskamp and she was then about thirty. (I cannot now remember what she looked like although I did see her once, a few years ago, hobbling across the Theatinerstrasse – she was then aged seventy-five or so).

In love I was, and handicapped by lack of funds when it came to entertaining Margarete in the style to which, surely, she was accustomed. So I uttered a dinner invitation, adding that I was a marvellous cook and would she dine at home? She would! Of course, had I known then what I know now I would have skipped the cooking. As it was, I counted my available cash and bought one tiny glass of Russian caviar, one chicken and one bottle of Henkel Silberstreif German champagne. Quite punctually, an elegant Margarete appeared at the flat I had borrowed from a friend – supposedly my digs – and the champagne cork popped. The caviar melted away and from the kitchen appeared a delicious looking roast bird. My carving knife sank into it and a ghastly smell escaped from the chicken – I had not cleaned it out! However, I think my German background asserted itself at this point. I had undertaken to feed the lady, and feed her I would. Margarete was bundled off to a nearby restaurant and fed. If she had planned to be seduced she never got to say so; and she was not seduced by me on that, or any other, day.

As I have said, Margarete showed less understanding than Hansi. At the end of our dismal repast in a dismal restaurant, she wished to head for home – without me. It then became clear to me that a delicious meal, served in the right place, is the gateway from the vertical to the horizontal. I swore that I would learn to cook, and I have. The lesson to be learned here is a simple one – if you have a teenage son, to be trained, send him to a whore and then to cooking school – he won't have a sex problem ever after.

# INSTINCTIVE CONCERNS

TWO EVENTS OCCURRED IN 1933 that forced me to discard the attitude of the twenty-year-old irresponsible youth that I was and to replace it with some immediate and careful planning.

The first event was when my father's will was opened. He had left me a gold watch and thirty-four bottles of rare wines outright. There was also a considerable sum of money. However, the will contained an unexpected and depressing clause: 'In order to force my son to grow up a responsible young man, this money will remain in trust until his twenty-eighth birthday. The interest will be cumulative'.

I was living in Munich with my mother at the time. Her income was not sufficient to take care of us both. I therefore had to immediately start earning some money.

The second event was the triumphant march of the Nazi hordes down Munich's beautiful Ludwig Strasse to the Feldherrn Halle[1,] which took place on the night of the 5 March and announced Hitler's coming to power.

I stood, wedged in by a huge crowd, facing the entrance to the Hofgarten[2] and felt considerable apprehension. I was 'Nicht-arisch', non-Aryan! My grandfather had been Jewish. Up until that day this had never been of the slightest importance, but I had read some extracts from Hitler's autobiography *Mein Kampf*[3]. I had also made myself familiar with the Nazi diatribes and had little doubt that this flaw in my family tree would soon lead to unpleasant consequences. I also remembered only too well the Nazi threats of the Beer Hall Putsch[4].

Instinctively, I refused to share the optimism of some of my Jewish friends who felt certain that the Nazis would permit anti-Semitism to become a secondary point of their political programme.

A few days earlier I had driven to Stuttgart with a friend of mine who had called on the American Consul for a renewal of his US Immigration Visa. The Consul had looked at my friend's passport and discovered that a previous visa had been allowed to expire unused. 'Hell' said the Consul, 'you're a Jew, aren't you? What are you waiting for?'

My friend declared that he was still hoping that the Nazis would permit the Jews in Germany to live in peace. Handing back my friend's passport, the Consul said: 'here's your visa. Stop being an Opti-Semit. Get out of here!'

I was remembering that conversation as I stood in the crowd on the 5 March. The torchlight procession could be heard approaching in the distance. Then it came into view, headed by a Nazi Brownshirt[5] who was bearing the Blood Banner, which had been carried during the unsuccessful Putsch in 1923.

There was the chorus of 'Heils' from the crowd and their right arms went up in the Hitler salute.

Before me stood a small middle-aged man dressed in Bavarian clothes. I could only see his back and greying hair, but his whole attitude seemed to be one of consternation. His head was slightly tilted and his shoulders were hunched up. His right arm remained hanging by his side. Suddenly a huge man in a brown shirt, with a swastika badge pinned to his tie, reached over and tapped him on the shoulder. 'Don't you give the Salute?' he asked.

The little man turned and looked at him. 'I don't know … What must I do? I mean – should I?' he stammered.

The big man pushed aside one or two people who were between them. 'I'll teach you swine what you have to do,' he roared and he hit the little man in the face with his fist. Down he went. Then there was a sudden push from behind and people began to trample on him. I saw him pulled up, bleeding and semi-conscious. Not one word was said to the big bully in the brown shirt. No one in that crowd came to the defence of the little man.

The whole incident had only taken a few seconds. I turned away and then I found that I was standing there with my right arm in the air. I was trembling, but at that moment I made two resolutions – I would leave Germany and, come what may, I would never again raise my hand in the Hitler salute.

As for the former, it didn't happen until four years later, and then only by force of circumstances. However, I managed to carry out the latter, although it entailed many miles of detours to avoid passing Nazi memorials, as well as some really quite unnecessary visits to the toilet of the Carlton Tearoom in Munich, which both Hitler and I frequented for our after-lunch cup of coffee.

Guests at the tearoom were compelled to rise and greet the Fuehrer on entry and exit, while a few of us would make a well-timed and rapid sortie to the door marked 'Gentlemen'. There were similar excursions each New Year's Eve when the National Anthem and the *Horst Wessel Song*[6] were played at midnight. The washroom of the Regina Hotel where I usually celebrated the New Year became quite crowded on such occasions.

## NOTES:

1. The Field Marshal's Hall.

2. The Court Garden in the centre of Munich.

3. *Mein Kampf (My Fight)* is a 1925 autobiographical book by Adolf Hitler. The work describes the process by which he became anti-Semitic and outlines his political ideology and future plans for Germany.

4. The Beer Hall Putsch, also known as the Munich Putsch was a failed coup attempt by the Nazi Party leader Adolf Hitler, in November 1923, to seize power in Munich.

5. The Sturmabteilung (SA) – Storm Detatchment – was the parliamentary wing of the Nazi Party. Its members were known as 'Brownshirts' because that was the colour of the uniform they wore.

6. The *Horst Wessel Song,* also known by its opening words, *Die Fahne Hoch (The Flag on High),* was used as the anthem of the Nazi Party from 1930 to 1945.

WOLFE FRANK
1913 - 1988
At the Nuremberg Trials in 1945/6

Plate 1

Wolfe Frank (right) and Judge Michael Musmanno (centre) interrogating SS-Obergruppenfuehrer (General) Karl Wolff – most probably during the Einsatgruppen Trial. The hand written inscription on the photograph reads: 'To Wolfe Frank – Ace Interpreter at Nuremberg International War Crimes Trials – and so far as I am concerned the whole world round. Most sincerely, M A Musmanno'.

Obergruppenfuehrer Karl Wolff was formerly Chief of Personal Staff Reichsfuehrer (Commander) and SS Liaison Officer to Hitler until sometime in 1943. At the end of World War II, he was the Supreme Commander of all SS forces in Italy and negotiated the surrender of all German forces in Italy, ending the war on that front in late April 1945. At Nuremberg, Wolff was allowed to escape prosecution by providing evidence against his fellow Nazis, and was then transferred (in January 1947) to the British prison facility in Minden. In this photograph it appears that Wolff's SS officer collar insignia has been removed from the lapels of his uniform jacket. Interestingly however the shoulder insignia is still attached.

Plate 3 (right): The Albert Frank, later Frankonia, factory at Beierfeld in c.1898.

Plate 2

Plate 3

Wolfe Frank's parents and grandparents

Plate 4

Wolfe Frank *c.*1915

Plate 5

Plate 6

Wolfe Frank in c.1915 with his half sister Olly who was about eighteen years old at the time. This photograph was most probably taken in the garden of Villa Frank (shown left – Plate 6) the family home that is thought to have been designed by the famous German architect Erich Mendelsohn. In honour of the family the road on which the villa is situated is now called Frankstrasse.

A bust of Olly (inset on Plate 6) is one of two carved into the fabric of the villa – the other bust is of her sister Maria who perished in Piaski concentration camp. Their mother Alice, Ferdinand's first wife, was taken to Thieresenstadt concentration camp where she died of 'A brain bleed and enteritis'. Olly however, in spite of being arrested, was never imprisoned. She survived the war and went on to live a long and happy life with her husband Richard Goyert, a well known mechanical engineer, and son Henry. She died in 1983 and although she lived in Germany all her life she travelled extensively as a most respected ambassador for UNICEF.

Plate 7

Above: Typical trade advertisement showing part of the Albert Frank range of lamps – which have now become sought-after antique items.

Right: The press announcement of the company's floatation onto the Berlin Stock Exchange in 1914. A later report indicated the company went into receivership in 1928. However in conversation (with his friend Mike Dilliway) Wolfe Frank indicated his father, in 1933, was concerned that whatever business he was then in was about to fall into the hands of the Nazis and that this was a contributing factor in his decision to take his own life.

THE HARDWARE WORKS, of Albert Frank, Beierfeld (Saxony), which principally makes automobile and bicycle illumination outfits and accessories for such, as well as household and kitchen utensils etc., has been transformed into a joint-stock company under the cooperation of the following Berlin Banks, viz. Messrs. Hardy & Co., Delbrueck Schickler & Co., National bank fuer Deutschland and bearing the name of "Frankonia" Aktiengesellschaft vormals Albert Frank.

The original stock is 2 millions of marks. The management of the new company remains as in the past in the hands of the former proprietor, Ferdinand Frank.

Plate 8

# HATRED AND DENIAL

I REMAINED IN GERMANY FOR AS LONG AS I DID because I loved Bavaria – I also had a good many friends who lived there and I loved skiing.

I found a job with the Munich franchise of a car-accessory firm and was given a small car and all of Bavaria as my field of operations. The owner of the firm, Herr Peter, was warned by various people that he was being rather stupid employing a non-Aryan. He was a kind-hearted old man from Saxony and he kept this to himself for quite a while. However eventually I couldn't help noticing that he had something on his mind. He owned up under questioning and I resigned.

A friend then supplied me with an introduction to one Dr Meyer, Director of the Munich branch of the Adler Works. When I presented myself to him I stressed the fact that I had had a Jewish grandfather. 'Never mind that' said Meyer. 'I propose to go on selling cars to Jews. You can take care of that.'

He assigned a demonstration car to me and for about three months I covered Munich and all of Bavaria without selling a single vehicle. Then Adler delivered the first specimen of a new 1.5 litre car with front wheel drive. I took it out a few evenings later and sold one over a large number of cocktails in the Bar of the Regina Hotel. Taking the customer home afterwards, I skidded and wrecked the only demonstration car we had. I expected to be sacked at once, but wasn't. Anxious to make up for the disaster, I made a special effort and sold seven cars within the next two weeks. After that my sales increased steadily.

This made my colleagues extremely angry. They called on Meyer – who had by then joined the SS – and they complained bitterly about the non-Aryan salesman's success. There was a nasty scene when one of them promised me that I would find myself in the Dachau[1] concentration camp if I, the Jewish swine, dared to sell just one more car.

The opportunity did not arise, because I was fired.

There then followed some months during which I tried to find a job but couldn't, before I eventually became an employee of a large garage that sold German and Italian cars and I took over its workshops as manager. The owner, although a member of the Nazi party, did not care about my ancestry. I stayed with him until I left the country in April 1937 in spite of the fact that he was repeatedly attacked for employing me.

Whilst my career, which I had in any case considered to be a very temporary one, was interrupted from time to time by the necessity of having to change jobs, it had produced a fairly satisfactory income. In addition, and this cannot be emphasized enough, I had no difficulties what-so-ever outside the business sphere. My friends remained the same with the exception of two or three Jews who emigrated. Life in Munich, on the surface, was as pleasant as ever. There was sailing on Lake Starnberg during the summer, skiing at Garmisch-Partenkirchen in the winter and there was the October festival with its beer-tents, roasted sides of beef and chicken. During February there was the Munich Carnival, with its studio parties and fancy-dress balls.

However, there were also frequent reminders that, for me at any rate, this delightful state of affairs could not be permanent.

There was the purge of 30 June 1934 when the alleged revolt by Hitler's Chief-of-Staff, Ernst Röhm, was supressed[2]. Two people I knew died in that: Schneidhuber, the Chief of the Munich police and a music publisher who was unfortunate enough to be called Willi Schmid – a most common name in Germany – his name had been given to a Gestapo squad who picked the wrong Schmid's address from the telephone book and shot him. The Fuehrer himself heard about it and was 'Most distressed'. So distressed in fact that he called on Schmid's widow and ordered a funeral at public expense. I knew Schneidhuber and Schmid only slightly, but their deaths brought a realization of things to come.

Then the brother of a Jewish friend of mine was taken to Dachau concentration camp. He was released after nine months because his US Immigration Visa had come through. I saw him at his home soon after his release and did not recognize him. Once a fit man of thirty-five, he was now a white-haired skeleton and he looked sixty-years-old. Before his release he had been made to sign the customary oath stating that he would discuss his experiences in the camp with no one. Not knowing this at the time, I could only look at him in horror and then ask him, 'My God, Alfred, what have they done to you?' He covered his face with his hands and sobbed out the answer again and again: 'Don't ask me. I can't tell you. I can't tell you …'

Part of my question however was answered shortly afterwards by another man from Dachau. I was driving from Munich to Heidelberg when an SS man waved me to a stop. When an SS man flagged down a car in Germany in those days, one stopped. So I did. Fortunately, he only wanted a lift to Stuttgart and we became quite pally on that trip.

He was, he disclosed, one of the guards at Dachau. 'The camp was full of Saujuden (Jewish swine)' he told me. Throwing caution to the wind, I suggested, 'No doubt they beat hell out of those Jews down there'. 'Well' he said, and then after extracting from me a promise not to tell anyone, 'officially the only permissible punishment we can give is twenty-five strokes with a whip. But we are compelled to count out the strokes aloud. Now, if we make a mistake in counting, we can't rectify such a mistake. We have to start again from the beginning. And, even if you find this hard to believe, only a few of us are any good at counting – ha, ha, ha! We get muddled when we're in the twenties. There's the Jew, naked, and bending down and we get to twenty-three and he thinks it's nearly over. And then we say, twenty-two – no, twenty-three ... alright, we made a mistake. One, two, three ...'

There were other warnings. A young man I knew had joined the SS early. He had been promoted quickly. One day his superior officer sent for him, then told him, 'You will have a new assignment from the first of next month; you will be adjutant to the Commandant of Dachau.' The young man turned pale. He went home and thought the matter over. Then he wrote to his superior and asked permission to 'Turn down the assignment'. He was told to report. 'You can turn down that assignment,' he was informed 'but you will still go to Dachau – as an inmate!' He accepted the assignment. One month later he was admitted to a Munich insane asylum.

These events occurred over a period of at least two years. At the time they did no more than convince me Nazism was evil and that I ought to leave Germany. I felt fear, but I was also aware that the Nazis had introduced considerable restrictions on the amount of money emigrants could take out of the country. I would have to leave with ten Marks (2.5 dollars) and my inheritance, already blocked until I was twenty-eight, would be lost. I kept postponing the decision.

Munich had been dubbed the 'Birth Place of the Nazi Movement', and to some extent it lived up to its new title. However, it did not lose any of its charm, and not for some time did the first unmistakable symptoms of life under the Nazis become noticeable. When they did, they were, nevertheless, very glaring. From the Röhn Putsch to the *Kristallnacht*[3] – when Jewish property was destroyed all over the city – there was noisy evidence of the new language the 'master race' was using to express itself. That language was loud and clear and it was quite impossible <u>not</u> to know what was going on, even if one was semi-blinded by the wishful thought that all this was a legitimate means to creating the new, great Germany.

There were the less blatant clues for those who wanted to hear and see. Jewish friends began to disappear in concentration camps or emigrated because they knew they had to. Mixed marriages became targets for blackmail and known political opponents of the Nazis were jailed, blacklisted, fired from their jobs and otherwise immobilized.

Years later – after the war and during the occupation days – in discussions with people I had known in the pre-war years, or who I had witnessed being interrogated, I became sick and tired of hearing the 'but I knew nothing' tale. (Probably the most outstanding performance in this respect was that of Ernst Kaltebrunner, Head of the notorious RSHA, the main Security Office, who claimed not to have known about the thousands of concentration camp detention orders bearing his signature).

I certainly heard and saw. There was the case of Dr Friedl Strauss, a Jewish customer of mine at the Adler Works and my lawyer. He had an Aryan girlfriend and made no attempt to hide her. He looked very Jewish and she very Teutonic. One night, Strauss was arrested and taken to the Dachau concentration camp. He had committed, so his mother was told, '*Rassenschand*'[4] the crime against the German race of a Jew having sexual relations with a German woman. When I came to work the following morning, his mother was waiting to see me. She begged me, as Friedl's friend, to ask the help of the Adler boss Dr Meyer, who was an avowed Nazi from way back who often wore his so-called 'Riding SS' uniform to work.

We had sold several cars to Strauss and his mother hoped Dr Meyer, who had bought his title at some obscure Austrian university, would help to arrange Friedl's release. Myer said he would try and two days later had instructions for me. The mother would, through Meyer, channel a very large donation to the widows' and orphans' fund of some part of the SS Organisation. A message would then be smuggled to her son in the camp, specifying the exact time and place where he could climb over the barbed wire of the Dachau camp and escape. There his mother was to wait for him, with his Adler convertible, bought of course from Dr Meyer, and he was then to get out of Germany.

The message obviously got through as, at the appointed time, Freidl ran to the fence and started to climb at the place indicated. Half way up, he was cut down by the burst from a machine-gun, not mounted in a watch tower but hidden somewhere, as his mother would later tell me.

14

In spite of this dreadful episode I stayed, mainly because, in spite of knowing subconsciously that I ought to be very concerned, I felt strangely outside events. I was also having too good a time in Munich to be very serious about anything.

## NOTES:

1. Dachau was the first concentration camp to be opened (in 1933) in Germany. It was located in Bavaria about ten miles northwest of Munich.

2. 'The Night of the Long Knives', also called Operation *Hummingbird* or, in Germany, the 'Röhm Putsch', was a purge that took place in Nazi Germany from 30 June to 2 July 1934, when the Nazi regime carried out a series of political raids intended to consolidate Hitler's power. Many of those killed were leaders of the Sturmabteilung (SA), or Storm Detachment, the Nazis' own paramilitary organization, colloquially known as the 'Brownshirts' due to the colour of their uniforms. The best-known victim of the purge was Ernst Röhm, the SA's leader and one of Hitler's long-time supporters and allies.

3. The name '*Kristallnacht*' comes from the shards of broken glass that littered the streets after the windows of Jewish-owned stores, buildings, and synagogues were smashed.

4. *Rassenschande* (racial shame) was a concept in Nazi Germany's racial policy forbidding sexual relations between Aryans and non-Aryans.

# AVOIDING THE NAZI SALUTE

MY FRIENDS AND ACQUAINTANCES fell into two very different groups. I was on the fringe of a set of people who included a very fine upright German from Cologne named Heinz Ickrath, who was considerably older than me and often took me flying in his private plane, and a remarkably brilliant woman who owned an antique shop in the fashionable Briennerstrasse. I also had friends who were actors, doctors and bankers with whom I would have coffee in the Carlton Tearooms, which were owned by Gabriele von Siebert. Hitler admired Gabriele and liked the Carlton Tearooms, which he continued to frequent after seizing power.

Whenever the Fuehrer was in Munich and had some time on his hands, he would arrive at the Carlton for coffee after his presumably vegetarian lunch. His arrival was signalled by a quickly gathering crowd outside and the shouts of 'Heil Hitler'. I would get up as rapidly and as inconspicuously as possible and disappear into the washroom. The other guests would rise upon Hitler's entry and would stand, facing his route of progress, with their arms raised until he had sat down. His party was usually small, perhaps four to six people and would invariably include his adjutant, Brückner, with whom I sometimes played tennis.

Once Hitler had sat down at his table in the left corner of the second of the Carlton's two rooms, I would return to my seat. This I usually managed to choose in such a way that I could also pretend to miss his departure which was always over very quickly since he left the place with fast long strides before anyone had time to get up and 'Heil' him. Thus, during my three years of visiting the Carlton, unlike all the other guests, I never once gave the Hitler salute as the Fuehrer went by.

Whenever necessary, we were also alerted by a marvellous waitress named Rita who had become quite famous for threatening Julius Streicher, the infamous Jew-baiter, with expulsion from the Carlton when he attempted to unwrap some home-made cake. 'This' she explained 'is a high-class tearoom and if you wish to act like a labourer you should eat elsewhere'. Streicher, blushingly, re-wrapped his cake and was not seen at the Carlton again.

The group around Heinz Ickrath sailed very close to the political wind in June 1934. Munich Police President Schneidhuber was, as I have mentioned, shot dead in the course of the frantic actions surrounding the executions of Röhm, Strasser[1] and others. Schneidhuber was a close friend of the Carlton group and whilst they did not attend his funeral they did make a collection on behalf of his widow which produced a staggering amount of money and some raised eyebrows in high quarters – I helped collect the money but was not then identified with the action. That occurred only much later.

My other group of friends was quite different, they were much more mixed, younger and more flamboyant. Included in this group was: Herbert Engelhardt, who was vaguely involved in selling used cars; Herbert Hemmeter, the son of the famous distilling family who because of his stature and features was known as the 'garden dwarf'; Fritz Schoettele, briefly the Bavarian downhill ski champion; and Fredy Goldstern who until his flight from impending concentration camp detention was my best friend. There was also Fredy's sister Alice, a very gifted sculptor.

At six feet tall however the outstanding figure in this group, in more ways than one, was an American music student named Gilbert Roe, who had come to Munich for six weeks to study piano under a famous teacher and stayed six years until he had his brush with the authorities over exporting cars, bought with Sperrmarks, (blocked marks – see Chapter 8, Note 1), which he had planned to sell in Switzerland for hard, Swiss Francs.  Gilbert had an annual income of something like $18,000, which was a fortune in those days, which made him the only member of our 'club' who always had liquid funds.

We often met at the Regina Hotel where the barman, Rosenow, reigned supreme. He was also an infallible message centre, counsellor on any subject from sex to travel, occasional banker and, as we discovered much later, informant for the Gestapo (secret police).

Two of Fredy Goldstern's brothers hurriedly left Germany but Fredy and Alice kept hanging on – Fredy because he was a ranking tennis player, and Alice because she was too absorbed in her work and her love for a Dr Otto Walter. The siblings were also trying to persuade their aging parents to liquidate their substantial property in Munich and get ready to go. This situation prevailed in many Jewish families. They found it hard to see the writing on the wall and they paid the terrible price of death for their inertia which, so often, was due to their love for Germany – their home, which they did not want to leave.

One morning, I found the Goldstern family in turmoil. Fredy had been summoned to police headquarters and the Rumanian Consul had warned him to get out at once. The whole family was in a pitiful state of indecision and I felt totally sure of impending disaster.

I cannot remember the arguments I used, but within no time Fredy and I were heading for Freilassing and the Austrian border in a second-hand two-litre BMW which I had planned to sell later that morning. I do remember that we left Munich eleven minutes after the Orient Express, which stopped at Freilassing for passport control, and I drove at an insane speed to get to the border in time for Fredy to catch the train. There were then, of course, no speed limits or controls and as we roared across the bridge over the railway before Freilassing station, the Orient Express rolled in underneath. Fredy ran, brandishing his passport, and they let him get aboard. I never saw him again, but I believe he went to Bucharest under the Communists, where he was probably unhappy, but alive.

His parents were murdered.

Alice left Germany when Otto Walter went to the USA with his new visa. (Some years later I loaned her my flat in Dolphin Square when I went into the army and she was tragically killed there in one of the first German air raids on London).

However, whilst it may have been underway, the Nazi terror machine needed breaking-in. The police, the civil service and all official organs of the country had to be converted to Hitler's frightful reign. This took time, as I was fortunate to discover, but when it had been done there was ruthless, murderous efficiency everywhere – total extermination of the Jews, total destruction of the opponents of the Nazi Regime, total preparation for war – and all of it carried out with total devotion by all those who could make their contribution, totally convinced that they would be victorious and would never be taken to task.

For all sorts of reasons, the warnings continued to be ignored, because to fully understand and interpret them was emotionally and intellectually beyond most of us; or was too uncomfortable, as in my case. That, certainly, was my frame of mind when I handed the BMW to its new owner that same day and went back to having a wonderful time.

**NOTE:**

1. Gregor Strasser was another prominent Nazi official and politician who was also murdered during the Night of the Long Knives in 1934 (see note 2 to Chapter 4).

# HALCYON DAYS

PART OF THE ENCHANTMENT OF THE TIMES was, thanks to Gilbert Roe's Dollars, the ease with which my friends and I could travel abroad, particularly to Grand Prix races, which we often did together with a variety of lady friends.

One of those eventful trips, to the Monte Carlo Grand Prix, is well worth mentioning. On route we suffered a puncture and found the spare was also flat. It was getting dark and we were somewhere in the mountains, miles from any town and garage and there was no traffic. However, there was an impressive, chateau-like building up a dirt road, so off we went, hoping it would be inhabited and hospitable. I knocked on the huge wooden door of the courtyard and, after some minutes, the door opened, slightly. We must have looked reasonably respectable because an old man, the epitome of the proverbial family retainer, decided to admit us.

We explained our predicament and he departed to consult a higher authority. This appeared shortly in the person of the Grand Seigneur, a man probably in his eighties who radiated courtesy and benevolence. He explained that the telephone did not function this late in the evening, 'But we must of course be his guests for dinner and stay the night'. With the token assistance of the family retainer, we returned to our car for some over-night things and were then shown, four of us, to separate bedchambers each complete with a four-poster bed, picture galleries of ancestors, washstands, chamber pots and tasselled ropes for ringing the bell. I threw open the shutters and had a breath-taking view of the mountains. The sun had already set and I felt quite elated by the beauty of the moment and the good fortune we were having in finding this experience, which, it turned out later, was to be unique and never-to-be-forgotten.

I cleaned up and went in search of our host whom I tracked down in the candle-lit salon, glass in hand, dressed for dinner and, clearly, radiating happiness. He poured exquisite old port for an aperitif and put us all at ease; which we needed badly in view of this very strange and over-powering interlude. We were, after all, in our early twenties and hardly used to castles and superbly gracious, eighty-year-old hosts.

Then 'Jeeves' announced dinner and served an exquisite, long-drawn out meal. Finally, we followed the chandelier-carrying retainer to the library for the worst coffee and best cognac I have ever tasted. At this point, our host raised his glass, welcomed us to his home again and mentioned, more as an aside, that this was one of the happiest days of his life. We asked the obvious question as to why that should be. 'You shall see shortly', said our host with a slight smile and continued to tell us about his house, his art treasures and his extensive travels. Jeeves reappeared, asked for our wishes and undertook to telephone the garage early in the morning to have them come up and repair our tyres (in fact, when I looked out of my window at 08.00 hours the next morning, they were just putting the wheel back on our Mercedes).

Much later, our host rose, took a chandelier with candles flickering romantically and indicated that we should follow him.

Up we went, to the first floor, across a sitting room – clearly that of a lady – through a tapestry-covered door and up a spiral staircase. We were obviously in a tower and went up a further floor where the old gentleman opened yet another door.

At first we saw only more candles and then, between them on a catafalque[1], we saw the body of a dead woman. She was quite old, looked quite aristocratic and, even in death, we expected her to pronounce some chastisement, or to issue orders to the effect that we must stop keeping her husband up so late, (and slightly intoxicated).

'Yes, yes', he said slowly, 'my wife! She died this morning. She was the hardest woman that ever lived. We were married sixty-two years. She was wonderful, in a way. But far too hard, certainly on me. Now I can relax. I will be at ease now, though not for long. I am happy today. I told you that.'

With that, he picked up the chandelier and we followed him down the spiral stairs. He bid us goodnight outside our rooms and slowly went down the long corridor.

Jeeves delivered his apologies the next morning, Monsieur was very tired and resting. It was hoped we had been comfortable. We were not invited to stay for the funeral. Maybe, after the previous night's

20

confession, any words spoken across the grave might have made us chuckle. I remembered my father's cremation!

There was, I reflected as we were driving towards the Cote d'Azur the next day, really only one moral to this story: if two people can't live together in happiness, they should call it a day. There is no use waiting for death, it might come very late indeed.

We joined Herbert Hemmeter (the Garden Dwarf) in the evening at our hotel in Monte Carlo. He had travelled down separately in his Bugatti. As usual, he was not interested in our adventures but felt that one would have to be moronic indeed to run out of spare tyres. All tickets for the Grand Prix had been sold. Standing room only – queue early in the morning – which we did – minus Gilbert and Herbert. They had vanished.

In those days grand prix racing was a very different kettle of fish to how it is now. There were of course the factory teams, but there were also private entrants, and instead of the engines being tuned electronically by teams of scientist-mechanics in the pits of the carefully sealed-off track, tinkerers were at work in rented garages in the town. No television, no artificially built-up heroes, just superb drivers, glorious machines and all of it one could touch, look at from close by and, if one went to the right bar, one could actually rub elbows with tomorrow's winner.

That Sunday we had to cope with something which, at least briefly, seemed incomprehensible. As we stood watching in the crowd, an hour or so before the start, the gates to the track were opened and Herbert's blue-and-white Bugatti appeared. It had large numbers '23' painted in the appropriate places. At the wheel, in racing drivers' dress, sat the Garden Dwarf. On the tail, long legs dangling nonchalantly, sat Gilbert in dirty overalls. The motor was being revved quite convincingly, and then the Bugatti was parked in a suitable spot from which our two chums watched the grand prix in extreme comfort and for very little money. For the price of a pot of paint and the assistance of a professional sign painter the Garden Dwarf had delivered another masterpiece. Nobody even asked, certainly not the man at the gate.

We had a very lively celebration that evening, spending the saved ticket money, particularly Gilbert who decided on a visit to a local brothel. Herbert and his girlfriend departed in the morning in Bugatti number 23 and we stayed on for a few days. We noticed that Gilbert had started scratching himself in certain places but didn't deduce that he had simply caught a dose of the crabs. He sneaked off to a doctor who prescribed something which should have been applied greatly diluted. Gilbert didn't understand the French instructions on the label and suffered badly from burns – a truly unique case of a racing accident – but, on the whole, it had been a lovely trip.

**NOTE:**

1. A decorated wooden framework supporting the coffin of a distinguished person during a funeral or while lying in state.

# THE PRICE, QUALITY AND
# QUANTITY OF LOVE

I LEFT THE ADLER WORKS and Dr Meyer of SS fame, not so much because I couldn't stand the anti-Semitic atmosphere but because I had wrecked the company's only demonstration model of a long-awaited new vehicle against a tree outside the Regina Hotel. I had the presence of mind the following morning, with the help of a mechanic friend, to simulate a faulty bake, leaving the left overs in the yard and my letter of resignation on Meyer's desk. This resulted in the all-important remark 'verlaesst die Stellung auf eigenen Wunsch' (leaves his employment by his own request) being included in an otherwise unusually brief testimonial.

I moved on to work at the Kolb Garage in the Bauerstrasse to sell their, and my own, used cars. I managed to take my tame, brake-fixing mechanic friend, Tony, with me and between us we produced some – outwardly – truly well reconditioned automobiles.

Tony also discovered a racing car for me he had found in a barn near Munich, for which I paid 500 Marks to a peasant whose son had left the thing behind without an explanation when he left to go abroad. Called 'Tracta' it had been made in France, had a 1.5 litre four- cylinder engine, was supercharged with front-wheel drive and was twenty years ahead of its time. The makers had disappeared, and rumour had it that none of the twenty cars they had built had ever been raced. Tony put the machine into tip-top running order and we polished the aluminium body to a high degree. We timed the car at 183km per hour, which was a lot for this sized engine in those days, and I entered it in a race, the Kochelberg Hill-climb in which three classes of drivers were allowed to compete; professionals (including factory drivers), drivers licensed by national associations and 'others' like me. In each class the top boys started first and the slowest last.

On the morning of the race the top of the Kochelberg was in the clouds. It so happened that there were no other cars between me and the last of the 'aces', one of Germany's top drivers, Ernst von Delius, who was driving something called a 'Zoller', which was so named after the designer of its supercharged 12-cylinder engine. The machine was turning at an unheard-of rate of rpms and they were having trouble with clutches, which kept burning out.

My practice times had been quite good and as I was screaming up the mountain that morning I was probably doing even better than the ace until I reached the wet part of the road where the clouds began. I came around a bend in second gear, with my foot on the floorboards only to discover von Delius, clutch obviously gone, trying to push his machine out of the way. In order to avoid the Zoller I had to take my foot of the throttle – a fatal thing with a front-wheel-drive car in those days. All I remember was the hiss of my tyres as my 'pride and joy' went skidding off the road. Somehow, I was thrown clear before my 500 Marks disintegrated on the way down the mountainside. My racing career had lasted just three minutes twenty-three seconds and I had to pay 200 Marks to have the debris taken away. Tony cried for days.

Hard work was necessary to recoup such losses and I took to deepest Bavaria in order to peddle my automobiles to trusting farmers. One night, in Passau, I spotted a truly lovely blonde with an unmistakeable mother and a nice little four-year old daughter. I established contact after dinner and the blonde promised to call me on her way through Munich; which she did three weeks later. 'I am staying at the Regina. Why don't you move in here', she said. The hotel was full, however my old friend Rosenow (the barman) was full of understanding and had a cot moved into a broom closet – no windows, no water, but lots of brooms –and that got me into the hotel. In those days, visits to guests of the opposite sex were difficult, especially late at night when eagle-eyed night porters would check all callers for their legitimacy. Today this seems hard to imagine, but it is totally true. Anyway, sometime later, I knocked at the lady's door. 'I am the 'night waiter' I said, with one eye on the cute child, 'will you require anything else?' It was an appropriate question, full of hope. The answer was negative, 'But was I comfortable?' 'Not very', I stated, 'having to sleep in a broom closet, two doors down on the left. Goodnight, Madam'.

For three nights we made breathless love in that unventilated hole, and for three more in a room I thereafter managed to obtain. Her name was Hedi and she had married, so she told me, a homosexual millionaire grain merchant in Naples who wanted children and a hostess. She was free to do as she pleased, and she wanted to see me again – often. This was the moment of a vote of thanks to Hansi, my superb instructress, who had rendered me worthy of such a sophisticated, and older, partner. Then she left, and after some months, I received a letter with a project for a joint holiday. I had to reply that I couldn't make it because of lack of funds, following which there was an immediate request to forget my handicap and come at her expense. Young, dumb and impetuous as I was, I declined to do any such thing at any woman's expense, and that seemed to be the end of it. However, my wallet later recovered, and I was in love with Hedi. My letters addressed to the Naples Post Office were returned unclaimed, so I decided to try and find her. I drove to Naples non-stop and started my search. There was nobody of the surname she had given me in the phone book or various registers and there was no information at the German Consulate.

I was wandering around Naples feeling rather lost and out of ideas, when I saw a queue outside what seemed to be a cinema. I looked closer and saw two prices above the cashier's box – something like five and fifteen Lira. It didn't seem much so I paid fifteen Lira and entered. To my surprise I was taken over to a lift by a chambermaid in a white apron who showed me to another floor. There she opened a door and half-shoved me into a bedroom where a very naked lady was adorning a rather functional looking bed. I was, as I discovered somewhat late, in a brothel!

There is no happy, or even satisfactory ending to this tale, however I did gain some very useful information. I had never been to a whorehouse and I was afraid, probably of infection, and being in love I was unprepared. So, trying my best Italian, I began to beg off. The girl however was from Bohemia and spoke perfect German. She was also delighted with the unexpected breather but asked me to stay the fifteen minutes I had secured with my fifteen Lira, so as to give her a bit of a rest. We chatted idly and I asked a question I had always had on my mind – how many clients in one day? Now, in the 'officers section' (fifteen Lira department) she explained, there was no problem, about four per hour, eight hours a day, so thirty to thirty-two maximum. But before, in the 'five Lira' department, she allowed only five minutes to a customer and, sometimes, she worked unlimited hours. Her record, she said, was ninety-five in one day! So now I had my answer and it was the only tangible thing I took back with me from my search for Hedi whom I never did find. Sometimes, when I can't go to sleep, I multiply ninety-five by seven inches. It comes out to one hell of a stretch!

# JOINING THE RESISTANCE MOVEMENT

ON MY RETURN TO MUNICH and the Carlton Tearooms Rita, the helpful waitress, continued to warn my friends and me of Hitler's impending approaches. She considered these visits from the Fuehrer to be partly a boon and partly a nuisance. She had benefitted by telling people what she heard him talk about, for which she would be well tipped, and on one occasion she had 'rented out' her apron and bonnet to a girl for twenty Marks, thereby enabling an adoring female fan to take the Fuehrer his coffee. Rita was however annoyed when Hitler occupied his usual table since that part of the establishment was then cleared of all but the most trustworthy guests, which meant a falling off of her tips.

My friends and I visited the Carlton daily and Rita would let us know what confidential matters were being discussed. These friends were all much older than me and included a banker, a wine merchant and several members of the Bavarian nobility who enjoyed a pleasant life of idleness. After some months I became particularly friendly with one of them who will have to remain incognito since, as I write this, he is still alive. One evening he came home with me and we drank a few of the precious bottles of wine my father had left me in his will. My friend asked a few apparently innocent questions such as 'Do you have a valid passport? Do you like to travel? Do you know Switzerland? Do you have any relatives other than your mother?'

The answers I supplied must have satisfied him because he approached me again a few days later and asked me if I would be willing to take a journey to Switzerland, which would ultimately help a Jewish friend of his. I asked for details. He told me that the Jewish director of an industrial concern in Berlin had been imprisoned by the Gestapo. They were however prepared to release him if he in turn was prepared to sell to a certain German bank his shares in one of his companies. A large sum of cash would also be required to 'straighten out matters connected with his release'.

The man didn't have that much cash and it was clear to all that he would eventually be forced into selling his business and still remain in prison. His friends were anxious to raise money to pay the bribe and enable them then to take over the factory.

Their plan was to smuggle German money into Switzerland and there exchange it for Swiss Francs. With these Francs, a Swiss agent of my Munich group of friends would purchase the so-called German 'Sperrmark'[1] funds, owned by Swiss holders, which were blocked inside Germany because of the currency restrictions.

Such Sperrmarks could only be used within Germany for the purchase of stocks and shares of German companies and this method could be applied to the share-holding of the Jewish businessman in Berlin. The increase in capital through the double exchange deal would be large enough for the Munich group to take over the factory. Once this was done the group would raise additional funds on that asset, pay the bribe, get the man out of jail and whisk him out of the country.

My task – if I was willing – would be to smuggle the German cash out of Germany into Switzerland, effect the exchange into Francs and pass the proceeds over to their Swiss contact. I agreed to do this.

The Munich group began to accumulate cash by making inconspicuous withdrawals from accounts all over Germany. Eventually they had collected the required sum of 102,000 Marks in notes of one hundred, fifty and twenty Mark denominations and they handed it over to me. Meanwhile I had begun to make enquiries about the extent of searching I might be subjected to at the German border. It became obvious that this would be considerable if I were suspected of being a smuggler.

Whether I would be a suspect or not, was a question that would have to remain unanswered, but the efficiency of the Gestapo was well known. They might already be on to me through linking me with those cash withdrawals – on the other hand they might not.

I realised that I had to try and find a place of hiding the cash in a car which would stand up to a thorough search. The inner tube of the spare tyre was out – that had been done too often and detected. The same applied to the upholstery, the roof, the radiator, the battery and the door cover. I experimented with a few notes concealed in the inner tube of one of the tyres on which I was running. After only a few miles driven at slow speed, I took off the tyre, removed the patch on the tube and looked inside. There was just some grey dust that had once been money!

So that was useless. Finally, the right idea dawned upon me – why not try hiding the money in the brake drums?

I decided I would dispense with the brakes on the front wheels of my car, take out the brake shoes and put the money there instead. This entailed a fair amount of work. I told my mother that I would be going on a trip to Switzerland in the near future and that I had to do some overhauls on my car before I went. I then sealed all cracks in the garage door with felt, painted the window black and went to work. I obtained a tool needed to remove the brake drums (the wheel is taken off, the tool attached to the bolts that hold the wheel and then a threaded bolt in the centre is turned until it exerts enough pressure on the axle-stump to withdraw a break-drum from its cone shaped seat.)

Once the brake drums were removed I was able to remove the brake shoes. Then I manufactured two round tin containers, which looked rather like cake-moulds, with a hole in the centre for the axle. I attached them to the bolts, which normally hold the brake shoes, put the brake drums back and went for a trial run. The idea worked although I had to go slowly since I only had the handbrake working on the back wheels. Two evenings later I transferred the money to the garage, removed the empty brake drums once again and started 'packing'.

It was a very hot summer night and after only a few minutes in the 'airtight' garage I was dripping wet. My mother, who must have been puzzled by my newly developed distaste for fresh air, came knocking at the door with an iced drink. I had to quickly cover up the piles of money before she opened the door, which could not be locked from the inside. I am quite sure she suspected a great deal but she neither asked any questions then or at any other time.

I had to fold the notes down the middle since they were too large for my containers. I then hammered them flat with a mallet and made parcels wrapped in oily paper and tied with catgut. I packed the tins as tightly as I could, but it soon became apparent that I would not be able to get all the money in. When they were full I had stowed away just over 60,000 of the 102,000 Marks. There would therefore have to be a second trip.

Early the following morning I set off for Switzerland, going via Kempten and using the ferry to cross Lake Constance. To ensure I did not arouse any suspicions at the border I dumped the special tool in some woods since this was not something that would normally be carried by a motorist.

As the customs barrier at Konstanz on the far side of Lake Constance came into view I felt slightly sick. There was one car ahead of me, this was checked and dispatched quickly. I survived the urge to turn the car around and return home. Then the customs officer stood at my car.

'Where are you going?'

'To Zurich'

'How much money do you have?'

'Ten Marks' (Something of an understatement.)

'Alright – pass.'

It was as easy as that. He stamped my passport and I was on my way. The whole thing was over in about one minute.

After passing the Swiss border control with equal ease, I drove on to the town of Winterthur and borrowed another break-drum removing tool from a garage, leaving my suitcase as a deposit. Then I drove out of the town and into a forest, removed the brake drums and unpacked the money. It was in perfect condition.

Back in Winterthur I retrieved my suitcase and went on to Zurich, feeling very light-hearted and satisfied. I telephoned my contact man and in my room at the Savoy Hotel we counted out the money behind drawn blinds. He would retain it, he said, until I returned with the balance and we would then do the whole exchange transaction.

The next evening saw me back in Munich after an uneventful journey. (I had bought another tool in Zurich and left it in a barn) We decided that it would be wise to allow a few days to elapse before my second trip. I set out again ten days later, having crawled around Munich slowly on half a brake.

Once again, I obtained the special tool, packed the remaining money and went off to Konstanz as before. This time however there was some commotion at the German border when I arrived. A large car was parked by the customs building. Its upholstery had been cut open and its two spare tyres had been taken off. The passengers, an old couple, were vainly protesting against further damage being done to their beautiful car. During the next twenty minutes I watched the customs men go over that car with a fine-tooth comb, but they found nothing. With the stuffing hanging out of the seats and the door covers, which had been unscrewed, stacked on the back seat, the two old people were eventually permitted to proceed.

Meanwhile I had debated with myself the advisability of submitting my car to a similar search. I decided to go on with my plans. That first car might be searched because it was suspect. But even if they were being meticulous with every car on that particular day, I still felt that my place of hiding was good. They certainly hadn't done anything to the wheels of the car in front of me. I might, so I thought, arouse further suspicion if I turned around after having waited for some minutes. When my turn came I was trembling and probably pale but outwardly I remained fairly confident. I asked the customs officer what they had been looking for.

'Never you mind' he said. 'We had orders.'

I grinned and said that I could guess. 'Money smuggling, wasn't it?'

He grinned back and didn't answer. He subjected my suitcase to a cursory inspection, asked me to show him my wallet, which contained the permissible ten Marks and then sent me on my way.

Once in Switzerland I had to stop and run off into the woods, as my insides seemed to be falling out. A few miles along the road I came across the old couple, they were trying to tidy up their ruined car. I stopped and asked them if they knew why they had run into trouble. The old gentleman, who was nearly crying, could only venture a guess. 'I have been taking rather large sums of cash out of the bank', he told me. 'Someone must have thought that I was taking it abroad and reported me, but I haven't got a penny over my travelling allowance with me. I was putting that money into jewellery.'

I could not have felt more grateful for the caution my Munich friends had used in withdrawing their money in the way that they did!

The remainder of that story can be quickly told. I contacted my man in Zurich once again and, with the cash complete, we went off to Bern. We met the cashier of a bank who carried the equivalent in Swiss Francs with him. We made the exchange and the Swiss contact man purchased the required amount of blocked German Marks on the following morning.

The German part of the transaction was completed with great speed. The Berlin factory was taken over by the Munich group, the bribe was paid and one of the group went to Berlin to collect the Jewish prisoner who was still held in the Berlin Gestapo jail. However, he failed to get him. Dr Goebbels, he was told, was interested in the case personally and it would be impossible to release the man against the Propaganda Minister's orders.

Fortunately, one member of the Munich group had gone to school with Gestapo Chief Reinhard Heydrich. 'I know enough about that bastard to get anything I want from him' he told us. 'What's more, he knows I've written it all down and left it in safe hands. He'll perform. Just you watch.' He went off to Berlin and re-appeared almost immediately – accompanied by the Jewish industrialist! He had walked into Heydrich's office and demanded a release order and got it. Goebbels hadn't heard of the man's release. When he did soon afterwards it was too late. The victim had left the country.

I myself was taken off the active list for some months during which it became clear that the entire transaction had gone according to plan and that not one of us had been linked to it by the Gestapo.

My confidence swelled, and I wanted action. There had been a feeling of shock every time the doorbell rang at an unconventional hour, but that fear soon wore off. By the time I was sent to Switzerland near the end of 1935 I had started to become careless and overconfident.

My assignment was very simple. I was to meet a guide in Zurich and arrange for him to meet a man, wanted by the Gestapo, near to the Austrian border. It was early afternoon when I left Munich and I would not reach Zurich until fairly late that evening. That would be too late to get hold of anyone who could give me some money and I wanted to go out to dinner and have a few drinks.

I decided to conceal a little extra money so that I would arrive with more than just the permissible ten Marks. A small price list of the cars I was selling seemed to fit the bill. I put two twenty Mark notes inside it and returned it to my wallet. That evening the customs men at Konstanz were in a bad mood. They carefully searched my bag and found nothing. Then they told me to empty my pockets. One of them leafed through the price list and there found the forty Marks!

The first thing they did was to arrest me and put me into a cell, which proved to be very handy. They left me alone for a couple of hours and that gave me time to cook up a story.

I was, I told them later, dealing in second hand cars and had sold one earlier that day. I had left the money at home but must have overlooked the two bills.

They informed me that they would check my story and returned me to my cell. There was no dinner out – in fact there was not even any dinner 'in' that night.

Early the next morning I was taken back and interviewed by the same customs officials. They had, they announced, decided to believe my story. I would be subject to one week's imprisonment, which would be entered in my penal register. However, the matter could also be settled with a fine, payable there and then. This would not be entered anywhere. It would amount to the forty Marks I was carrying illegally plus a further sixty Marks which I had better obtain from Munich by cable.

We understood each other perfectly. I left my passport with them and phoned my mother who cabled me the sixty Marks, which arrived two hours later. Back at the customs, I settled my debt without bothering anybody about a receipt and I was allowed to pass. Luckily, I had run into officials who needed some ready money.

When I returned to Munich and reported the incident to my friends, they frowned. There might be a leakage. Frank had become a known quantity at that border and had therefore ceased to be employable. My 'resistance' days were over!

31

I did not think I had done anything heroic, rather, I thought I had given free rein to two dominating traits of my character which have stood me in bad stead forever after – irresponsibility and adventurousness.

However, I had assisted people who were in great need of help. I felt good about that then and have done ever since.

## NOTE:

1. The German Government placed the liquid assets of German Jews in special blocked accounts known as 'Sperrmarks' which could only be used in Germany. Those Sperrmarks held their value internally but had much less value (perhaps as low as 25%) outside the country. To purchase goods (such as cars) in Sperrmarks and then sell those goods abroad was one way of getting a better exchange rate – however such transactions were soon made illegal by the Third Reich. Similarly smuggling banknotes out of Germany – which could be exchanged at true market value for Swiss Francs was also a crime that carried the severest of penalties. Francs obtained through such transactions could then be used to buy Sperrmark funds in Switzerland at extremely advantageous rates. Those Sperrmark funds could then in turn be used to pruchase shares in German companies. This was a hugely profitable, albeit highly dangerous, way for German Jews to use the financial system to their advantage.

# TRUE LOVE AND MARRIAGE

FOR A FEW MONTHS I CONTINUED TO SELL CARS and went skiing and nothing unusual happened, except that occasionally a friend would get into trouble with the Nazis and disappear into a concentration camp, whilst others left the country as emigrants.

Then in the spring of 1936 I met a girl that I had admired from a distance. She lived opposite the garage in the Bauerstrasse where Tony and I were beautifying old cars. She was a beautiful blonde and I would watch her move about in her first floor flat. It appeared that there was no man in her life. I decided to change that. We met and immediately fell in love.

Her name was Maditta von Skrbensky and her father, a Baron, owned estates in Silesia and bred horses in the Rhineland. He was a member of the 'Herrenclub' in Berlin, a sort-of political, social, sinister assembly of nobles, industrialists and political grey eminences of Germany who were of considerable importance to Hitler and were tacitly absolved from giving proof of their faith in the Fuehrer through Nazi Party membership.

After every self-inflicted German disaster, the members of the Herrenclub have managed to emerge in remarkably fine shape to get ready for their next vital, patriotic contribution. (The Americans attempted to bring some of them to justice during the so-called Subsequent Proceedings at Nuremberg, where such giants as Krupp[1] and Flick were tried, but their sentences were absurd in the light of what they had done, and their return to wealth and honour was rapid. Alfried Krupp, for instance, was found guilty of crimes which, had he been tried by the IMT, would have meant a death sentence.)

For a girl in Maditta's position I, a non-Aryan, was therefore the worst possible choice she could make. Although we agreed on this, we continued to see a great deal of each other. We would, we thought, eventually leave Germany and get married abroad.

On making enquiries the replies we received were always the same. We would not be breaking any law and the marriage would definitely be legal. As for other consequences – that was up to the Nazi Party and the Gestapo.

We decided to try. There was however one serious obstacle. In those European countries for which travellers' cheques could be obtained in Germany a lengthy stay was required prior to the marriage and we could not take with us enough money to cover such a period. The one country in which marriage was possible after only a few days was England and that was financially inaccessible.

However, in February 1937, the problem was solved for us during a skiing trip we had taken to the Italian Alpine resort of Sestriere. There we had met a charming English couple on their honeymoon – Humphrey Sykes[2] and his wife Grizel. When they heard our story they immediately invited us to stay with them in the garrison town of Tidworth in Wiltshire, where Sykes was serving with the 9th Lancers, and they told us we could get married from their house. We accepted gratefully, and details were settled; we would travel to England in April for the sole purpose of getting married.

Back in Germany, we thought the matter over and decided it would be wise not to let too many people know about the impending wedding. Only our best and most reliable friends were told before I went off to Breslau to discuss the plan with Maditta's father, Baron Skrbensky. He was, he explained to me, 'Far from enthusiastic about the idea'. Did he propose to intervene I asked? No, he did not – after all, his daughter was of age and it was her business – but he would warn her of the consequences that might arise from a 'mixed marriage of this sort'. Certainly Baron, please do that. Good-bye!

Before I left Munich for England the Garden Dwarf arranged a truly imaginative event to end my days as a bachelor. We were driving up the Maximilianstrasse in his car when he spotted a very sexy looking girl in a very tight-fitting skirt. She had long, black hair and exceptionally good legs. Herbert pulled up at the curb and offered her a lift, which she accepted. She was Hungarian, not that young, but a real sex bomb. We adjourned to Osteria Italiano, our favourite bistro where the food was excellent. Soon after Herbert and the girl disappeared having instructed me to organise a farewell party. I concurred and went off with some of my friends to my pied-a-terre near the garage. Herbert appeared a couple of hours later, with the girl in tow. He looked as if he had been run over by a tractor – scratches everywhere, deep circles under his eyes, and he seemed to be staggering, not walking. His Hungarian discovery looked happy and benign – even when Herbert named her the sex-maniac author of his dilapidated condition. The others then took turns with the lovely, including Gilbert, and eventually I too succumbed to her charms.

That was that, no regrets, no comment until three days later – the night before my departure for London. We were all at the Regina Bar, looking funereal over my impending exit when Gilbert rose to go to the toilet. A few moments later he was back: 'I've got the damned clap' he announced. We all applauded. 'Don't you look so gleeful, Wolfe,' said Gilbert, 'you've probably got it too – from that Hungarian nympho'. He then showed me what it looked like. I felt giddy. Within twenty-four hours I would be in England, in Maditta's bed, and I was bringing her the clap as a wedding present.

Then the committee of experts went into session and, to my great relief, finally explained that the Garden Dwarf and Gilbert were the authors of a splendid prank. Gilbert had obtained some mayonnaise at the Regina and introduced it, carefully, to make it re-emerge under my horror-stricken eyes. It was a good joke, depending on where you sat. They then drove me to the airport and waved good-bye – it was the last time I saw them all together.

Maditta, who had travelled to London ahead of me, and Humphrey Sykes met me at Croydon and we were dropped off at a small hotel in Knightsbridge, with separate rooms, of course. We wanted to see how the other half lives and spent the night apart, feeling very virtuous and, in my case, recovering from my monumental hangover.

The next day we travelled to Tidworth for another night of virtuousness, and then to Andover Registrar Office, where everything had been organised. Humphrey and Grizel were our witnesses and we had a splendid lunch somewhere, after which they dropped us at their house in Tidworth – for the young couple to be alone, at last. We felt duty bound not to disappoint them. Much later, I told Maditta the VD tale and she laughed for days.

## NOTES:

1. The Krupp Trial (officially, *The United States of America vs. Alfried Krupp, et al.*) was the tenth of the twelve SP trials at Nuremberg. Twelve former directors of the Krupp Group were accused of having: enabled the armament of the German military forces; actively participated in the Nazis' preparations for an aggressive war; and used slave labourers in their companies. Wolfe Frank indicates elsewhere in his papers that 'Alfried Krupp was found guilty at

Nuremberg and sentenced to twelve years in prison of which he only served five! However even as his trial was approaching its climax, the Germans were busy restoring him and their "elite" to their un-lost glory'.

2. Humphrey Hugh Sykes, born in 1907, was to become a very important figure in Wolfe Frank's life. He was the son of Major Herbert Rushton Sykes and Hon. Constance Harriet Georgina Skeffington. He married, firstly, Grizel Sophie, daughter of Air Vice-Marshal Sir Norman Duckworth Kerr MacEwen, in 1936, from whom he was divorced in 1948. He married, secondly, Muriel Hooper, daughter of Colonel John Charles Hooper, in 1958. He was educated at Rugby School and gained the rank of Major in the service of the 9th Lancers. He died in 1991 after having travelled from Scotland to the home of Mike Dilliway in Dorset in search of Wolfe Frank's manuscript and other documents.

# GESTAPO AT THE DOOR

MADITTA AND I WERE MARRIED AT ANDOVER on 12 April 1937. Four days later we were flying back to Munich. I had a feeling of foreboding; which proved to be justified.

When we unlocked Maditta's flat in the Beuerstrasse, I immediately saw the official looking letter on the floor. I tore open the envelope which was addressed to me. Dated 14 April (two days after the wedding) it read as follows: 'In matters of your marriage to Maditta von Skrbensky in England you are requested to appear at this police station at your earliest convenience. The Certificate of Marriage is to be brought with you.'

The game, I knew, was up. My wife did not, of course feel the same way. She knew nothing of my previous, rather indiscreet journeys to Switzerland.

We trotted off to the police station and were received by a policeman I had known for years. He congratulated us in broad Bavarian and then proceeded to copy the Certificate, letter by letter. When he was through I asked him what the whole thing was all about? Who had made the inquiry? It had come from 'Police headquarters' he said, 'and probably didn't mean anything at all'.

That didn't ring true. No-one, but my most trusted friends, had known of our plans. Someone must have caused inquiries to be made, and that someone could only have been Maditta's father.

As soon as possible I called on a member of the anti-Nazi group who had, I knew, contacts at Gestapo headquarters. He promised to be in touch with me. There followed the most nerve-wracking honeymoon imaginable. I jumped every time the doorbell rang. I woke up in the middle of the night, bathed in sweat. Then on the 22 April the uncertainty was over. The call came from my friend. He would meet me in the evening. He had some news for me.

The Gestapo were indeed after me. The upshot of it was that, while we hadn't broken any laws, I had violated the German national feeling – 'verstossen gegen das gesunde deutsche Volksempfinden' was the German phrase. This was to be rectifiable by means of an educational course I was to undergo. The place was Dachau. The time was 05.00 hours the following morning.

I decided I would not attend.

I went home to Maditta and told her that I would have to leave. We didn't have much time to waste. After a brief discussion we decided that I would go alone. She would put our affairs in order, draw as much money as possible and follow me. It never occurred to us that she would be prevented from carrying out the plan.

Ten minutes were spent in throwing a few things into a suitcase. There was a quick 'auf Wiedersehen' and no time to get emotional. We didn't see each other again until nearly ten years later.

Maditta's passport was impounded and her accounts blocked. My financial affairs went haywire after my departure and there was no money she could lay her hands on. After six months her father reappeared on the scene and indicated that all this would be put right if she agreed to divorce me. For another month Maditta put up a fight. Then she signed on the dotted line.

(On 8 January 1938, in London, I received my divorce decree. The marriage had been dissolved, it stated, because 'a German woman of the standing of the plaintiff could not be expected to remain married to a man of the defendant's type and character'.) The defendant hadn't known that divorce proceedings were in progress.

At any rate, I anticipated none of this as I drove towards my mother's house around 21.00 hours on the evening of 22 April. Having to say farewell to her was more difficult. I told her that I was going on an unexpected business trip to Switzerland and would return within a month. She believed none of it. Mothers have an uncanny way of knowing the truth on occasions like that. Mine cried a little and wished me luck and when we met again, two years later in Switzerland, she told me that she had known that I was in deep trouble.

Once again, after the ten-minute stop at mother's house, I was on the familiar road towards Konstanz and Switzerland. It was a horrible night. A gale was blowing, and rain mixed with snow was pelting down as I drove through the Allgau. I was driving an American car, a supercharged Graham convertible that held the road badly. But I felt like going fast. At 04.50 hours the next morning the Gestapo would receive a telephone call informing them of my departure – an arrangement I had made before leaving. We were hoping to prevent their arrival at my wife's flat; but it didn't work. In any event, I had to be out of Germany before that hour.

I splashed to a stop outside the customs house at Konstanz. The time was 02.40 hours. A small window opened, and a large hand reached out for my passport. The window slammed shut. The wind was driving the rain against the building and howling in the telegraph wires. A lamp over the black-white-red barrier was wildly swinging about. Outside its circle of light was blackness and dozens of footsteps seemed to be coming from all directions. Then the catch of the window snapped open. I whirled around. The large hand was returning my passport. 'Thank you. Good night'

'Heil Hitler!'

Starter. Handbrake open. Headlights on. First gear. A sentry stepped out of his box. The barrier rose. Under it. Passed it. I was out. I had done with Germany. I had lost a wife after just six days of marriage, parted from my mother, and left behind everything I owned – but I was glad!

After passing the border I took stock. I was wearing ski clothes. In addition, I owned: five shirts, four pairs of socks, underwear, one suit, one Graham Page supercharged convertible with sixty litres of petrol and ten German Marks. I also had 500 Swiss Franks in an account in Zurich. That was all I had in the world.

I went to Zurich and took a room in the cheapest boarding house I knew – which was used mostly by variety artists and unemployed actors – and I began to write letters to friends and acquaintances all over Europe, telling them of my unwanted departure from Germany and asking for their help in finding me work. From Belgium and Holland, France and Luxembourg, Denmark and Sweden came the same depressing answer: 'We would like to give you a job, but it would be impossible to get you a working permit in our country.'

I descended upon a well-to-do uncle in Milan with whom I had had little contact in the past, walking the last sixteen kilometres into the city from the spot where my car had run out of petrol. Horrified, the good man offered his hospitality but made it very clear that there was nothing else he could do for me. So, I returned to Switzerland.

My contacts seemed exhausted. All but one. I had not written to Humphrey Sykes in England. I felt that he had done enough when he had enabled us to get married in his house and I felt guilty because his generosity had been rewarded with this disastrous outcome. However, as a last resort, I wrote to him. Could he advance travel money and write a letter that would get me into England? Once there I would sell the Graham and pay him back. Also, there ought to be enough money left over for me to hold out until I could find a job, hopefully with his help. I also indicated that if I had not heard from him within ten days, I would know that he could not help me, or did not wish to do so.

I sat back and waited, helped by five lovely young Austrian girls – a dance team – who had just come back from an engagement in England where they assured me working permits were hard to get. Some small mechanical trouble with the car absorbed too much of my cash reserve and I found I had less money than I needed to last out the ten days.

It occurred to me that I might make some use of that non-Aryan portion of my family tree and I decided to call on the Rabbi of Zurich for financial aid. I rang his bell. A maid opened the door. No, the Rabbi was at the Synagogue. He wouldn't be back until the following night. I claimed urgent business. Then I could certainly visit him at the Synagogue, but of course I would need a hat. I didn't own one. She suggested I should buy one. As that was too much of an investment, I dropped the matter.

Then the dance team made a collection and financed the remainder of those ten days that quickly elapsed, but still there was no answer from Humphrey Sykes.

I made a decision. I would not become a money-less refugee. I would go back to Germany and face the music.

On the following morning I donated my suitcase to the dance team who stood around my car with tears streaming down their faces. Then as I pressed the starter button a Swiss postman appeared around the corner. He had a telegram for me. It read 'Yes certainly – money and letter following – Love Humphrey'. My suicidal journey back to Germany was cancelled.

Then came fifty pounds and the explanation for the delay. He had been away and found the letter on his return. Would I make my way to Tidworth, to arrive there not before 22 May?

So, on the 20 May I set out for Southampton, the port nearest to Tidworth. The dance team who had been repaid were waving a cheerful farewell.

On the way to Le Havre my motor blew a cylinder-head gasket. After paying for the repair I arrived at the port with just enough money to pay for the passage. Unfortunately, the ferry was fully booked that night.

The next one would leave three days later. I took a room at the cheapest hotel I could find and made arrangements with the Royal Automobile Club for paying some of my fare to England. I left myself no money for food. I stuffed my pockets with fresh rolls at breakfast when the waiter wasn't looking and then sat on a park bench all day, reading books from a library and eating a dry roll when my stomach became too noisy.

During the second afternoon I was joined by an attractive blonde girl and we began to talk. When she heard my story, she laughed and insisted that I should be her guest for dinner. We adjourned to a pleasant boarding house and I stuffed myself with large quantities of delicious food served by a smartly dressed maid.

At 11.00 hours that night my hostess regretted that I would have to leave, as it was time for her to start work. I had been entertained, generously and enjoyably, by a prostitute in a brothel. On my way back to the hotel, my thoughts wandered back to Hansi and the establishment in Naples and I came close to saying a silent prayer for all the lovable whores of this world.

The following evening I loaded the car and made the night crossing to Southampton. There the car had to be left in bond since I had no customs documents. The trusting RAC bought my ticket to Tidworth on the strength of Sykes' invitation and put the cost on the bill.

# ENGLAND

AS I SETTLED DOWN IN MY SEAT ON THE TRAIN I felt extremely hungry once again. The train was due in at Tidworth at 12.50 hours and Sykes would, I knew, lunch at 13.00. I had visions of steaming dishes. At Tidworth I jumped out of the train and almost ran to their house at 4 Hampshire Cross.

Humphrey Sykes received me joyfully. He was dressed in white. 'I'm glad you got here in time,' he said 'I'm just off to play Cricket at Winchester College. You'll be interested in seeing that, I'm sure'.

The maid passed us with the lunch dishes. Vainly, I tried to put across the fact that I was very hungry. I failed. We went off to Winchester. I have hated Cricket ever since, and I am sure that even today they talk about the silent guest at Winchester College who, during the tea break of a certain match, ate more sandwiches than the two opposing teams between them.

At the match I found myself sitting next to a teacher who wanted to practice his German. For some time, I gazed at a group of men who, at first, seemed to be in doubt about what to do with themselves. They finally started to throw a ball about half-heartedly and now and then one of them seemed to arouse himself from his lethargy, to take an awkward swing at the ball with a large, clumsy lump of timber. Finally, I felt that I required an explanation. I turned to my neighbour and asked him when they would start to play? 'Heavens' he said with an expression of complete horror on his face, 'what do you mean? They've been playing for over an hour … and this is a frightfully exciting match!'

Back in Tidworth that evening, I managed to convey to the Sykes the essential details of what had happened to me, and my marriage. They felt that I must try to get Maditta over to England as quickly as possible. However, I had learned in Switzerland that her passport had been taken away.

Humphrey knew Lord Mount Temple, the Chairman of the Anglo-German Fellowship – that is how it came to pass that he and I visited his Lordship's home at Romsey the following morning where the conversation concerning the return of my wife's passport, which I reported in the Prologue of this book, took place.

Soon afterwards, I managed to sell the Graham Page and I settled down to polish up my English by reading mostly murder stories and going into lengthy sessions with Allan, Humphrey's batman, who taught me the kind of English that cannot be found in any dictionary. This was quite essential. For instance, he taught me to say, 'Chase a bug around a tree,' quickly. He then assured me I was doing fine 'why,' he said, 'you've nearly lost your accent'.

Travelling back from London by train soon afterwards, I encountered some officers' wives from Tidworth. They admired my perfect English, but I submitted that I still had a lot to learn. However, it didn't seem to me that saying, 'chase a bug around a tree' quickly was a necessary step in the right direction. Clearly, the ladies could not see it either and the conversation ceased abruptly. That night after dinner I tackled Humphrey's uncle, Sir Sidney Barton, former British Ambassador in Addis Ababa. 'Ahem; never mind that sort of nonsense,' said Sir Sidney, 'that won't further your studies'.

Allan, the batman, was more constructive: 'Sir,' he said, 'there's a lot to this here English language that you won't never pick up in there,' and he pointed at the house, 'but you'll use it sooner or later. I reckon I'd better give you some lessons.' When, two years later, I joined His Majesty's Forces, I was therefore an equal in any barrack room conversation.

Soon after these events a German officer, Major Monzel, visited the 9th Lancers – Humphrey's regiment – in an exchange that had seen one of the 9th's officers go to Germany. I was asked if I would help Monzel a bit as he didn't speak a word of English. Only too happy to meet someone who was worse off than myself, I set out for the officer's mess.

Major Monzel was expecting me. 'Heil Hitler,' he said. '*Falsch* (wrong),' I replied, 'I'm not that sort of a German'. The Major looked over his right shoulder, then his left. Nobody was listening. 'I'm sorry' he announced, 'neither am I, but you know what it's like – I have to keep my job in the German Army'.

I looked him over. He was wearing a dark blue suit of uncertain vintage. It was a little tight; something which would improve after a few weeks of British Army food. The sleeves and trousers were on the short side. Later I discovered that he had also brought a bowler hat,

1923 model, and an umbrella, as he had heard that officers in England wore civilian clothes a great deal of the time.

After a few weeks I encountered Major Mozel on his solitary evening stroll. He was glad to see me. He had seen a number of interesting and puzzling things. But what puzzled him most was the attitude of these English officers towards soldiering. 'They aren't taking it seriously at all,' he confided, 'they never do any work but play all the time. Good God, to them, polo or cricket or hunting is more important than duty. That's where the German Army is different, we're all experts'.

Another month later he called on me with the request that I should write a farewell speech for him. He would be leaving in a couple of days and wanted to thank his hosts for their kindness. Speeches, I explained weren't customary in England on such occasions. He wanted to make one just the same. So, I agreed to draft it. He had something on his mind and I managed to extract it. He felt that he had been wrong in his judgement of British Officers.

'Perhaps these Englishmen are far wiser than I thought,' he opined. 'Yes, we in the German Army work more and harder. At the beginning I felt that the British would make a poor opponent in a war. Now, I'm beginning to wonder. We've worked so hard that we are tired. These men here are just playing at soldiering, but they enjoy it. Maybe, if war came they would have the great advantage of being fresh and enthusiastic while we would be "*pfichtgetreu*" – faithful to our duty – and tired.'

I told him that I hoped that he was right. I wanted to see Hitler defeated. He said nothing to that but stood there a minute and then left, reminding me to write his speech. He never got it. Someone saw it after I had concocted it and accused me of the most cold-blooded brutality for wanting to expose Major Monzel to much ridicule before British officers. Monzel would certainly have made a fool of himself if he had read it, not more so, though, than when he had Heil-Hitlered me amongst the lovely hills of Hampshire.

As for his hosts, the 9th Lancers, he may well have come across them again. They were part of that ill-fated British Expeditionary Force which ended up on the beaches of Dunkirk. He may even have met them again later, in Africa. They made quite a comeback when the German Army was beginning to 'feel very tired.'

# LEARNING THE ROPES

THOSE DAYS AT TIDWORTH, when I seemed between lives, were also days of emotional stocktaking. I knew where I had been, but I did not know where I was going.

My stormy transfer from an artificially carefree life in the very troubled world of Nazi Germany to the serene atmosphere of a British cavalry garrison headquarters seemed to me to have been like a lucky jump, without a parachute, from an aeroplane which was about to crash not knowing what might happen on impact.

What I felt was by no means regret over leaving the land from which most of my forefathers had not in any case come, but sorrow over the end of my marriage, or my life, with Maditta.

This period of introspection was terminated when Humphrey Sykes offered me a job[1]. He had invested money – far too much – in a development scheme at Cape Canaveral in Florida. Materials needed to be sourced from England and Humphrey required a selection of contacts with suitable suppliers. I was hired to make those selections and having a job enabled me to move into a pleasant boarding house in Earls Court, London. From the sale of the Graham Page I had also been able to pay back the loans Humphrey had advanced to me.

I immediately purchased those items that I considered were necessary to distinguish myself as a business executive, such as an umbrella and briefcase, but I balked at the bowler hat – into which I am convinced one has to be born. At the same time, I bade an almost tearful farewell to certain rather colourful continental items of clothing that I could not possibly have worn around the City of London in 1937.

My disguise was convincing. Soon after acquiring my new attire I was returning by train from a weekend at Tidworth when two sedate looking young gentlemen boarded and entered my compartment. Having looked me over – most of me was hidden behind *The Times* –

they decided that anything so British-looking would not understand a foreign language and they began speaking in German.

One of them was obviously Dutch, the other English. I found their conversation fascinating. They were homosexuals and they were re-living their lovely weekend in much detail. I got a touching picture of the technical and emotional aspects of their relationship, plus some interesting information on members of their sect who happened to live in Germany.

When we pulled into Waterloo station, I lowered *The Times* and asked, in German, for the best way to Piccadilly. One of them, the Dutchman, took off like a flash, the Englishman however walked along the platform with me. I had, he supposed, overheard their conversation? I had. I would not, he hoped, make any use of the names of their German friends? (Homosexuality was a crime in Nazi Germany, and German tennis ace, Gottfried von Cramm, was serving a year in jail at the time having been found guilty of such an offence.)

All the time I was learning – and I loved it – about British business and the men in it, about the people in the pubs and nightclubs, about British decency and neighbourliness, and about the greatest of British traits – the understatement!

I relate here a particularly good example of the last mentioned.

I spent a weekend with a friend at a flying-club. We drank a great deal of beer and I got to know the man who was the secretary of the club. One Sunday morning I took my hangover for a walk and ran into him. Would I like to do a little flying with him? I certainly would.

As we were walking towards a Tiger Moth, I asked him how much flying he had done? 'Eighteen hours solo,' he told me. Not much, I thought, but enough for a harmless circuit over the aerodrome. We had been flying for ten minutes when his voice came over the intercom: 'I say, old boy, do you mind if I try a loop?' We were 2,000 feet up, without a ladder. I gulped. 'Of course not,' I replied, 'please do.' For the next five minutes, while we climbed to 5,000 feet, my life passed before my eyes in the proverbial manner. Then I heard him say, 'Here we go!' We went. There was the sky where the earth ought to have been and ground where I expected to see clouds. He did half a dozen loops and a spin before making a perfect landing. The only thing that had been trying was the understatement.

Back in London, my boarding house, the Raeburn Club, turned out to be a winner. It was full of amusing people and was run by a man called Dudley Hodgeson who became a close friend during our joint pursuit of a lovely Swedish girl named Marianne Cornelius. She had been sent to the Raeburn by a friend of Dudley's and loved the place, although she could have afforded to stay at the Savoy.

Dudley and I had simultaneously become infatuated with the lady. She wanted some excitement, so we took her night clubbing every night. Dudley and I always said goodnight to her at her bedroom door. Feeling more and more exhausted – physically and financially – and getting nowhere – except in each other's way. Dudley, whose working hours were more regular than mine, finally conceded. The next night, Marianne and I went out alone, returning in the early hours. I was invited into her room.

I finally held her in my arms. Then the telephone rang. No, it wasn't Dudley, it was Marianne's mother calling from Sweden. When the call finished, everything that had risen to the occasion had irretrievably fallen down on the job. I slunk off to my lonely digs and the following night Dudley was 'in'.

Soon afterwards however Marianne's even more beautiful seventeen-year-old sister turned up and we four – Marianne with Dudley and me with Ulla – went to Paris for the weekend. The price was something like £13 for the round trip including the sleeper train and a night in a nice hotel. Unfortunately, Ulla became pregnant immediately and returned to Sweden for operational reasons, followed soon after by Marianne – Dudley and I were glad to be able to 'rest up'.

My love life became intolerably dull, being limited, I don't remember why, to a member of the Jewish faith who was married to someone in the garment trade. I was in love with Maditta. I met a well-known lady expert on contraception[2] at a cocktail party and asked her, as a poor conversation piece, about the safest method for preventing pregnancy. 'Young man,' she said, audible for miles, 'you must wear a preservative and use one of my cubes. You must practice coitus interruptus and drink a glass of water.' 'A glass of water?' I wanted to know 'when? Before or after?' 'Instead, you fool, instead,' she thundered as she left me standing there, looking every inch a fool and red in the face. I realised then that cocktail party conversations are an art.

**NOTES:**

1. The Canaveral Land Corporation of Cocoa, Florida.

2. Dr Violet Randall.

# INSULTING THE FUEHRER

EARLY IN 1938 HUMPHREY SYKES got stuck with a sandpit. It was the only tangible thing he managed to extract from the assets of a bankrupt cousin to whom he had lent money. A few days before Humphrey was due to leave for Cape Canaveral he handed me a map with a cross marking the location of the sandpit and said, 'I think it isn't much more than a hole in the ground. You had better find out if we ought to fill that in or dig deeper ... and you had better become a director of the company'.[1]

For the lack of something better to do I consulted an encyclopaedia. Under 'sand' I made a startling discovery – it was not only used for making mortar and pits in children's playgrounds, it was also used for making glass. There was a glass industry in England, according to the encyclopaedia, which obtained its sand supplies from Belgium and Holland where the right kind of sand was lying about the beaches.

At that point I stopped reading and started thinking. If war came, and I was sure it would, those sand supplies from the continent would surely be cut off. If any of the sand in our hole in the ground could be used for glassmaking we were in business. An analysis proved that it could be used after some rather expensive treatment, so we started pestering the bottle makers for contracts. They told us to go home as the continental sand was much cheaper, and better. War? There wasn't going to be one. However, we got into our stride and when things began to look black in 1939, our hole in the ground became quite a busy place.

There then arrived a letter from Sykes who was busy making big deals in Florida, telling me that his American friends were offering me a job over there and that they were expecting me to arrive sometime during 1939. Humphrey however had some misgivings with regard to my German nationality, there was going to be some considerable involvement of the US Government in Canaveral and Humphrey felt it best that I did not turn up there as a German! I had already tried, and failed, to find some trace of my father's British citizenship; although I did discover he and my mother had been married in England.

'You will be better off as a stateless person,' said Humphrey in his letter, 'and I have found out that there is a way to accelerate the cancellation of your German citizenship. You can, so I am told, work it by abusing the German Government on German soil. In other words, go and insult Hitler in the German Embassy in London. But you'd better contact … first, he's a high-ranking official in Scotland Yard and is a good friend of mine. Perhaps he'll take the necessary steps to prevent the Germans from becoming a nuisance.'

Up until that time I had heard nothing about the loss of my German citizenship from Germany, although this would certainly follow in the case of anyone who had 'quit' the Third Reich under a self-made cloud. However, there were so many of us the *Reichsanzeiger* (the official gazette) was lagging behind in publishing names – a necessary pre-requisite for being '*ausgebuergert*' (de-citizenized.)

I had heard from a lawyer friend in Germany that all my traceable assets had been confiscated and that the money my father had left to me in trust had been blocked. That money vanished together with the executor, a Jewish Berlin lawyer. No trace was ever found of either him or the capital, consequently my debts exceeded my assets. I could not have cared less. (Many years later Maditta told me that she had been forced to pay some of my debts, but it was really her father the Baron's money and she considered the losses to be a minor evil in the face of everything else that had been done to us.)

My lawyer also warned that I would be declared, 'Hostile to, and an enemy of, the National Socialist German Reich' – a bad blow which I would manage to overcome.

So, Sykes' 'abusive' scheme was to be put in operation. The Scotland Yard man opined that I wouldn't need his help, 'After all,' he explained, 'they could hardly spirit you out of the German Embassy and England.' As a matter of fact, the whole thing went off very nicely.

I went to Ribbentrop's Embassy in Carlton Terrace and demanded to see the Chief of the Passport Section. I believe his name was Dr Kraft. I had to convince a receptionist of the highly important and confidential nature of my business before I was allowed to enter the office of the Herr Doctor.

Adolf 's portrait was hanging over a huge desk in the large and exquisitely furnished office. Kraft was a man in his late forties with a duelling scar[2] across his face and he had a typical Prussian square skull.

'Heil Hitler,' he said.

'*Quatsch*' (best translated as bullshit) said I. Lord Birkenhead had put it more elegantly by calling it 'plural, and they bounce.' Kraft thought he hadn't heard right. I didn't repeat myself but said: 'Don't you Heil Hitler me. I'll tell you what I think of your blasted Fuehrer'.

Kraft was absolutely speechless. His face was turning purple and he displayed a very nasty expression while I rattled off a list of adjectives for his Fuehrer – all of which are unprintable.

As the Fuehrer looked down on his faithful servant, I gave the thing a finishing touch. I walked around Kraft and spat in Adolf's face. '*Nazi Schwein*' I said, running out of adjectives and imagination. I then got out of there fast. Kraft hadn't said a single word but now he started shouting, 'Stay here – *dableiben*! (you, come back here!)' – I could hear him roar as I reached sunlit Carlton Terrace. Oddly enough, a police constable on the opposite pavement, upon sighting me, turned on his heel and went 'off' like Ogden Nash's Glow-worm, 'to an appointment in somebody's ointment', now that he was not needed in Dr Kraft's!

The scheme worked. Forty-eight hours later I received a registered letter from the German Embassy. It said: 'You are deprived of your German citizenship with immediate effect. Your passport is confiscated. You will return it to this office forthwith'. I reported the matter to the British Home Office and on 12 May 1938, the *Reichsanzeiger* published my name as that of an individual, 'Hostile to, and an enemy of, the National Socialist German Reich.'

## NOTES:

1. Ace Sand & Gravel Company Ltd of West Malling, Kent.

2. A duelling scar or 'bragging scar' was seen amongst upper-class Germans and Austrians, especially those involved in academic fencing, as being a 'badge of honour' that emphasized one's class and status in society. German military laws permitted men to wage duels of honour until World War I, and in 1933 the Nazis legalized the practice once more.

# THE IMPRESARIO

THE HOME OFFICE SUPPLIED ME WITH a harmonica-like
structure document entitled, 'Certificate of Identity' in lieu of a
passport. It was not a very satisfactory document and I needed a visa for
every country I wanted to visit. Switzerland even required a deposit of
£100 before they would issue a visa.

The certificate gave me a feeling of being a second-class human being
every time I crossed a border and there was always a great deal of
questioning about the length of my proposed stay. No country was in
the least bit ready to admit someone they could not get rid of, if ever
that person chose to stay. I could not, of course, be deported to my own
country, since I didn't have one.

The Home Office never admitted that I was 'stateless'. Later, when I
joined the Army, it turned out that the War Office, for reasons on which
I will elaborate, did. Whenever I registered at hotels during the war, I
ought to have put 'German' in the 'nationality' column although I wore
the King's uniform, I didn't. I put 'stateless'. However, a friend of mine,
who was in exactly the same position, did enter 'German' on his
registration form in an Edinburgh Hotel. The ancient porter, who had
probably returned to his desk from retirement when war broke out,
looked at this for a moment. 'Just one minute, Sir', he said. The young
corporal sat down and waited. A short time later, the riot squad arrived
and arrested him. The old porter had 'phoned them with the startling
news that a German soldier had just registered, and they came to grab
the spy.

Of course, when I had called on Dr Kraft in 1938, I did not think of
myself as a British soldier. I was thinking only of a journey to sunny
Florida and a job at Cape Canaveral. Once there, I thought, I would
apply for American citizenship and, when war came, I would be
assigned to something where I could use what I had learned. I was,
quite utterly, wrong.

Two events occurred at this point which constitute indelible and treasured memories. I became a theatrical producer briefly and, in so doing, met the most enchanting person ever. I should have hung on to her and didnt, which ranks me high amongst the proverbial fools born every minute.

Humphrey had a cousin, the Honorable Jock Skeffington[1], later Lord Massereene and Ferrard, to whom he had lent money that was never to be repaid (this was the incident that had resulted in the take-over of the sand-pit). Skeffington was stony broke and one day I was having lunch with Humphrey and found him distraught. He told me 'Cousin Jock' – Humphrey's mother, Lady Constance, and Skeffington's father were brother and sister – 'needed more money'. He had bought the English performing rights, for an operetta by Hungarian composer Emmerich Kálmán. The operetta was called *Countess Maritza*. It was, so Skeffington had been assured, a huge success on the continent of Europe.

Not many people in England, so it seemed, knew that this was, indeed, one of the most beautiful operettas of all times – household word, ever-green, call it what you like.

To Skeffington, it was 'a thing to do'. To Humphrey it had become, of necessity, a cause worthy of salvation. Skeffington, the worst stutterer I had ever encountered, had also assured Humphrey that to drop his option on *Maritza* would be tantamount to 'killling the goose that would lay the golden egg.'

There was some sort of deadline on the day when I was lunching at the Landsdowne Club[2] in Mayfair with Humphrey, for Skeffington to exercise his option – and somewhere, some bank manager was deciding at that very moment whether the Sykes/Skeffington combine was worthy of additional credit. I remember Humphrey trotting out a chessboard and offering to teach me the game while we waited for the good word. Then the bank called. Humphrey could have £5,000 more as an overdraft, 'If he would put all his assets in hock'. He did, and we had *Countess Maritza*. More precisely, since Humphrey's presence was urgently required in Florida, *Maritza* was mine!

Skeffington had already put together some sort of a ghastly mess that he insisted on calling a 'production' of the operetta. He had also leased London's outstanding house, the Palace Theatre. Question for Wolfe Frank, the English theatre's latest tycoon: 'Would it succeed?'

Answer from Wolfe Frank, the uninitiated amateur producer, after seeing the try-out in the provinces: 'No, certainly not'. For the benefit of the do-it-yourself potential producer I will spell out why I reached that conclusion.

It was in fact, spelled out for me by a good friend, England's great singing star, Evelyn Laye, who came to Birmingham with her husband Frank Lawton to see *Maritza* on tour. 'Darling,' she said, 'whoever put this together ought to be shot'. I agreed entirely.

The bad things in the show outnumbered the good overpoweringly. Lucie Mannheim, a brilliant dramatic German actress was the leading lady. She could not sing and did not try – she 'spoke' Kálmán's music. Her leading man had a great voice, but he couldn't have acted his way out of a paper bag. The libretto was ghastly and devoid of any humour. Douglas Byng and Shaun Glenville, two of England's best-known comedians, were as funny as a clown without make-up. The orchestra sounded anaemic and played Kálmán's fiery, Hungarian music like a minuet by Boccherini.

For a bunch of top-notch professionals, their imitation of a local amateur drama group was startlingly realistic. The man 'who ought to be shot' had, indeed, earned his verdict. Since I could not shoot him, I fired him that evening, after the show. I then spent the rest of the night talking to every member of the cast. They all knew, and admitted, that this pre-congenitally malformed *Maritza* could not be allowed into the Palace. Everybody, that is, except Miss Mannheim. Our verbal battle was endless, heated, emotional, full of theatricals and pointless We sat in her airless dressing room, terribly brightly lit by high-powered, naked bulbs and we went round in circles, until Lucie threatened to have me thrown to a past husband of hers, a German director called Jurgen Fehling, who had become a high-ranking SS Officer in Germany – Lucie's premature desire for 'Wiedergutmachung' (restitution) was a trifle illogical – 'SS Officer in Germany downs escaped enemy of Reich on behalf of Jewish actress?' was hardly plausible I thought! My late-night animosity towards our 'star' hardened, as did her appearance, in view of its considerable mileage and the bright lights. She was disintegrating rapidly at the expense of any charm she might have had.

Claiming some interest in her career as a dramatic actress in England, I explained that everybody's notices would go up on the board here and now unless she relinquished the lead in *Maritza.* Finally, in the early hours of the morning, she exited in the footsteps of our so-called producer. The final scene of her departure was proof of her great talent as a dramatic actress, as were her many successes in London's theatre later on.

*Countess Maritza* was re-vamped, rewritten and re-cast. Mara Loseff, Richard Tauber's 'nth' wife, became the lead. John Garrick remained in the cast and Tauber, while cajoling his wife into some sort of an acting performance, propelled Garrick along with it.

The script was redone and Byng and Glenville became very funny. The orchestra was taken over by Walter Goehr and the music sounded beautiful. Someone was directing it all but I cannot, now, remember who. I do remember though, that during the dress rehearsal, I felt a. great thrill because we had a beautiful show and I felt certain that it would be a hit.

The opening night at the Palace had the audience on its feet. We lost count of the curtain calls.

The notices next morning were ghastly. *Maritza* closed after eleven weeks. Kálmán himself had been there for the premiere and had predicted success. He came up with a truly constructive explanation for our misfortune: 'London,' he said, 'was not yet ready for *Maritza.*' During the many times I went back to see the show I vainly tried to detect the cause of our failure. I couldn't. Of course, people are ruthlessly dishonest when they talk about a show to somebody who is involved in it, and nobody failed to bemoan the injustice of the critics in the face of a performance which could have given boundless joy to thousands had it been kept alive until it made it over the hump.

However, the Sykes/Skeffington/Frank consortium decided not to provide the crutches. We closed with a very minor deficit, probably only because the accommodating bank manager had had so many free tickets. My personal feeling of frustration, in any event, was not permitted to last. There was one feature in the Palace production of *Maritza* that had made my investigative attendances sheer pleasure. She danced and sang her way through the show with tremendous charm and talent, looking young and crisp and golden and very, very sexy – her name was Patricia Leonard[3]. She was also, fortunately, unattached.

It was love at first sight, for both of us. It was also the marvellous experience of an old-fashioned courtship, which lasted for some weeks, before we became lovers.

In our case, at the end of one particularly enchanting evening, Pat and I returned to my Earls Court haunt hand-in-hand. We kissed long and passionately and then, suddenly, Pat stood before me, very naked and very beautiful, with skin like gold. Smiling, she raised her arms and said: 'Do you like my body?' It was a safe question to ask. Pat had the most perfect body I have ever seen or held in my arms and she knew it, of course. She was not tall and would not have made it as a Hefner bunny. However, she had a dancer's body and moved beautifully and her mouth was sensuous and perfectly shaped. Her blonde hair was long and lovely and her voice was unusually low – and always a little hoarse – which made her singing something out-of-this-world.

Because of our long, gentle courtship, we were mentally and

emotionally completely adjusted to each other and it was no wonder, then, that our lovemaking was of immediate perfection. Neither of us, so we discovered, had known love like this before and it is only through intensive auto-suggestion that I have persuaded myself that some moments, afterwards, have ever been as good.

## NOTES:

1. John Clotworthy Talbot Foster Whyte-Melville-Skeffington, 13th Viscount Massereene and 6th Viscount Ferrard (1914–1992) was a politician and landowner. He succeeded his father in 1956 and regularly attended the House of Lords.

2. The Lansdowne Club is a private London club that was established in 1935. It is located in Berkeley Square.

3. Patricia Leonard was born in Fulham on 9 November 1914. Her father, Theodore, was an actor from South Africa and her mother, Elena, was a well-known opera singer from Australia. Patricia was a starlet at seventeen and became a leading lady in many West End productions in the 1930s and during the war years including *Hi Diddle Diddle* (1935), *Red Peppers* (1938), *A ship at Bay* (1939), *The Little Dog Laughed* (1939), *Scoop* (1942) and *I See a Dark Stranger* (1946). Soon after the war she married the noted American philanthropist Francis Francis, heir to the Standard Oil fortune. The couple purchased Bird Cay, one of the Berry Islands, and transformed it into 'one of the most developed islands of the Bahamas'. They also had a home on Lake Geneva. Patricia retired from the stage in the late 1940s to raise a family and devoted much of her time to animal and children's charities. She died in 2008, aged ninety-three, at her son's home in Switzerland (see photograph at Plate 22).

# THE JOLLY BOATMAN

MOST OF THE FRIENDS PAT AND I HAD during this period were involved in the theatre and included stars and starving kids alike. We saw all the shows, went to all the clubs and we ate, it seems, in all the restaurants in the West End.

The sandpit was paying me a reasonable salary, the Canaveral project contributed a little more. Also, Humphrey had acquired a small furniture factory in the East End of London that he christened the Cygnet Furniture Company – because the Sykes' family crest included such a bird. The managing director left when Humphrey bought out the owner.

I know not why Sykes wanted to make furniture, nevertheless he appointed me managing director of this company also. The sales manager was an unforgettable cockney character, Dennis Blakely, who was completely bald at the age of twenty-six and he wore a red wig that must have come from Woolworths. He frequently found the wig bothersome and shoved it to the back of his head like a gangster would wear a hat in a bad movie.

I moved from Earls Court to Dolphin Square[1], a new and well-conceived block of flats in Westminster. I furnished my new abode with Cygnet's best furniture and used it as a showroom. It was this flat that I lent to my old friend Alice Goldstern when she fled from Munich. Tragically she was killed there during a German air raid on London.

Dolphin Square had one of the finest sports centres I had seen. So, every morning at a quarter to eight I would take the lift down and do twenty minutes of exercises in the gymnasium, followed by half-an-hour's squash and a swim. This I did no matter how late or how drunk I had gone to bed. By the time I hit the pool I was sober and any hangover had gone. Pat and I would then eat a huge breakfast and I would be in my office by 10.00 hours – which was quite early enough for London.

Much to my regret, Pat and I never managed to live together. She had a pretty autocratic mother, a retired singing teacher, and a nosy brother whom I got off our backs by employing him at Cygnet as a salesman.

Mum however had to be lied to when her darling daughter wanted to stay away for the night, and we came up with some priceless stories. Strangely enough, mother Leonard never objected when we went on holiday together, but the odd night in London had to be camouflaged.

By this time, I owned a boat that, after renovation work, Pat and I set sail in, or rather cranked up the engine of, for the first time at Easter 1938. As Pat was unpacking crockery below deck, I approached my first Thames river lock, near Maidenhead. I had never driven a boat before and put it into reverse far too late. I hit the far gate of the lock, which was of course closed, with a tremendous wallop and the tinkling of breaking china and glass from below deck went on for an unreasonably long period – rather like a sound effect on a radio comedy show.

Twenty-four years later I entered Boulters Lock again, this time with a chartered cruiser. The lockkeeper stared at me, then walked off to operate the gates. He came back, stared some more, scratched his head and said: 'Wuurrent you the Gentleman who troyed to knock me gate down a while back?' 'I wurr,' I replied. Clearly an impression made with a bang appears to be a lasting one – Confucius, he say.

We made some lovely trips on that old boat. It slept four and we had the most enjoyable company. One particularly memorable excursion took us down the Kennet-Avon Canal from Reading to Bristol. The canal, though no longer used by freight barges, had to be kept in navigable condition because of an ancient piece of legislation.

There were four of us aboard, Pat and I plus Hugo Rignold[2], who was the then musical director of the London Casino, and his exceedingly glamorous girlfriend (and later his wife) Phyllis Stanley who had played the leading nun in Reinhardt's *The Miracle* and was then an up-coming star under Charles Cochrane, the famous London producer of musicals. Phyllis called the much-shorter Hugo 'The Woozle' and their nightly activities in the forward cabin made almost as much of a bang as my collision with the lock gate.

It took us twelve days to make the 105-mile journey and we were hanging over the stern of the boat most of the way cutting off the weeds which were wrapping themselves around the propeller. When we arrived at a spot a few miles before Bristol, where I had arranged to meet a pilot who would take us across the mouth of the River Severn and up-river, Phyllis and the Woozle returned to London and another friend of ours was due to join us. I was to pick him up at Bristol station at 01.50 hours, but when I tried to start the car I had rented I found the battery was flat. The village was sleeping peacefully and I was reluctant to disturb anyone.

Looking around I spotted a light in a railway signal box and clambered up the stairs. The lone occupant who was making tea greeted me without surprise. I explained my predicament – there was this friend coming down from Gloucester on the night express and he expected to see me at the station. He didn't know where the boat was moored. Was there a way to get a message to him on arrival at Bristol? 'Before we go into that you'd better have a cup of tea' said the signalman 'aye – there'll be something we can do. No hurry, though. Train'll not be here for forty minutes'.

He poured me a cup of strong, sweet tea from an enamel can on the stove. 'I reckon your friend can get off right here', he said. And when the express approached half an hour later he set the signal for his sector at 'closed'. The train stopped. I got aboard and quickly discovered my friend in a first class compartment. A few seconds later we were off the train and the signal went up. My tea-making friend refused a tip. 'I like to do things for people.' he said. 'Have another cup of tea'.

They liked to do things for each other in England then, and what a change that was from Germany where people were busy doing things against each other most of the time!

One wonderful aspect about Pat's and my relationship was that there was no jealousy – we were simply too close for that.

There had been one rather surprising incident at the Cafe de Paris when a hop-headed Swedish nightclub singer, Inga Andersen[3], made a rather obvious pass at me. Pat accompanied her to the ladies' room and poured a lot of cold water over her head to stop her from 'getting too hot about Wolfe'. I never saw the doused Miss Andersen again.

When Pat was in a show I saw a lot of the actor Ferdy Mayne[4], and his several girl friends. In fact, his charmingly dynamic activities in that area earned him the nickname of 'The West End Stallion' and I have sworn statements that he deserved it. My nickname was 'Big Bad Wolf'.

**NOTES:**

1. Dolphin Square is a block of luxury flats, favoured by members of both Houses of Parliament and the Gentry, which were built between 1935-1937 near the River Thames in Pimlico.

2. Hugo Henry Rignold (1905–1976) was an English conductor and violinist, who is best remembered as having been Musical Director of the Royal Ballet and conductor of the City of Birmingham Symphony Orchestra.

3. Known during the Second World War as 'The Blackout Girl', Inga Andersen was a Canadian actress and singer who entertained troops in Italy and was known as 'Hildegarde of England'. She was also a record-holding speed skater, and an accomplished violinist.

4. Born Ferdinand Philip Mayer-Hocrckel in Mainz in 1916, Ferdy Mayne appeared in over 230 films and countless West End productions.

# GATHERING STORM CLOUDS

TIME WAS MOVING FAST, as it always does when life is full of joy and worry free. Then, in the autumn of 1938, came the Czechoslovakian crisis[1] and my first performance as a simultaneous interpreter – I translated one of Hitler's maddest radio speeches for a group of friends. We dispersed, shattered, to burn the candle at both ends before disaster struck.

In February 1939, I made one last pre-war skiing trip to Davos[2] and, on the last day, I skied the whole of the ten miles downhill from the mountain's top to the station to catch the train back to England. It was a glorious winter morning and fresh snow had fallen during the night.

The world was white and blue and golden. I stopped in the sun for a while and, leaning on my poles, I let my eyes wander over the endless ranges of the Alps.

Not fifty miles away was the German border. As I stood there, breathing it all in, I had a strong premonition that I would not see this beautiful picture again for a long time. It seemed unbelievable to me that men behind that border were planning war and destruction. There are moments in life one will always remember very clearly – that was one of them for me.

I thought long and seriously about freedom and decency and how fortunate I had been. I pictured England at war and thought of the friends I had left behind in Germany, who were now in German uniforms, and I sought to visualize the long, long road to victory. I thought about myself and I knew that I wanted to be in that war and yet had no idea how it would be done. To the British authorities I was a former German. What would I be allowed to do in this war to come? Would I be interned? Surely, with my political past and my father's citizenship, which would have to be unearthed, this could be avoided.

During the train journey back to England I made plans to get into the British Army there and then. On my return I began to pull strings. The answer was utterly discouraging in every instance. It ranged from the reply that, 'I was being silly since there would be no war', to the statement that, 'once a German always a German and I had no business trying to get into the British Army'. There were 40,000 similarly placed Austrians and Germans in England at that time, all of who shared my status.

Towards the middle of August 1939, I walked into the War Office and began asking where an alien could enlist in the British Forces. After wandering around the building for some time I reached a backroom where an official produced a form that, he thought, might apply to a case like mine. I filled in the form. It was the only form I have ever completed in England that didn't, at some time or another, catch up with me again. It probably ended up in the wastepaper basket.

I called on the officer in Scotland Yard who knew me as the, 'Hitler-abusing friend of Humphrey Sykes'. I wanted to know if I would be interned. No, he thought, certainly not. 'Scotland Yard,' he explained, 'had all enemy aliens well taped'. There were no arrangements to intern anybody if war were to break out, and more useful information could be gathered by watching us whilst we were free – and anyway Scotland Yard had my dossier and I would be the last to be affected even if internment were to come.

A few days after war was declared on 3 September 1939, the orders affecting 'enemy aliens' were published. All would have to go before Aliens Tribunals[3] who would base their decisions on the police file, a personal statement and a testimony by sponsors who had to be British.

There were three categories of Enemy Alien – A, B and C.

Category A meant immediate internment.

Category B placed restrictions on movements and required regular reporting to the police.

Category C (friendly enemy alien) meant no restrictions except notification of address.

In October 1939 I went before such a tribunal and was classified as being Category 'C'. I continued running the two companies for Sykes but the job in Florida was now out of reach, as I could no longer leave England.

A friend of mine from Munich, Wolfgang Schlittgen, was far less lucky than I, and his story is so weird that it must be told. I had known Wolfgang in Munich for years. His appearance indicated that he was Jewish, but he was pure Aryan. One day, in 1935, he and a friend had taken their girlfriends to lunch in a restaurant near Munich. There was a table with SA men – storm-troopers – who kept glancing in their direction. When the group left the restaurant the SA men had beaten the hell out of Wolfgang, in order to, 'teach him, the bloody Jew, to lay off running around with German girls'.

Wolfgang decided something had to be done. He had heard of a Nazi organization which could be joined and would issue a membership card, to be shown if such an incident threatened to re-occur. Wolfgang, having obtained his *'Ariernachweis'* (documentation establishing his pure-bloodedness) joined what turned out to be the motoring section of the SS. He got his membership card and forgot about the whole thing. Then he began to get instructions to report for drill, which he ignored. An officer called and told him he had better show up – he ignored that too. The officer came back. There would be a special parade the following Sunday. Herr Schlittgen was to be there, in SS uniform, or there would be disciplinary action. There might even be concentration camp detention. Wolfgang borrowed a uniform and got drunk. Then he staggered on parade and ruined the whole thing. When he was marched before an officer and severely reprimanded, he invited the officer to 'kiss his arse'.

When he sobered up he very wisely left the country and went to England. There he made a lot of friends and dined out on his story which was considered to be extremely funny by everybody who heard it. We all knew that Wolfgang had been a bit of a fool but was certainly anti-Nazi. When he appeared before his tribunal with his friends however he was asked: 'Were you ever a member of a Nazi organisation?' 'I was, on paper' admitted Wolfgang, and went on to tell his story. 'Too bad' said the tribunal chairman, 'to us you were an SS man, Category A' and Wolfgang went straight 'inside'.

He went to Liverpool and embarked on the *Andorra Star* that was sunk by a German torpedo. He drifted in the water for seven hours and was then shipped off to Australia and an internment camp. There he stayed, felling trees and building roads for almost six years. He came back in late 1945, feeling, understandably, lost and bitter. Subsequently, to round off the tale, HM Government bestowed British Citizenship upon him.

**NOTES:**

1. The German occupation of Czechoslovakia began in 1938 with the invasion of the Sudetenland, the former German-Austria border regions.

2. Davos, an Alpine town in Switzerland, was Wolfe Frank's favourite place. He loved skiing and visited Davos often over much of his lifetime. He eventually

had homes there and hoped that would be where his ashes would be scattered.

3. Aliens Tribunals were set up in September 1939 to make certain that no one who ought to be interned remained free. They also dealt with the proper disposal of all aliens whose activities, status, general character and disposition towards this country were investigated.

# ARREST AND INTERNMENT

BESIDES LIVING VARIOUSLY AT MY LONDON APARTMENT and on my boat on the Thames I also rented a large property, known as 'The House on the Creek' in Maidenhead where Pat and I often stayed until Maidenhead was declared a 'protected area in which enemy aliens, even friendly ones, were not allowed to reside'. I had been keeping my boat nearby, so I loaded my two radio sets and my bicycle onto the boat whilst a friend, Jimmy Harwood, drove my car to the White Hart Hotel at Sonning on Thames, a few miles up-river and out of the 'protected area.'

Our timing was quite perfect. I tied up my boat and Jimmy arrived a few minutes before opening time. 'Two pink gins' we said.

'This is the six-o'clock news.' crackled a voice on the radio over the bar. 'With immediate effect enemy aliens are prohibited from owning or using motorcars, boats, bicycles and radio sets.'

'Ch ... ch ... cheers' said Jimmy 'I suppose you'll be allowed to keep your shoes on.'

To do justice to the Chief Constable of Berkshire, it must be said that I applied for and was granted an exemption from that order.

Five weeks later however, on the glorious, beautiful morning of 26 June 1940, I emerged from my bath whistling and ready to travel to London for lunch with a particularly nice and attractive young woman when I found two large gentlemen waiting for me in my room.

'Good morning sir,' said one. 'I suppose you know what we're here for?' I confessed I had no idea. 'We've come to detain you,' he said cheerfully.

I sat down. Then I asked a lot of questions. 'Yes,' I was told, 'every enemy alien in England was to be detained.' Did they think I would be detained for long? – 'Definitely not, only for a few days.' Could I telephone? 'No, unfortunately.' Could I take luggage? 'Certainly. But it would be silly to take too much, since I would soon be back.' I told them about my lunch date. They promised to let her know and trotted off to the telephone.

I packed as much as I could get into a fairly large suitcase and was taken in a police car to 'a secret location' – which turned out to be Wokingham Police Station – where I was put behind locked doors.

A police constable entered to enquire if I had had breakfast? I hadn't. He took some money and returned a few minutes later with a tray on which I found tea, toast, butter, marmalade and a boiled egg under an egg warmer in the shape of a chicken's head. I could not help but laugh – that egg warmer seemed to be a ludicrous touch under the circumstances.

During the hour I spent alone in that room, I took stock. I had preserved my freedom by fleeing from Germany but had lost out to the British. I had got rid of my German nationality and would remain stateless for the duration of the war, whist my naturalisation application remained suspended.

I stared at the locked door of my private suite – the way through it into the British Army looked quite impossible. The ground had, very effectively, been pulled from under my feet. I felt scared, mistreated, victimised and extremely angry. However, I also resolved that I would emerge undamaged and triumphant, in fact the victor, over all these injustices and those who created them.

Both the principle and the methods used to intern those of us who had fled from Nazi terror – whom the British had conveniently labelled 'enemy aliens' – became the subject of much criticism in England, and elsewhere. That criticism could be heard in Parliament and read about in the Press and it will always remain one of the less glorious chapters in the history of a nation that is generally so very humane; but which can, at times, also be extremely cruel.

It was foolish for anyone to expect plans to be ready for the internment of 40,000 of Hitler's arch enemies in a country which was altogether unprepared for war and did not have enough anti-aircraft guns to hold off enemy planes. It was also quite unreasonable to think that this was the way to control enemy aliens and make a Fifth Column[1] in England impossible, and to then demand the immediate internment of those aliens in order to be certain.

Those in authority should have realised much sooner than they did that the aliens were themselves enemies of the same regime the British were fighting and included amongst their number racial and political refugees many of whom had already suffered in Hitler's prisons and concentration camps. It should also have been obvious that, properly employed, we could make a considerable contribution to the war effort of a country desperately short of manpower.

Yet instead of using us to the limit, we were antagonised to the limit. For over two years, expert workers in every possible field of science and production, as well as young fighting-fit men, wasted their time behind barbed wire fences or in digging holes in the Pioneer Corps.

Much later, of course, we were allowed to do our share and not one single case became known which might have justified the ill-advised 'caution' that had been applied, and the lack of understanding and generosity continued even after we had become fully-fledged members of the British Armed Forces. We could not apply for British citizenship during the war, yet officers and men in some of the finest regiments in the British Army had earlier been classified as enemy aliens. Germans were running the risk of being taken prisoners by Germans. British medals were pinned on German chests.

Finally, at the end of the war, those who joined the armed forces were given priority for naturalisation. However, they first had to be approved by an 'Inter Service Naturalisation Board' – men who had fought in the front line for the British Army were vetted by a panel of staff officers to see if they were suitable to become British Citizens.

Seething as I was that day in June 1940 I had been re-assured by my friendly police escort that my discomfort would be all over in just a few days. My dismay only increased however as more internees began to arrive and eventually some fifteen of us were transferred to the army barracks at Reading where preparations for our arrival had not been well planned. Each man was issued with two trestles, three boards and some blankets – to be used as a bed – and it soon became clear that the Army personnel had no idea who we were, nor did they have any instructions regarding our treatment. They did not know whether we could write or receive mail or even notify family or friends as to our whereabouts.

I looked closely at the other men in the group, which had grown to over a hundred. It included all ages, from eighteen to sixty-five years. Some of the older men were sitting on their beds, head in hand, unable to grasp what had happened. Many were former inmates of Nazi concentration camps and they were unable to remain rational in the face of this renewed imprisonment after what they had already suffered.

We sat about dejectedly for the rest of the day and I eventually managed to persuade a young Private to take some of our money to the camp canteen, where he bought essentials for those who had brought none with them. The night was spent, rather uncomfortably, on wooden boards without mattresses.

Early the next morning I was called out. Humphrey Sykes, who had come back to England at the outbreak of war and had been through the Dunkirk evacuation, was waiting for me. The owner of the White Hart Hotel had kindly called our company office to tell them what had happened to me and Sykes had traced me to Reading. He knew the Commandant of the camp who gave his permission for us to meet. However, Humphrey had only bad news. He had contacted everybody he knew in an attempt to get me out but had been told 'all aliens were IN and they would stay IN.' We were given just half an hour to settle our affairs. I gave Sykes authority to process my resignation from the boards of our two companies and he left, looking dejected and guilty, uttering the most unbelievable platitude I had ever heard. 'The darkest hours,' declared Humphrey, looking every inch the priest in cavalry officer's clothing, 'are always those before the dawn', thus providing me with the first good laugh since the chicken head egg warmer incident.

That afternoon, we were transferred to a school in Southampton that had been turned into a 'Prisoner of War Camp[2]'. There were boos and hisses from the crowd as we marched into Reading Station. At Southampton our group was joined by other groups and our overall number grew to about 250.

The officers in charge of the camp were extremely kind and courteous. In a brief speech the Commandant expressed regret at our 'temporary predicament', which he indicated he felt certain would not last long. He then asked us to choose a 'camp leader' and to make our own arrangements for the carrying out of essential services such as cooking and cleaning. I volunteered to take over the kitchen since I was anxious to keep busy. During my time at that camp I started cooking breakfast at 04.30 hours and kept cooking until 18.00 hours. My helpers were detailed by the internee camp leader and changed daily.

There was nothing particularly unpleasant about that camp, except that one had to get used to being locked into a room at night with a toilet bucket and taking shelter from the occasional air attacks by the Luftwaffe. After ten days we were ordered to prepare to move. We clambered aboard a train at Southampton and immediately noticed a change of atmosphere.

From that point on we were heavily guarded. Soldiers with rifles and fixed bayonets stood on duty at each compartment door and they started fiddling with the safety catches of their weapons as soon as one of us moved. They treated us as very dangerous people and refused to tell us where we were going. In fact, whoever was commanding had read the book on rules for the transportation of 'prisoners of war.'

The train took us to the town of Bury in Lancashire where, carrying a motley collection of luggage, we were shepherded towards a tall chimney belonging to a disused factory that had been entirely surrounded with barbed wire.

Further carriages had been added to the train along its route and about 1,000 of us 'marched' through the gates of the compound, which was a disused cotton mill, that had been condemned as being unfit for production by the Ministry of Labour.

Carrying my suitcase, I began to look for a suitable place to park myself. The floors in all the factory halls were covered in grease and the glass roof with many panes missing had been painted black, presumably as an air-raid precaution. At this point, we were herded together and lined up for 'search and registration.' This entailed being taken to one of several tables manned by an NCO who took down our name, assigned us an internee number and then passed us on to a private soldier who went through our belongings and pockets with a degree of thoroughness that would put any of to-day's airport checks to shame.

Our cash, cheque books, cigarettes, cigars, drinks, medicines – in fact everything except clothing and toiletries – were impounded. (Most of our belongings were never seen again and some years after the war, the Commandant of the camp was kicked out of the Army and jailed for the theft of our belongings.)

I grabbed some boards and trestles and staked a claim to a bed space in one of the halls. There were no lights at any time during the three weeks I spent at Warth Mill Internment Camp[3].

Opposite me, about twenty Catholic priests were setting up home. I walked over to them and found them wonderfully calm and confident. Some of these 'highly learned, dangerous holy enemy aliens' stayed with me throughout my internment and I don't know what I would have done without them. Their unshakeable trust in the ways of the Lord was certainly preferable to our resentment of the treatment we were given. One of the priests, Father Aschenauer, an Austrian, provided proof of the flexibility of the Jesuit education in the form of the following limerick, which he whispered to me during one of our endless walks around the camp:

*There was a young monk from Siberia.*
*Who got wearier and wearier and wearier*
*One day with a yell he broke out of his cell*
*And eloped with the Mother Superior.*

Perhaps the Lord objected, as one night, during a terrific thunderstorm, a blocked drainpipe on the roof snapped and a large jet of water poured directly onto the group of priests. They were soaked through in seconds and the water began to rise in their section of the hall. In pitch darkness everybody was trying to help them move to a drier place. The priests took it all in excellent humour.

## NOTES:

1. A fifth column is a clandestine group of people whose objectives are to undermine a larger group from within.

2. Officially numbered 402a or C19, the PoW Camp at Southampton was one of hundreds set up throughout the UK during the Second World War.

3. Warth Mill Internment Camp, Bury, Lancashire, eventually became a PoW camp. However, it was originally a camp for enemy aliens where the conditions were every bit as harsh as Wolfe Frank describes them.

# THE CAMP LEADER

MY INITIAL ASSESSMENT WAS that there were about 2,000 of us interned at Warth Mill (1,837 as it turned out later). A collection of soya boilers in one of the halls represented our kitchen. There was a total of four – I repeat FOUR – cold water taps for washing ourselves, our laundry and kitchen utensils.

There were fifty toilet seats arranged in two rows. They faced each other and were separated by a long urinal. This 'facility' was located outside the factory and, since no one was supposed to leave the buildings after dark, guards were always on the verge of shooting a person trying to reach the toilets during the night.

Rations began to appear mysteriously, and we had to make arrangements for their preparation. We therefore formed a camp administration.

In the beginning the kitchen was manned by volunteers, but we later set up a labour office and detailed cleaning and cooking duties from a roster of all the internees.

I became the assistant to the Camp Leader, however he suffered a nervous breakdown almost immediately and I found myself running the camp. Our immediate concern, after getting the kitchen going, was to create a hospital. Somehow, we obtained a few beds, but we had no medicine, so we sent a message to the Commandant who immediately appeared on the scene.

His name was Major Braybrook and he was one of the most unpleasant Englishman I have ever encountered. He was a Military Police Corps officer who had lost an eye in the First World War and he had been a PoW in Germany. He hated all things German – and that certainly included us.

Major Braybrook had been commanding the camp for some time and before our arrival it had housed Italian internees. I discovered this when I was working in the document centre where I found tea chests filled with the Italians' personal belongings, which had been confiscated, and placed in individual sealed envelopes bearing the owner's name. Most of these envelopes however had been torn open and a collection of articles such as wristwatches, razors, prayer books, wallets and family photographs, were falling out all over the place.

'The discipline in this camp,' announced the Major 'would be strict.' To him we were PoWs and he wasn't concerned with our past history. We had better not make any trouble, or there would be plenty of trouble for us.

There was no mention of the medical supplies we had requested and running that camp under such a Commandant was far from easy. Many suffered nervous breakdowns and there were attempted suicides, threats of a rebellion and hunger strikes to deal with.

Many of Braybrook's officers however were on our side. The interpreter, Major Carstairs, did what he could for us, including obtaining some urgently needed drugs behind Braybrook's back. For our own sakes, he begged us not to make any more complaints. I remember his reasoning to this day: 'The man is a bloody sadist who revels in your sufferings.'

We managed to smuggle a telegram of protest to the International Red Cross and a representative of that organisation put in an appearance shortly afterwards. He walked all over the camp, accompanied, of course, by Braybrook and whilst we could tell that he was visibly shocked he told us there was really nothing he could do. We were not German PoWs and the British Government did not have to answer to the German Government for anything happening to us, even if that involved violations of PoW conventions. He could, he said, 'Do no more than make unofficial recommendations.'

After the Red Cross man had left, and during a meeting of all internees, a hunger strike was proposed and almost started. I got onto a table and made my first public speech, with a Sergeant sent by Braybrook listening.

'This,' I told the gathering, 'is not England. We are the victims of one man who is exploiting his temporary powers. Ways can and will be found to put things right. However, if we stage a hunger strike, it will be Braybrook who makes out the report and it will most certainly turn the authorities against us. We might not have an opportunity to state our case and we would run the risk of being regarded as a bunch of troublemakers.' I went on to suggest we should wait until the right opportunity presented itself at which time we could raise our grievances. I must have made a certain amount of sense because the idea of a hunger strike was dropped.

One of the officers came to our aid by suggesting we write a letter of complaint to the War Office – which Braybrook, under Army regulations, had to grant – we did but the result of that complaint never became known.

We were then ordered to prepare a nominal roll of all internees, to be made up by age groups: 18-25 years, 26-35 years, 36-50 years, 51-60 years and those over 60. Meanwhile Braybrook had hit upon an idea that he thought would torture us. He called us together at regular intervals to tell us of the latest successes of the Allied Forces, thinking we would hate to hear of defeats inflicted upon the Germans. He was quite surprised at the applause that greeted each of his announcements.

When the list of internees was complete, the Commandant addressed us once again. 'The War Office,' he pronounced, 'had ordered the camp to be dissolved. Some of you will be sent to Australia, some to Canada and some to the Isle of Man. Transport will be leaving, according to age groups, starting tomorrow'.

The implication of this arrangement, I realised at once, was that every family in the camp would be split up. As Camp Leader I raised this point immediately. 'That,' said the Major 'would be too bad and those are my orders.'

There were some heart-breaking scenes as we left the camp. An old blind man begged Braybrook to be allowed to stay with his son who led him about. Refused! An invalid, tears streaming down his face, implored the Commandant to let him remain with his two sons. Refused!

I stood near two of Braybrook's officers whilst this was going on. 'The bastard,' said one of them, 'he's lying about those War Office orders.'

Thank God this all ended well. There ensued the most colossal muddle in connection with the shipments to Australia and Canada. In the end, nobody went, but a lot of luggage did. It was far better to lose that than a father, or a son, and they all were reunited on the Isle of Man.

For some of us however our troubles did not cease immediately.

We were put on a train to Glasgow, transferred to buses and taken to a camp that was beautifully situated in the hills of Scotland, near Dunoon. *Glenbranter* had been a forestry camp in the grounds of a fine old country house belonging to Sir Harry Lauder, the Scottish comedian. My group reached the camp at 21.00 hours. We de-bussed and were ordered to fall into ranks of three. We remained standing there for well over an hour, in the pouring rain. Then the Commandant appeared with a group of officers, all well protected by raincoats.

He inspected us, a roll was called and finally, after another forty minutes, we were designated huts, which contained the usual boards and trestle beds with one blanket each and no mattress.

The interpreter, Captain Smith, addressed us the following morning and introduced the Commandant Major Dunne. Then came a familiar note. We were told to behave. There was a war on. We had been locked up for good reasons – and 'for the duration.' We would be alright if we kept the discipline.

We did 'keep the discipline' but we weren't alright. The food was appalling. We were refused a canteen and for weeks we were denied the right to write letters, and there was no sight of any incoming mail.

We complained to the interpreter and were immediately ordered on parade.

'You had better stop complaining if you know what's good for you,' announced Smith sardonically. 'You have every reason to be satisfied. If you were locked up in a Nazi concentration camp in your own country, you'd not be complaining. You'd be dead.' All this was said in German in case we forgot who we were, and Dunne was standing by, loving it.

This time I got good and angry. A couple of days later we were given the special notepaper we were to use for letters, and I sat down and wrote to a Member of Parliament whom I knew, Sir Thomas Moore.

'Is it necessary,' I wrote, 'that, because of the short-sightedness and ignorance of some officers, people in this camp, men who are genuine enemies and victims of the Nazi regime and true friends of this country, should be turned into embittered men and made to feel that Britain's cause is no longer theirs?' I then elaborated on the particular complaints we had.

Less than twenty-four hours later a sergeant burst into my hut. 'Frank,' he roared, 'get outside the Commandant wants to see you.' I got outside with a soldier with fixed bayonet either side of me. 'Quick march,' commanded the sergeant. I was careful not to be out of step. We went out of the gate and up to Sir Harry Lauder's family seat, Dunne was seated behind a desk.

'Are you internee number 12345, Frank?'

'Mhm,' I went.

Did you write this letter?' and he read out all of it in a voice which was growing louder.

'Definitely,' I said.

'Why do you make yourself the spokesman of a bunch of whining, complaining idiots who don't know how well-off they are?'

No answer. I stared at him.

He put down the letter and leaned forward on his desk: 'If I had my way I'd put the lot of you against the wall. You, Frank, belong in solitary confinement. What do you have to say?'

No answer. I stared at him.

'I'll tell you something Frank. I saw this letter when I censored it. You can insist on it being sent to the addressee. If you do, a copy will be sent to the War Office with my report that will show that you are a troublemaker, an anarchist. What's your decision?'

I thought things over.

I knew that my goose would be cooked if Dunne wrote such a report. It would be his word against mine and if Sir Thomas decided to act on my letter, he would draw a blank.

I picked up the letter and tore it up.

'Take him away,' ordered Dunne, looking extremely satisfied.

I returned to my hut and copied the letter (I had kept a duplicate, of course) this time onto ordinary stationery. Another inmate of the hut removed the heel from his shoe and produced a stamp and a ten-shilling note.

Late that night, I crawled up to the barbed wire. I picked a little Scotsman who was doing guard. 'Hey, Jock,' I whispered, hoping that he wouldn't shoot me immediately. Jock was a lousy soldier – he didn't shoot.

'Aye,' he said and ambled over to me.

'Listen, Jock, we're having trouble with the Commandant. Will you help us?'

'Sure,' said Jock, 'anything to get that bastard into trouble. We hate him just as much as you chaps,' and he agreed to post that letter (and to buy himself a drink with the ten shilling note).

A week later, we observed unusual goings on at the house. A number of staff cars arrived and some officers got out. Luggage was unloaded. An hour later, luggage was put into the staff cars, followed by Dunne and his staff. They didn't say goodbye!

A sergeant arrived and asked the internees to meet the new Commandant in the dining hut. He made a speech. There had been some misconception with regard to our status. We were being addressed as 'Gentlemen' and told that, due to a misinterpretation of the rules, our mail had been withheld and had accumulated in the office. It would be submitted to only the most cursory censorship before reaching us. And could we not arrange for a 'social evening', a friendly get-together that evening, to meet the new officers? We were delighted to do so.

That afternoon, our mail came down – hundreds of letters, masses of parcels, plus telegrams, announcing the births of children and the deaths of relatives. Whether or not this radical change of our treatment was due to the good offices of Sir Thomas Moore I have never been able to ascertain.

Then, once again, we were to be transferred to another camp and the circumstances were somewhat hilarious. We boarded some buses and travelled about fifty miles. The buses were late picking us up and we lost more time through breakdowns. We missed the train to Liverpool so special coaches were laid on to transport us and were parked inside the station while the officer in charge went to get new orders. It was stifling hot. We stood in that station for four hours, until 23.00 hours, when it was finally decided that we were to return to the camp. Meanwhile, the guards had been given permission to go off, in relays, for refreshments. When we finally departed most of the officers, who had been marooned for weeks in that remote camp, had made up for lost time and had got nicely stewed, including the young Scotsman in charge of the transport. We reached *Glenbranter* camp at 03.00 hours and a roll call was ordered. During my internment I had already noticed that very few NCOs in the British Army seemed to be able to count, however that morning's roll call beat anything I had known. There appeared to be three internees too many, and one guard was missing.

The puzzle was solved later in the day.

Whilst we were parked in the station, a policeman had approached the conducting office. He explained that they had arrested three young Italians that morning who had to be interned. The police wanted to get rid of them. Would it be possible to attach them to our group?

'Shertainly,' the officer had said, (he was fairly carefree by this time) 'the more the merrier'. He had stuffed the newcomers' documents into his briefcase and promptly forgotten the matter. The Italians, rather enjoying the whole thing, had kept silent and were, in any case, too tired to notice or care. The missing soldier had got very drunk and gone AWOL. I am glad to say that it was not Jock spending our ten-shilling note.

The next day we made the journey to Glasgow once again, this time without a hitch. At Liverpool we embarked for the Isle of Man, landed at Douglas and were taken by train to Peel on the west coast of the island.

By now – September 1940 – conditions had begun to improve. The Home Office had taken control of the internee administration away from the Army which remained however responsible for running and guarding the camps. Many of the Isle of Man's seaside resorts had been turned into internment camps including Douglas, Onchan, Ramsey and Peel.

Requisitioned groups of boarding houses, surrounded by barbed wire fences, were our accommodation. We were given a completely free hand in making our own arrangements inside them and we started running canteens, cafes and schools. We were even allowed to go swimming under guard and for those who wanted a job, there was agricultural work at the fabulous salary of one shilling per day.

# JOINING THE BRITISH ARMY

THE OFFICERS AT PEEL CAMP[1], headed by Commandant Major Hawkey-Shepherd, included Captain Eden, the brother of Anthony Eden[2], and they were all very good to us. I shared a room with Dr Otto Seifferta, former Austrian newspaper editor and Schuschnigg's[3] press officer. Fritz von Tschirschky, von Papen's[4] former adjutant, was our neighbour. Their conversations, or rather arguments, were on a fascinating level and I learned a great deal. Unfortunately, none of this compensated for my loss of freedom.

Mail began to catch up with us and I discovered that, at this point in time, no amount of string pulling would get me into the Army. It began to look as if I would spend the whole of the war behind barbed wire. In due course 'barbed wire sickness' set in and has been written about by men far more qualified than me, such as long-term prisoners of war.

There were, though, certain aggravating circumstances in our case. We had been interned simply because we were Austrians or German, yet we were as hostile towards Germany as the British were – even more so – and in spite of a very bad beginning and the grave injustice we were suffering we were still pro-British. In fact, we were quite fond of our jailers. Moreover, whereas a soldier accepts imprisonment as one of the dangers of war and will suffer whilst fighting for a cause – the cause of his country – we had no cause at all. In order to find a simple term to explain this confusing situation I would say that we were rotting away in those camps for absolutely nothing.

This began to eventually dawn on the British Government who, in the autumn of 1940[2], began to publish a number of directives that explained how our release might be possible. Those directives included health reasons, taking up employment in war essential industries, and the possibility of joining a special unit of the Army called the Auxiliary Military Pioneer Corps (AMPC)[5]. We discovered that those who joined the AMPC would become fully-fledged members of His Majesty's

Forces. Together with many others in Peel Camp I volunteered at once. I completed a huge form in triplicate and passed two medical examinations conducted by an internee doctor who merely asked me whether I could stand on my head. When I answered in the affirmative he rated me A1.

I was told I would be serving in some sort of labour corps, and I had no intention of remaining in it. Once out of internment, I resolved, I would continue my efforts to join a combatant unit.

On the 18 December 1940, I appeared before a recruiting officer and was sworn in. I was paid half-a-crown (twelve and a half pence in today's money) per day and I was a soldier.

The following morning the gates of the camp were opened for ten of us and we were free – or so we thought!

We got off to a nice, wrong start. Aboard the ship taking us to Liverpool we discovered that we were under escort. This made me angry and I stayed angry all the way across. At Liverpool we were received by an officer who had orders to take us to a transit barracks. I sat down on my suitcase and informed him that I wasn't going anywhere – this rather horrified my comrades.

I then informed the officer that we had been sworn in as members of HM Forces and were, as he might realise, now privates in the same army in which he was an officer. We could not therefore be internees at the same time. We had not committed a breach of any regulations, so there was no justification for an escort. If he couldn't send that escort off himself, he had better get hold of someone in authority that could.

The officer took my speech rather well and saw my point and we set off towards the barracks – not escorted, but 'guided' by a soldier who had travelled with us – where I got a look at our movement orders. These referred to us as being, 'One other rank (OR) and ten internees.'

I went on strike again and I was taken to see the officer in charge, to who I repeated my argument. He too was very sensible and not only altered the movement orders but also gave us the next twenty-four hours off; in spite of the orders stating 'confined to barracks'.

So, the time had come to mix with 'free' people again. I walked out of the barracks and into Liverpool a free man – six months had passed since the egg warmer incident in Wokingham police station.

I had wondered if it would take long to get used to that freedom. In actual fact, it took less than five minutes to return to normal; at least as far as meeting people, ordering a meal and latching on to an acquiescent young lady was concerned. Psychologically, though, the effects of spending six months behind barbed wire did not wear off for as many months.

I spent that day lunching at a hotel, going to a cinema, then to a show and finally to a dance hall where holding a girl in my arms after six months of total abstinence was a most unbalancing experience. When I finally adjourned to the apartment of the consenting, adult female I felt exceedingly nervous, but what's natural comes back naturally.

We, the latest additions to the British Army, set off for Ilfracombe in Devon the following evening. On the way to the station our party was caught up in a hell of an air raid. In those days Goering's bombers were having it all their own way and Liverpool, on 21 December 1940, experienced the worst air-raid it ever had[6]. We were hugging the buildings as shrapnel fragments flew around us and every pane of the station's glass roof was totally shattered. Since that was the first raid I had ever experienced it was all quite frightening. (Later, in London, raids became a routine affair.) Our train was four hours late when it finally steamed into Liverpool and lost another three hours on its journey to Devon.

In order to be fair to the Army I ought to describe the condition I arrived in at the Ilfracombe training centre. I had taken only one suit of clothes with me when I was arrested in June. I had slept in it for many nights at the Warth Mill and Peel internment camps and I had never quite succeeded in restoring it to its former respectable self. Over this suit I was wearing a camel hair coat and I carried a rather expensive looking rawhide suitcase.

Worst of all was the state of my hair. The camp barber at Peel had been released at a time when my haircut was already overdue. The first sergeant major to see me when I arrived at Ilfracombe nearly suffered a heart attack. 'Blimey,' he said 'wot's this? Jesus Christ,' followed by, 'haircut, you!' So, before anything else, I went off to the barber and had what is known as a 'pudding basin' – which derives its name from the legend that the barber places a pudding basin on the victim's head and cuts off all the hair showing below it. In my case the man did extremely well without the basin and I saw a stranger in the first mirror I came to.

Then I received my uniforms, two of them. We filed along a counter and picked up boots, socks, shirts, underwear, gaiters, haver-sacks and, finally, two battle blouses[7] and trousers. A corporal had a look at me and threw the garments on the counter. 'Are you sure they're my size,' I enquired naively. 'Sure I'm sure' came the reply. 'We never make mistakes'.

I had received two suits of different sizes and made of different material and for several months afterwards I had the choice of the following outfits:

1. Blouse and trousers of the same material, trousers ridiculously small, blouse too large.
2. Blouse and trousers of the same material, trousers far too large, blouse too small.
3. Blouse and trousers of different material, both far too large
4. Blouse and trousers of different material, both far too small.

We gallant fighting men of the AMPC were quite a sight, particularly if we donned our overcoats (called greatcoats) that made our resemblance to a potato sack complete.

The seven days I spent in Ilfracombe were fairly evenly divided between hanging about aimlessly, kitchen fatigue and a little foot drill. I let Hitler have it right there and then by washing, in tepid water, 4,000 tin plates in one day!

Our status was clarified a little more during those first few days. The Unit would have British officers and aliens could hold NCO ranks up to quartermaster and staff sergeant. We were to remain unarmed but would get the same amount of leave as any other soldier. However before going on leave we would be required to state the address to which we were going and, once there, report to the local police. This last regulation was soon dropped.

We moved out of Ilfracombe on the 29 December. Those seven days represented the total basic training we received. We had a vague idea of how to salute and stand to attention. As for the rest, we were terrible. We marched like no uniformed body of men had ever marched before, which must have broken the hearts of the NCOs, some of whom had actually been transferred to the AMPC from Guards regiments.

Before we departed for the station there had been a speech given by the commanding officer. We were, he told us, 'Going out to do a very special job of the very greatest importance'. This turned out to be carrying flour and potato sacks.

We were moved to Catterick[8] in Yorkshire as 240 Company, AMPC. There we were split into sections and sent off to our various duties in small detachments. My section was attached to a Company of the Royal Army Service Corps (RASC), which was operating a Command Supply Depot in West Auckland, where we got on splendidly with both officers and the rank and file. With our own officers and NCOs the situation was slightly different for several reasons.

In those days the Pioneer Corps (PC) was the most unpopular unit in the Army. Its members included men who were too old or unfit to serve in fighting units and men released from jail on the condition they volunteered for military service. There were also so called 'Q' or 'Queer' companies that, in those days, meant those men released from mental institutions. Finally, there were we former enemy aliens.

For obvious reasons every officer in England tried to stay away from such an outfit for, in addition to commanding such splendid human material, they would have to spend endless days supervising manual labour, which would be alright for a short period but would be soul-destroying if it were to last for a year.

Much later some sugar coating was applied to the picture. 'Auxiliary' was dropped so the Corp's title became Military Pioneer Corps (MPC). After the war the crowning glory ensued when the word 'Royal' was added to make it the Royal Military Pioneer Corps and its members were even armed.

In its later days the corps had its fair share of excellent types, however in 1941 at West Auckland we were considered to be a bottom-of-the-barrel-scraping operation. Billeted in a draughty memorial hall, we were commanded by a roughneck sergeant who was proud of his Royal Navy record – having been held in detention barracks and jailed for, amongst other achievements, being a criminal homosexual.

The duties were tough, particularly for those of us who had become physically unfit during our six months in an internment camp, but we didn't mind that too much and went about our work with a sort of sporting enthusiasm. However, our situation was aggravated by the existence of some pretty despicable types who cow-towed to the sergeant, assisted him with his black-market activities and got themselves some of the more comfortable jobs.

To get these concerns off my chest I wrote a long letter to Humphrey Sykes who had the brilliant idea of sending a copy, complete with my name, to the War Office, addressed to the King Pioneer – a general whom he knew. Humphrey probably felt that such action would accelerate the end of the 'darkest hours that precede dawn'. He also observed that this kind of thing was detrimental to the reputation of the British Army (with which I heartily agreed) and he assured me that there would be absolutely no repercussions for me.

The King Pioneer's office copied my letter and sent it to my own CO and the Deputy Director of Labour (DDL), the top Pioneer in the Army Command where I was stationed.

The CO, an outstanding case of an 'Officer and Gentleman,' having read my letter swore, according to a friend of mine who was a clerk in his office, that he would see me in the 'Glasshouse' (military prison). Fortunately, the DDL decided otherwise. By now we had left West Auckland and moved to Nissen[9] huts in the grounds of Hoddom Castle (usually referred to as either Sodom or Goddamn Castle) near Ecclefechan in Scotland. The work had changed from loading sacks to digging a ditch for a pipeline.

I was submerged in this ditch when an NCO called out to me 'The DDL wants to see you immediately' Hell, I thought, this means trouble.

The DDL, Colonel Innes, a huge man, was soon waving a copy of the letter to Humphrey in my face and asked, 'Are you the Frank who wrote this silly letter?'

It was not said unkindly, so I took the bull by the horns.

'Yes sir,' I replied, 'and if I may say so, sir, I don't feel that it is a silly letter. It is stating facts as I am sure you will discover if you go into the situation.'

'That' stated the boss 'may or may not be so, but one doesn't go and write letters like this all over the place. I'll look into it. Be more discreet in future.'

The interview was over.

Shortly afterwards our beloved sergeant disappeared to be followed by the CO. There were, indeed, no repercussions for me. On the contrary, I was 'given a stripe' – made a Lance Corporal – by the new CO and my name went forward as an officer's candidate. The War Office had decided that we former internees could, after all, be commissioned, though only in the Pioneer Corps. This was not for me and I declined the honour.

I then got wind of a new regulation under which we could be commissioned in certain fighting regiments. I asked my CO to put my name forward and was sent to a selection board for an interview.

Another seven candidates went with me, and the whole process started badly – one candidate went before the board whilst the next waited in a small office. Somebody had accidentally dropped a teargas bomb, and by the time I entered the boardroom I was crying bitter tears.

There were no less than five colonels present. Two took no part in the proceedings. Of the other three one was cross-eyed, the second almost deaf and the third, who conducted the interview, stammered badly.

'W-wwwhat rrr—rank a-a-are you?' he enquired.

'Lance Corporal, Sir,' I sobbed.

Then I was asked a lot of questions about my past: where I came from? what school had I attended? what experience did I have? what were my hobbies?

After some minutes the semi deaf colonel fixed me with an icy stare and said, 'I say, Frank, why aren't you an NCO?'

'But I am, Sir,' I said after a quick look at the solitary chevron on my sleeve, 'I am a Lance Corporal.'

'He should have been made an NCO before coming here,' said the hard-of-hearing colonel.

'Thahhts w-w-w-hat he i-i-is' announced the chairman, 'a-a-a L-l-lance C-c-c-corporal.'

'Oh, is he? Good.' Then there was sustained silence.

'Thank you, Frank,' someone said, 'that'll be all. We'll let your CO know the result'.

The result was that none of us passed. However, I kept making applications for a transfer to a fighting unit and was interviewed by two very inquisitive gentlemen from Military Intelligence when aliens became eligible for transfer to paratroop regiments – I was turned down as being too old – I was then twenty-nine!

## NOTES:

1. Several alien civilian internment camps were set up on the Isle of Man during the First World War and they were used for that purpose again during the Second World War. The one at Knockaloe, near Peel, was a small, self-contained, township that accommodated male internees only.

2. Robert Anthony Eden, 1st Earl of Avon, was an MP and pre-war member of the Cabinet. During the war he held the rank of major and was appointed secretary of several Government departments, then Foreign Secretary and Leader of the House of Commons. In 1955 he succeeded Winston Churchill as Prime Minister. Eden was in fact Secretary of State for War from May to December 1940 – the period his brother, Sir Timothy Calvert Eden (attached to the War Office) was an officer and Wolfe Frank was an internee at Peel Camp – and it was during that period that new regulations were brought in granting some aliens their freedom and their right to join the British Army. (Editor: Is it possible therefore that Wolfe Frank's continual representations as Camp Leader at Peel – which demanded the above rights – somehow reached the notice of the Secretary of State for War via his brother and that those representations came into Anthony Eden's thinking when he was considering changing the Government's position on aliens?).

3. Kurt Alois Schuschnigg was Chancellor of Austria from 1934-1938.

4. Franz von Papen was Chancellor of Germany in 1932 and Vice-Chancellor under Hitler from 1933-1934. He was one of the defendants at Nuremberg who Wolfe Frank later interrogated and for whom he interpreted.

5. Members of the Auxiliary Military Pioneer Corps performed a wide variety of tasks in all theatres of war ranging from handling all types of stores, laying prefabricated track on beaches and stretcher-bearing. They also worked on the construction of harbours, laid pipes under the ocean, constructed airfields and roads and erected bridges. In 1940 the Corps' name was changed to the Pioneer Corps and, following the war, King George VI designated it to be the Royal Pioneer Corps.

6. Referred to as the Christmas Blitz, 365 people were killed in Liverpool between 20 and 22 December 1940.

7. In the British Army a blouse was a short jacket made of wool serge that buttoned to the outside of high-waisted wool serge trousers.

8. Catterick is the largest British Army garrison in the world.

9. A Nissen hut is a prefabricated steel structure, made from a half-cylindrical skin of corrugated steel. Invented by Major Peter Nissen, the huts were used extensively during the Second World War.

# AN OFFICER AND A GENTLEMAN

IN MAY 1943, 240 COMPANY WAS DISSOLVED and I was transferred to another Company at Northampton. Shortly after my arrival I was informed that I would, at last, be transferred to a fighting unit.

I attended another selection board, filled in endless forms and went through various intelligence tests. The result was a transfer to the Royal Armoured Corps (RAC) Training Regiment at Farnborough in Hampshire, where I arrived at the end of July 1943. After two years seven months my hole-digging days were over, and I had to learn to be a soldier.

For sixteen weeks I drilled, learnt a great deal about armoured vehicles, wireless, rifles, bombs, revolvers and map reading and I received a heavy dose of physical training. The CO then selected me as an officer candidate. I attended a special course, run by the regiment in order to equip me for a War Office Selection Board (WOSB) that I was told I would have to pass before going to an Officer Cadet Training Unit (OCTU). For weeks I did special PT, went over obstacle courses, did night exercises, endless route marches and attended countless lectures.

Then, in February 1944, came the selection board. With it the War Office had found an excellent solution to a difficult problem.

At the beginning of the war one had to be born into the right families to become an officer. Men with the proper background and education could be fairly certain they would receive a commission. By 1944 however the country was running out of such elite types and a system had to be devised to draw on the rank and file of 'ordinary' human beings in order to find the men who were psychologically, physically and intellectually suitable to hold a commission.

The system of interviewing boards consisting of deaf, stammering or cross-eyed fogeys was, wisely, scrapped. To accept a Cockney[1], for instance, who had perhaps received only an elementary level of schooling, was more than could be reasonably expected from an 'old school tie' staff officer.

It became the responsibility of officers commanding training units to select potential officers from amongst their men. These candidates then went before the WOSB, not as good or bad soldiers or even NCOs, but as a number. All badges of rank were removed, and names and past history were unknown to the testing officers. Candidates then went through three days of gruelling tests compiled by experts, including psychologists. At the end of the three days there was enough information to decide if the candidate was officer material and possessed the essential qualities of leadership, intelligence, adaptability, integrity, and courage.

The Board was housed in a beautiful country house near Godalming in Surrey where the accommodation and food were excellent. We were taken over by an NCO as soon as we arrived and, before being assigned quarters, we each of us received an armlet with a number that was pinned on the sleeve and covered all traces of any badges of rank.

Having selected our bunks, we were then conducted to a classroom for the written tests. For fully five hours, and without a minute's break, we answered intelligence-test questions that became progressively more and more intricate and time limits had to be strictly observed. At dinner that night we were joined, in the pleasant officer's mess, by three military testing officers (MTOs) who stayed with us every minute during the board. They not only knew at the end therefore what our qualifications and abilities were, but also if we had a semblance of decent table manners and what sort of conversationalists we were.

The second day was devoted to practical tests in the open and the third to tackling obstacle courses. There was one last interview with the officer in charge, this time not as a number but under one's own name and rank. He asked in which unit I would like to be commissioned if I had passed. I told him that I wanted to remain in the RAC. He told me that this would be impossible. The age limit, strictly observed for the Corps, was twenty-five and I was exactly thirty. There was therefore no hope of an RAC commission for me.

I argued fiercely, pointing out that I had had all my military training in that branch of the army and that I had a technical background. It was no good.

The colonel suggested that I should select Infantry Support – a newly formed unit where I would be able to use my background. I gave in.

The news that I had passed reached the regiment two weeks later. I would be sent to a pre-OCTU where I would undergo infantry training until I had reached the standard of an Infantry NCO. From there I would go to the support OCTU at Alton Towers in Staffordshire. Following this I spent further periods of strenuous training at Wrotham in Kent and then at Sandhurst – the home of the Royal Military College and Armoured Corps OCTU – and we thought we were going to share in its comfort. We were quite wrong and ended up in tents half a mile away from the college.

I was finally commissioned on 22 December 1944 and at last stood on parade as a Second Lieutenant in a fighting regiment –The Royal Northumberland Fusiliers. The Passing Out (Army lingo for graduation) was taken by a rather ancient and, apparently, totally senile general who, when he came to me, stopped and looked me over. After ascertaining my name, he arrived at the standard questions used on all such occasions:

'What were you doing in civilian life?'

'I was a managing director of a sand pit, Sir.'

'I see. Where?'

'In London, Sir.' (keep it simple I thought.)

'I see,' he said and passed to the next man. Then he stopped, pondered, and came back to me.

'I say, there isn't any sand in London, is there?'

There we were. One should always be accurate in one's answers. Now I had to say, 'No, Sir, there isn't. Our pit was located in Kent and the offices were in London. Sir.'

'Yes. Ah. Quite. Thank you,' said the general and went on his way.

Then it was all over. There was a dance, when officers and NCO instructors became utterly human and when we equipped them, cold-bloodedly, for a major hangover – we weren't there to see it – we were well on our way home for ten day's leave.

This leave happily coincided with Christmas and New Year. I spent both with Phyllis Stanley-Rignold. The Woozle had been sent abroad, leaving her pregnant in a flat just across from the *House on the Creek* in Maidenhead and she had invited me to spend my leave there provided she wasn't giving birth just then. I turned up, suitably equipped with some booze and Phyllis introduced me to a female friend staying with her whose looks, mind and performance were so totally insignificant that I would not have remembered her had she not tried to blackmail me, years later, as being responsible for a pregnancy – for the termination of which she thought I ought to come up with £300 pounds, please. I was happily married when the letter came, and my wife made me take it to a solicitor whose letter to the bitch ended the affair.

The war was still on when my leave was over, and I was still in it. There was a training period during which I had to show I was able to live up to the great tasks and responsibilities of being a Second Lieutenant who, it is said, 'knows nothing and does everything whilst a major knows everything and does nothing.'

For some weeks I drilled troops, took them on route marches and gave them lectures. The time of my departure for the war was getting near. Then I was called to the adjutant's office. This, I thought, was it. However, I found him staring at a form that I had filled in about four years earlier, just after joining the Army. It contained every scrap of personal data from the colour of my grandmother's hair to the size of my socks.

'I see, Frank, that you speak French,' said the adjutant.

Thoughts began to race through my head. Liaison officer with some French outfit, perhaps? Some very special assignment? I felt worried. I had put 'fluent' in all three columns regarding my knowledge of French – 'Read, write, speak' In actual fact, my French had been quite good, though entirely non-military, but it was now almost non-existent. Perhaps there would be time to put this right.

The adjutant interrupted my thoughts.

'I'm jolly glad I found out about you. I have a special job for you.' (Airborne? Liaison? Interpreter?)

'The Belgian Army is forming machine gun battalions. They will be using our Vickers machine-gun.' (Liaison after all, damn that machine-gun, don't know an awful lot about it, really.)

'Some officers and men are arriving here tomorrow. You, Frank, will teach them the Vickers.' (Crash! This is the worst thing that could possibly have happened.)

'Yes, Sir,' I said, and staggered out.

The Belgians turned up the next day. They were headed by a colonel and there were seven sergeants. I headed for the Mess to face the music, but Colonel Viatour, a professional soldier, saved the day. I bought him a couple of whiskies, worked up the necessary courage and told him the truth.

'I am,' I told him, 'supposed to teach you the Vickers machine-gun, however I lack two important qualifications for the assignment. Firstly, I couldn't really teach the gun in any language, not even English. Secondly, I do not know the name of a single one of it's several thousand components in French. Where do we go from here?'

Viatour looked at me kindly. Apparently, he had understood most of what I had been saying. Then he grinned and told me his own story. He had been in the Belgian Army since he was fifteen and had completed almost forty years. He also had more medals on his chest than I had ever seen on any officer below the rank of general.

When the Germans had invaded Belgium in 1940 he had, somehow, fallen into the hands of the Gestapo and had been treated very badly. The same applied to the NCOs who had come with him. He fully understood my predicament but did not think that it was serious. Then he said, 'I myself, and my men, have only one target and that is to fight the Germans as soon as possible. Learning the machine-gun is the first step in that direction but, as we are machine-gunners, specialists, we won't have a problem. All you will have to do, Monsieur Frank, is to get hold of some pamphlets and we'll work the rest out together.'

And so we did. To begin with we worked out what might be called 'the public appearance act.' We agreed to talk much and rapidly when within the earshot of others. There were to be no clues that I did not understand him or was talking horrible French. This act was always entirely successful.

Then we found a Nissen hut on the perimeter of the camp to which we adjourned daily, at the very reasonable hour of 10.00 hours, which was two hours after the regiment had started on its daily tasks. In order to make up for this we went home an hour before they did, at 16.00 hours.

My conscience might well have pricked me if these men had not been such excellent pupils. They taught themselves. They had forgotten more about machine-gunning than I would ever know. All I had to do was to make them familiar with British drill in connection with the use of the weapon since they would be working in close co-operation with us. The rest they learnt themselves.

After five weeks – a week ahead of the adjutant's timetable – they knew all there was to know. The CO made enquiries as to progress.

'We will be through in another week, Sir,' I said. Following which the colonel thought they ought to be given a test.

'I'll tell you what we'll do,' announced the Old Man. 'I'll write down some questions and you'll translate them into French. I'll have the adjutant attend the test. Then you'll translate the answers and I'll compute the results.'

This set-up was, of course, quite perfect. I took the questions to our Nissen hut and between us we worked out the answers. I told the Belgians that we could not possibly turn in 100 per cent correct answers. I suggested we make a few mistakes. They wouldn't hear of it. Finally, Colonel Viatour asserted his authority. He made a list of convincing errors and we drew the victim's names out of a hat.

Under the eyes of an admiring adjutant my gallant men produced a score of 89 per cent. It was the best result ever attained in the regiment. Naturally.

**NOTE:**

1. A Cockney was at one-time defined as a person born within the sound of the bells of St Mary-le-Bow church in Cheapside, City of London.

# OH, WHAT A LOVELY WAR

AFTER A FAREWELL DINNER for Colonel Viatour and his men, I was again summoned to the adjutant's office. 'I'm frightfully pleased with that Belgian cadre you've been running,' he announced. 'take a long weekend and when you come back you'll be on your way to France.'

It looked as if I might get into the war.

I went off to London with feelings ranging from elation to apprehension and fear. They presented an excellent excuse for man's favourite remedy against such an emergency. I got very drunk indeed and stayed that way for seventy-two hours. I met a very lovely new friend at the Mayfair Club by the name of Sylvia. She was endowed with outstanding measurements and a cosy, old-fashioned flat in Kensington. I took no time off for sleeping.

Pale and hung over, I arrived back at camp just in time for the first parade. I staggered into the Company Office and arranged with a friend that he would take over my duties so that I could go to bed. However, I encountered the Company Commander on the way out.

'Ah, Frank! Good morning. Glad you're back.' He smiled. 'I have a job for you, old man. Would you mind taking B and C platoons for rugger touch?'

I did mind, but he wouldn't have been interested. I changed into PT clothes and, shivering, I went out into the cold morning air.

Rugger touch is a game with very few rules. It is part of the toughening-up programme for British soldiers. There are two goals, marked in this instance by tin canisters, and the object of the exercise is to shoot goals, no holds barred. The particular attraction for the men in that training regiment, was that the game provided an opportunity for them to beat up their officers. Of course, it was all done in the best of fun.

B and C platoons got cracking. For a minute or two, I ran up and down aimlessly, thinking of Sylvia. Then I suddenly remembered what

I had been taught relentlessly for many a month – 'Officers will be an example to their men at all times and display leadership and initiative.'

I put my head back on and got hold of the ball. B platoon set out to tackle me. C platoon attempted to protect me. All at once about thirty men descended upon me and I found myself at the bottom of the heap. I was still clutching the ball. The two opposing teams pulled hard. What they were pulling happened to be my leg. There was a rather audible crack. The leg had broken.

I was out of the war!

Later that day I drew up a temporary balance. (I had just lost a one-pound bet to a sergeant who said my leg was broken and I said it wasn't. This was before the sixth X-ray produced a reasonably clear picture).

I had been in the Army four years and two months, or one thousand five hundred and thirty days to be exact. Discounting the useless days of digging holes, I had spent eighteen months being trained as a tank driver, an infantry soldier, and, finally, an Infantry Support Officer. The object had been to get into the war as a fighting soldier. Now, in February 1945, with the war nearly at an end, it was fairly obvious that it had all been in vain, every bit of it. The doctor's verdict was one month in plaster followed by one month of physiotherapy – and I would not be fully fit for four to five months after that.

Moston Hall Military Hospital at Chester was a very busy place. They put the leg into a plaster cast (it was done by a private soldier and no doctor had seen me) and then took the cast off again because they didn't like the look of it. They then ordered my immediate transfer to a convalescent home, however when I got out of bed and put some weight on the walking plaster I passed out with pain and it was decided that I should stay a bit longer.

The next morning, a newly operated case was wheeled into the ward. When he came to he immediately put his hand under the blanket obviously checking something. He sighed and went back to sleep. Later, I asked him what it was all about. He told me he had been lying on a stretcher outside the operating theatre, quite doped, when a medical orderly walked up to another semi-conscious type next to him. 'You're next, Captain Watson,' said the orderly. My friend's name was Watson. The other fellow's name was Wilson.

Watson had a hernia on the right. Wilson had time to murmur that he had a hernia on the left. So, all the way through the anaesthetic, Watson was worrying whether Wilson, mistaken for Watson, would be sliced open on the wrong side, and he, Watson, also. All was well, however, the holes were where they belonged. My other neighbour, a young guards officer, was one of those cases of a man who, according to the book, ought to have been dead. He had been run over by his own machine-gun carrier. His insides, according to his own version of the incident, 'Were hanging out all over the place, but some chap had labelled them, numbered the lot and put them back in.'

In Roger, the Guards officer's, opinion, 'The chap had made a slight mistake,' for his bowels functioned at least eighteen times a day, which, he felt, 'was a shocking waste of time.' He had come to the hospital to have his insides 're-arranged'.

One afternoon a group of Medical Officers (MOs) drifted into the ward and displayed great concern for Roger's case. They prescribed a huge quantity of castor oil for the poor chap for the following morning whereupon he would be X-rayed at two in the afternoon. Roger, rather reluctantly, postponed his date with a pretty girlfriend. He swallowed the castor oil and was X-rayed. However, the MOs had departed, and a new batch turned up that afternoon and didn't like the look of the X-rays. They ordered a repeat performance. Roger phoned his girlfriend. This thing dragged on for five days. Finally, they sent him home on leave, having decided that they could do nothing for him.

I was released from that hospital after ten days and sent to a lovely country house in Shropshire which had become an Army convalescent home. I played a lot of bridge with the CO and he took a liking to me. He felt that I could do better than just sitting around the place but said they couldn't do anything for me whilst my leg was in a plaster cast.

Then some general came to visit the place and, to mark the occasion, some of the inmates were given home leave. The CO, giving up a bridge partner with considerable regret, added my name to the list. I was to go on home leave for a month until 16 March 1945. The leave orders stated that I was to proceed to my home address and would be notified when and to where I was to report back.

I called Sylvia and she was willing to receive the wounded. I moved in and practised two of my favourite hobbies (the other was cooking).

At this point, the Army chose to forget me altogether. Came the end of March, and I hadn't heard from them. I contacted a friend at the War Office who told me that I wouldn't be hearing from them for at least another month since all officers' convalescent depots were overcrowded. April passed, the war ended. I was still on sick leave.

I would also have been in a cast, still, if I hadn't taken the initiative to have it taken off at St. George's Hospital. I wanted to claim the cast which had hundreds of autographs and some nice drawings on it. 'Sorry,' said the Doctor, with a twinkle in his eye, 'we have to keep it for our records.' My assertion that they were unlawfully seizing War Office property didn't impress him.

A week after VE Day, and the ensuing five-day shindig, I went back to see my friend at the War Office. 'Good God man', said he 'don't be an idiot. If we send you back on duty now you'll be posted to some training regiment. You'll spend your days drilling recruits. Stay on leave until they send for you.' He was my senior. I obeyed orders.

My pay kept coming, punctually, at the end of every month. I had acquired an old but worthy automobile and Sylvia and I were enjoying life and each other's company. She was working during the day, I can't remember at what, and I was fairly stationary because of the post-plaster condition of my leg. I spent a lot of time on the telephone, but the problem was that it was in the bedroom on the first floor of the duplex flat and by the time I had limped upstairs to answer its ring, the caller had usually hung up. So I got hold of some low-tension wire and built my own extension. Somehow, it didn't quite correspond to Post Office specifications. When I dialled a number, I found myself listening to somebody's conversation as often as not. This became a pastime and I heard some fairly priceless talk. One day a couple of War Office colonels were debating on what date an article, 'By this fellow, Huxley,' should appear in some Army publication. One of them suggested May, the other September. I inserted my opinion. 'Maybe, old chap' I said, 'we shouldn't print the stupid thing at all. Nobody will want to read it.'

There was a lengthy silence. 'Really?' said one Colonel 'well …' but the other had hung up!

# THE BRITISH WAR CRIMES EXECUTIVE

O N 28 JULY (1945) I WENT TO THE WAR OFFICE once again and asked them to give me a job. They said they would see what they could do.

The telephone was ringing when I returned to Sylvia's flat. 'Officer Posting' was on the line. 'Frank' said a bored voice, 'you've just been posted to a thing called the British War Crimes Executive (BWCE). I haven't a clue as to what it is all about. They're having a meeting in a couple of hours. You'd better go and find out'.

I proceeded to the meeting forthwith. Half a dozen officers and thirty or so other ranks were waiting. Then a major of the Coldstream Guards raised the most bored voice I had ever heard. His announcement was brief and to the point. 'This unit will be engaged in collecting material for the prosecution of the major war criminals. That's Goering and others, you know. We leave on Sunday.' (This was Wednesday).

There followed some frantic efforts to get hold of my Army kit that was still with the regiment in Chester. The adjutant despatched it at once. It reached me five months later. My new unit was assembling in a transit camp on the coast. Our departure was delayed by two days and I took a staff car to come up to London in order to search Euston station for my kit.

It wasn't there so I decided to look in on Sylvia and have a bath. I still had a key.

She was having a grand old time with a gent who, judging by his clothes hanging over the bedroom chair, was serving in Uncle Sam's Navy. At least he was an officer. The following evening, having returned to camp minus kit, minus girlfriend and minus key, I boarded a landing craft as a newly promoted staff captain and in charge of this latest holiday excursion. As I drove my car into the huge belly of the ship I saw a neatly painted inscription on her stern, 'Is this journey really necessary?'

BWCE had no orders beyond going to Ostend in Belgium where we were to await developments. The crossing, normally a matter of a few hours, took more than a day. Then we rumbled into the badly bombed Belgian port. For the first time in six years I was back on the Continent.

The memory of the Germans was still fresh in everyone's mind. During the next month I collected enough information to discount the German claim that they had behaved no worse in the countries they had occupied than the Allies in Germany.

We spent a lazy week in Ostend, mostly on the beach, and then received orders to proceed to Paris. There the Americans seemed to have made a start on sorting documents for the forthcoming trial of war criminals. The BWCE, we were told, was to work with the Americans.

Things were chaotic when our convoy arrived in the French capital. BWCE had been assigned a magnificent suite of empty offices in the Boulevard des Capucines, totally empty of furniture. We had precisely one document in our possession. It was Hitler's infamous '*Nacht und Nebel*' decree,[1] ordering the execution of Allied fliers. In order to keep busy, we translated this document, edited the translation, poof-read it and mimeographed[2] it. Then we translated it back into German and came up with something totally different from the original text.

We started from scratch.

Fortunately, my office could boast a long balcony on which I could spend most of my time gazing upon the carefree crowd passing by below. One of those corrugated rotundas, aptly named pissoir[3], was situated below my balcony. Its roof was missing. I was able to make extensive and conclusive studies of man's behaviour during the minute he spends in a pissoir, more or less alone. In the evenings, we were all over Paris. My French got a face-lift that could have been most beneficial to my machine-gun squad, which now seemed a matter from a far-distant past.

My constant companion was Captain Leslie Hill, who had been taken prisoner at Dunkirk. He had been drafted into BWCE as a linguist. Leslie's German, which had an unbelievable English accent, was grammatically impeccable. His French was hopeless, but his Russian – self-taught during his imprisonment – was, someone told me, nearly perfect.

Having spent most of the war in a camp, and then his PoW leave with his mother, Leslie was ripe for some good old French amour, and there was no lack of opportunity. The Americans had been in Paris long enough to make us, the British, the most welcome of Allies. We were constantly having the most desirable of contacts with such people as restaurant owners, hotelkeepers and girls, girls, girls!

Unfortunately for Leslie, it took him so long to disentangle his French from his German and Russian that the damsel at whom it was being aimed had left to catch her last train before he could say, 'voulez-vous coucher avec moi?' (Do you want to sleep with me?). Fortunately for me, whilst my French was grammatically impossible it did have the benefit of a rapid-fire delivery. Consequently, and for the duration of our stay in Paris, I maintained a truly good relationship, or rather two of them, with a pretty blonde hairdresser, who worked until 21.00 hours, and a member of the world's oldest profession who, obviously, worked nights.

I therefore needed to maintain three abodes: one, the Hotel Bedford, was my officer's billet, one was a small hotel in Passy where I spent many nights having my hair done, and the third was the apartment of the Basque, dark haired, dark skinned and 'fiery' lady of the night.

Fortunately, I could claim the 'Nacht und Nebel' order as an alibi for some hours of respite during the day, during which time I rested up by watching my fellow men doing their stuff in the rotunda below.

Of course, none of this brought Goering any nearer to the gallows.

After a couple of weeks of case studies I was sent to Justice Jackson's[4] headquarters in the Rue Presbourg where the Americans were sitting on, literally, mountains of German documents. Jackson was heading the US team at Nuremberg and he had been one of the architects of the London agreement between the Allies which produced the Charter setting up the International Military Tribunal.

The Americans had done an amazing job finding these documents, which were often poorly hidden, often of monumental impact on human history, and often quite absurd and comical. Knowing how serious I would have to be about all this in due course, I concentrated on the latter.

There was for instance, Frau Scholtz-Klink,[5] the German Women's leader forever writing letters to Hitler's philosopher, Alfred Rosenberg, trying to sign him up for a speech to her women – and he was forever ducking out. In one such indignant letter she wrote, 'German women have stood solid behind the Fuehrer in everything he has done. Their contribution to our war effort has been great and invaluable. They deserve recognition.'

Then there were some files from an SS court, trying wayward leaders. One of them had been looking after young boys. Whenever one of them had erred, the SS officer had him get up on a ladder and the lad was ordered to pull out a prescribed number of pubic hairs as punishment. Such ingenuity!

After three weeks of all this productive studying, we were ordered to Bad Oeynhausen, headquarters of the British Occupation Forces in Germany.

## NOTES:

1. *Nacht und Nebel* (Night and Fog) was a decree, issued by Hitler in 1941, which dealt with the elimination of persons in occupied territories. Victims of the decree were said to have disappeared into the night and fog without a trace.

2. A mimeograph was a duplicating machine that forced ink through a stencil.

3. Public urinal.

4. Lord Justice Robert H. Jackson was the US Chief of Counsel at the IMT.

5. Gertrude Scholtz-Klink. later known as Maria Stuckebrock, was a Nazi Party member and leader of the National Socialist Women's League.

# THE BAD AND THE GOOD IN OEYNHAUSEN

**B**AD OEYNHAUSEN, A CHARMING SMALL German health resort about 80km from Hanover, had quickly and justly earned an unpleasant reputation. For some reason the centre of the town had been surrounded by a barbed wire fence. Inside the Army lived and worked and the ban on fraternization was very much in force when we arrived.

As we approached Bad Oeynhausen (the 'a' in Bad is pronounced as in bath) we spotted an interesting sequence of Army signposts that read, successively, 'Bad Curve', 'Bad Road' and 'Bad Oeynhausen' – It was!

All the way across Germany I had tried to converse with Germans and failed. I was intensely curious about their frame of mind, of course. We had crossed the Rhine on a provisional bridge, which were few and far between. It was a one-way bridge and the line of vehicles and people crossing it was several miles long. Allied military traffic had priority and as we crept slowly towards the bridge I had studied the faces of the Germans who were watching us as we went by.

I hope that somebody has recorded these scenes and faces. 'This,' such a record would say, 'is what a beaten nation looks like.' There they were, men and women and children of all ages. They were standing in line for hours, pulling little hand-carts and every one of them in search of food or fuel.

It had taken them perhaps five hours to get across the bridge in the morning, all day to find a few potatoes, and as many hours to get back. They were mostly just staring into space, without expression. They looked totally, frighteningly hungry, desperate and downtrodden.

It was, to me, eerie and incomprehensible. I had not seen Germans in Germany for eight years and then they had been the master race, inspired by the thundering Fuehrer to deeds which history had recorded as being frightful, inhuman and often heroic. The swing of the pendulum was more than the eyewitness could comprehend and no imagination could have pictured any kind of tangible future for them.

Yet, a few days later, I saw them crawl out of their roofless ruins and go to church or for a Sunday walk among the ruins. Somehow, they had managed to get hold of a clean shirt and a reasonably decent suit of clothing.

I felt that I wanted to walk up to them and ask them hundreds of questions, but the orders were, 'Only essential contacts with Germans.' It was quite foolish. Obviously, we were there to stay and we would be talking to them eventually. Why not now? Would we not have been a great deal wiser today if we had been able to penetrate their minds then? Would we not have understood better what had made them serve Hitler to the terrible end in everything he demanded from them?

We retired behind the barbed wire instead, prepared for a resistance movement and acts of sabotage. The 'book' said that occupying forces would have to expect that from the beaten enemy, so our vehicles were equipped to cut wire barriers secretly strung across the roads, to trap Allied drivers. We were armed to the teeth and there was a strict curfew for Germans.

However, there was no sabotage and there was no 'resistance.'

We had many hundreds of Germans working for us in the compound, as cooks, cleaners, drivers and office staff. Eighty per cent of them were women. They were young and many of them were very pretty.

My group were positively straining at the leash and, after a few days, noticeably sex-starved. Our three weeks in Paris had got us back into the habit but now, it seemed, the strict non-fraternisation rule would keep us from getting a whiff of defeated Germany. This splendid unit which I had the honour to command had no military duties, no documents to study and, worst of all, no transport to get out of that compound. We had too much comfort and all this was clearly demoralizing. So, when my men had divested themselves of their morals sufficiently, it was time for me – their leader – to act. I decided to forget about the rules.

The several hundred Germans working at the camp were called the 'indigenous personnel'. They had been security checked carefully and had to show their passes to the military guards when entering and leaving the compound. The checkpoint was directly outside my office window. It took me very little time to realize that our German help included a very high percentage of attractive Frauleins. Such happy statistics, the result of the war, were nationwide and continued for quite a few years.

As I was watching this procession of slim and neat German girlhood going by, I ceased being the good soldier who should have looked the other way and began to design the sinister plot to infringe upon General Eisenhower's[1] no-fraternisation rule for the benefit of my brave troops. My 'you-only-live-once' humanitarian instinct won out.

Three officers were sharing my villa with me and we agreed on immediate action. We drew post-card sized maps showing the location of our villa at the far side of the camp, and right by the fence. On the map it said 'Goethe Strasse 9' (marked by a cross) 'A party here next Thursday at 20.00 hours. You are invited. Hole-in-fence HERE (marked with a cross).' I then enlisted a young German, who hastened to help in exchange for a carton of cigarettes, and we stationed him just outside the gate where he could see me at my office window. Every time I raised my arm he gave one of our maps to a young lady who was passing him and he thus got rid of fifteen cards in three minutes flat. No chorus line has ever been selected faster and with greater success for the quality of the chosen candidates.

It must be said in our honour that we actually did arrange a party for Thursday night. We pooled our liquor rations, sent our batman home and made sandwiches. We had flashlights to guide our guests through the hole in the fence, and we had music.

Six ladies turned up between 20.00 and 20.03 with true German punctuality. They didn't know each other which, I think, helped. They were all very pretty, very young, very shy and very hungry. We took care of the last two problems very quickly – our sandwiches vanished. The first corks popped. The effect of the booze was staggering. These girls – the oldest was twenty-three and the youngest nineteen – had not tasted alcohol for years, if ever.

Shyness disappeared and the numbers problem – six girls, four boys – ceased to matter. I think we were years ahead of the rest in the field of Anglo-German 'rapprochement', language crash courses and, in a nice, embarrassed sort-of way, group sex.

My own conquest was beautiful Lorelei. She had long blonde hair, was twenty-two years of age and a schoolteacher. After the two ladies who had enhanced my days in Paris she seemed inhibited at first, but some more Moselle melted the ice and I became the beneficiary of that shortage of males in Germany – which meant that a German girl had to be very good if she wanted to hang on to a play-mate.

I was so entranced by her that I hung on to my schoolteacher for the rest of my stay in Bad Oeynhausen. So did my mates to their friends, only they had five for the price of three, whilst I was busy being a one-woman lover. I also recovered some sanity in my feelings about

Germans in the process. It helped a lot during the grisly days of Nuremberg. The memory of the beautiful, slender body of my first post war German girlfriend detracted from many horrific impressions that were waiting for me.

**NOTE:**

1. Dwight David 'Ike' Eisenhower (1890–1969) was the 34th President of the USA (from 1953 until 1961). During The Second World War he was a five-star general and Supreme Commander of the Allied Expeditionary Forces in Europe.

# BECOMING AN INTERROGATOR

IWAS ASSIGNED TO A FIELD SECURITY SECTION, the equivalent of the American Counter Intelligence Corps (CIC). It was engaged in rounding up, interrogating and jailing the active Nazis of the town of Munster. Most of this work was being carried out by a black-bereted sergeant, who became known as *'die Schwarze Schmach'* – the Black Curse.

Hundreds of printed postcards were mailed to various functionaries of the Nazi Party, ordering them to report to us at a certain time. They were all in the 'automatic arrest' category because of their rank in the party or an affiliated organisation.

It became known that no-one ever returned from a visit to our pleasant little suburban villa where the entire card filing system of the Nazi Party, the SA, the SS and the Gestapo had been left intact by those organisations who had had to get out in a hurry.

The Black Curse only sent for those men in the files who were due for immediate arrest. In this he was, of course, infallible, thanks to the files.

So, at 09.00 hours each morning the two benches arranged outside the house would be occupied by dejected looking men who, invariably, carried a battered briefcase, the contents of which were always the same – long underwear, shirt, collar, shaving kit, soap, bread, some apples and a family photograph. Oddly enough, our 'customers' in the photos they showed us were never in uniform.

One by one they would then file into the sergeant's office, where I spent many hours attending these sessions. The Black Curse would look at each man before him in a friendly sort of way and say:

'Your name is Schultz?'

*'Jawohl, Herr Obergefreiter,'* and the German then invariably stood stiffly to attention.

'You held the rank of *Blockleiter* in the Nazi Party?'

There then always followed the same story. The rank was purely nominal. The man had not carried out any functions for years. He had only refrained from resigning from the party because that would have been too dangerous in Germany. Instead, he had done everything in his power to help people who had got into trouble with the Nazis.

Sometimes the Black Curse picked up a letter from the huge pile on his desk. It was one of hundreds of anonymous denunciations that we received daily. He would then read part of the letter to his visitor. It usually accused him of ill-treating Jews or being brutal to non-Nazis. The man would then display an expression of complete consternation and re-iterate his innocence, or his long-standing anti-Nazi activities.

At this point the Black Curse usually produced the file card – kept up-to-date until very recently – complete with the man's photograph.

'This would not, by any chance, be you?' he used to say. The *Herr Blockleiter* would then turn pale and shrug his shoulders in a gesture of defeat.

'Take him away' said the sergeant – and another Nazi would be on his way to an internment camp.

To see the way these men behaved was the most sickening display of bad lying and cowardice imaginable. I thought at the time it had to be unique. I was wrong. Later, during the Nuremberg trials, such performances were surpassed by the leaders of Hitler's 'Thousand Year Reich'[1].

My first experience as an interpreter at an interrogation came whilst I was still at Oeynhausen. I had met Colonel Gerald Draper in the officer's mess. He was clearly very sick (he had tuberculosis, I later discovered) and he had the air of a man who had something to take care of before it was too late.

Draper, who had been a barrister before the war, belonged to the Judge Advocate's Office and had been assigned to the case of one Dr Bruno Tesch, now in custody, who had been one of the two owners of a Company called Tesch & Stabenow in Hamburg. They were manufacturers of a gas called 'Zyklon B' (or Cyclone B) – which was used to exterminate the inmates of Hitler's death camps. Tesch was to be tried for his contribution to this, the most heinous crime in modern history. However, there was another side to our investigation. The Russians had requested Tesch's extradition and had filed a prima facie case.

This led to a very subtle consideration. If Tesch was to be found guilty by the British, he could be condemned to death and executed. The Russians had abolished the death penalty and would, it seemed, in all probability sentence him to life imprisonment – obviously a fate worse than death.

I must admit that Draper and I, together with another interpreter and a sergeant, were not overly gentle with Tesch. He was a repulsive type. He was heavy set, dressed in an expensive suit, a little the worse for wear after some months in jail, and sure of himself to the extent of being conceited.

We had a lot of documents showing him as visiting the camps and letters from Himmler[2], asking for adequate supplies of Zyklon B so that the '*Ungezieferbekampfung*' – the vermin extermination – could be carried out expeditiously. There were also letters from Tesch to the RSHA containing good advice as to how blankets could be used to make gas chambers airtight – to exterminate the vermin in them, of course.

We started the interrogation at 06.00 hours and Draper kept at Tesch for eight uninterrupted hours, with me as the interpreter. Tesch was given water to drink but no food. At 20.00 hours in the evening, Draper had himself replaced by his colleague, again with me as the interpreter. We kept going until 04.00 hours the following morning, then we went to bed, while Tesch was kept awake, sweeping his cell and working in the kitchen.

The interrogation was resumed at 06.00 hours. Draper was back, and he stayed on the job until 05.00 the following morning, when Tesch confessed.

We hadn't touched him, but there was a glaringly bright light on him throughout. Only once, when he nodded off during the second night, had the sergeant thrown a mug of tea in his face. Apart from that we had mollycoddled him compared to what Gestapo would have done to him had they been in our place.

Tesch confessed that Zyklon B had been developed to kill people. He knew who he was helping to kill and he saw it done. He also assisted Otto Ohlendorff, of whom we will hear later, in designing the mobile gas chambers used in Eastern Europe.

We just sat there after these admissions had poured out of the prisoner. We were dazed, drained and nauseated. I informed Tesch that his confession would be typed up and that he would be asked to sign it. He nodded, slowly and rose to be returned to his cell.

Gerald Draper covered his face with his hands. He was sobbing.

After some minutes he thanked me for my help. I had done much more than interpret questions and answers since I was now a member of the interrogation team, sensing the moments when the pressure needed to be applied, or when understanding needed to be displayed. I had been rather effective.

As Draper and I were walking back towards our billets he told me the reason for his emotional outburst. He had been engaged to an

Austrian Jewess who had been killed in a camp where Zyklon B was being used.

Shortly before I left Oeynhausen Draper asked me to accompany him to the camp where Tesch was being kept. A decision had been sent to Draper from London to the effect that the Russian request for the extradition of Tesch had been granted. I read the text to him in German. He broke down completely. We left the room while he was still jabbering disjointed pleas for a change of this dreadful decision.

## NOTES:

1. In June 1934 Adolf Hitler stated to a British journalist: 'At the risk of appearing to talk nonsense I tell you that the National Socialist movement will go on for 1,000 years! Don't forget how people laughed at me 15 years ago when I declared that one day I would govern Germany.' At the Nazi Party Congress in Nuremberg in September of the same year the Fuehrer also declared: 'It is our will this state will endure for a thousand years!' In fact it endured for just twelve years. However Hans Frank, one of the defendants tried, found guilty and executed at Nuremberg, declared at the IMT: 'A thousand years will pass and still this guilt of Germany will not have been erased'.

2. Heinrich Luitpold Himmler (1900-1945) was Reichsfuehrer (Commander) of the SS and a leading member of the Nazi Party. Hitler appointed him a military commander and later Commander and administrator of the entire Third Reich. Himmler was one of the most powerful men in Nazi Germany and one of the people most directly responsible for the Holocaust. He was arrested by the British at the end of the war and committed suicide in May 1945.

# A DEAL WITH DIELS

O N MY WAY OUT OF THE CAMP I encountered the captain who was the official interpreter. He told me he had heard I would soon be going to Nuremberg. He then informed me that they had a man in camp who might be of interest, not only to me, but as a witness for the prosecution at Nuremberg. The captain knew this man to be a relative of Goering and that he had been a high-ranking officer in the Gestapo. He said he would send the man over, if I was interested.

That is how I came to meet Dr Rudolf Diels, one of the most fascinating men I had ever encountered. He was brought into an interrogation by the Camp Interrogator who then left us alone. I took a look at my new customer. He was tall, very dark haired and had heavy duelling scars on his face (see Chapter 13, Note 2). He was extremely intelligent and spoke beautiful cultured German. He was also emaciated, dreadfully nervous whilst being sure of himself, and he was courteous without being servile or afraid. His face showed the weariness he expected from yet another interrogation.

I told him who I was and that I would be involved in the trial of Goering and the other top Nazis, and I asked whether he might have anything pertinent to contribute to the picture we would be developing of them. He said he did have. He wasn't suggesting that he would be of considerable value to us at Nuremberg. He merely, in a few sentences, gave an outline of his activities in the Third Reich, which were as follows:

He was married to a cousin of Goering and he had been Chief of the Prussian Gestapo at the time of van der Lubbe's burning down of the German Reichstag[1]. He had been Chief of the Shipping Division of the Hermann Goering Works (a national industrial unit engaged in a multitude of economic and production activities) and also Lieutenant Governor of the City of Hanover. He had been denounced as having been involved in the 20 July 1944 plot against Hitler[2] but had been spared execution following Goering's intervention. Instead he had been sent to the Russian Front as a private in a '*Strafkompagnie*' (penal company) where he ought to have been killed. He had however escaped to the West and had been captured by the British.

This potted history was delivered in the briefest of terms and in less than five minutes. I could not detect any improbabilities or any attempt to promote my sympathy or compassion. I decided that I would hang on to Diels. The question was – how? I asked my friend the interpreter.

'Why that's easy,' he said. 'Sign for him and take him with you.'

Diels was told to be ready the following morning but not where he was going. I signed a piece of paper stating my name and rank and that, 'I had received one prisoner, Rudolf Diels.'

I then took him back to my billet in the Oeynhausen compound. This was, of course, monumentally irregular and pleased me enormously since breaking rules was, and still is, one of my favourite pastimes.

We didn't talk much on the way, but I could see that his face twitched when the gate to the compound was flung open and we drove into yet another camp. His expression changed to incredulity, however, when I took him to a nicely furnished bedroom and told him to make himself comfortable.

'Come down for lunch,' I told him, and left him to it.

We were alone at lunch (my two colleagues were off on some assignment) and I noticed that Diels was totally tipsy after a small aperitif. He hadn't had a drop of alcohol in nearly two years and his stomach was, obviously, rather empty. It had also shrunk, and he ate very little for a day or so, after which he raised his intake by leaps and bounds.

Our conversation centred around the problem of how this unorthodox arrangement between him and me could be continued. I asked him to give me an undertaking not to run out on me. He did, and he kept to it scrupulously.

Then he came up with a list of names of those people who, he thought, would be involved in the administration of the trials at Nuremberg. This was the first time that I discovered his uncanny ability to remember names, situations and to assess people's characters.

There were, indeed, two names on his list who did eventually turn up at Nuremberg – Dr Robert Kempner, German-born Assistant Prosecutor for the USA, and General William 'Wild Bill' Donovan, former head of the Office of Strategic Services (OSS), the USA's famous cloak-and-dagger outfit. Donovan had been involved in some intelligence activities in Berlin where Diels had met him when he was in the Ministry of the Interior and before he became a Head of Gestapo.

Kempner had been in the same Ministry under Wilhelm Frick, the Nazi Minister of the Interior who had thrown Kempner, the Jew, out of the Ministry and Germany. Kempner later had himself assigned to Nuremberg as chief of the prosecution team against Frick, who was hanged.

I got hold of both Kempner and Donovan and found them entirely agreeable to my scheme of bringing Diels to Nuremberg. A request to the British in Bad Oeynhausen to have Diels transferred into US custody was approved and he was picked up from my villa.

The story Diels told me, during a long night, his tongue loosened by Rhine wine and *Steinhager* (German gin), ran as follows:

He had met Goering's cousin in Berlin shortly after Hitler had come to power and Goering, who had taken a liking to him, indicated that he would look favourably upon a marriage into the Goering family. The marriage did not last long.

Goering arranged Diels' nomination as first Chief of Gestapo in Berlin and the Reichstag Fire had happened whilst Diels held that position. However, as he was not a member of the 'inner circle' the investigation was taken out of his hands and fabricated charges were brought against van der Lubbe, a young Dutchman, in order to achieve the desired political objective.

As far as they go, Diels accounts of the events of those days may be considered correct and he later wrote a book about his life during the Third Reich, *Lucifer ante Portas*, which is remarkably analytical so far as these events and the leading figures amongst whom he lived are concerned, but it is almost schizophrenically un-analytical regarding Dr Diels. He did not however claim ignorance of the horrors of the time, only the impossibility for anyone to swim against the monstrous tide. Nor did he – and Kempner and Donovan made certain of this – commit any act of his own that would have made him a guilty contributor.

Goering kept up his patronage of Diels until a grotesque mishap occurred at Karin Hall, the Reichmarshal's vast hunting domain in Schorfheide. Diels, a keen hunter and an excellent shot had been invited to a boar hunt. Goering was holding court in his capacity as '*Reichsjaegermeister*' a title bestowed upon him as the 'Supreme Master of the Hunters of the Reich' which entitled him to wear a variety of uniforms depending on the prey to be pursued, or the season, or the weather, or the time of day.

It was in such a fancy dress that Goering loomed up in front of Diels. To add to the impact, the head of the Luftwaffe was also wearing heavy make-up. '*Um Himmels Willen*,' exclaimed Diels '*eine Taucheruniform*? (For heaven's sake – a diver's uniform?)'

Goering stared at him for some seconds, then he roared, '*Reisen Sie ab*' (leave at once) – and so Diels departed from Goering's orbit and patronage.

Diels was first sent from the Goering Works into a non-political activity with no future, then he became Government President of Cologne, another job of little consequence, then down another step to Government President of Hanover and finally he was implicated in the attempt on Hitler's life on 20 July 1944. It was never ascertained how all these demotions were arranged since Diels – as he now had reason to regret – had nothing whatever to do with the assassination plot. What is known however is that Goering, as a last act of generosity for a man he once liked a great deal, had Diels' name taken off the list of death candidates and he had him sent, instead, to a penal company of the Waffen-SS (the fighting section of the SS) which was being decimated on the Eastern Front. Diels made his getaway from there and had been taken prisoner by the British Army.

As our guest in Nuremberg and as a source of information Diels proved himself to be inexhaustible, infallible and completely accurate. He had a photographic memory as far as channels of command, responsibilities, positions, officeholders, terms of office and organisational charts were concerned. He did however refuse, from the very beginning to the end, to implicate any of his former friends, colleagues or enemies in the Nazi hierarchy. This so angered some of the American prosecutors that at one stage they had him re-arrested – although this was quickly corrected on Donovan's intervention and another way was found to extract the information from Diels. In other words, someone might have asked Diels if so-and-so had ordered such-and-such an atrocity, and Diels would disclaim any knowledge of such an act. However, if asked if the same man had held the position in question at the time of the crime Diels would answer yes or no.

As long as Diels was in our charge the Germans had no jurisdiction over him and de-Nazification[3] proceedings against him remained suspended. His property near Hanover, a beautiful seventeenth century farmhouse and farming operation had been confiscated by the British and was held by the Property Control Office in Hanover. I went up there with him on one occasion – I was still in uniform and didn't have to ask anyone's permission. Diels had telephoned ahead and all his former employees and neighbours kept calling in to see him. It was quite a touching scene. They had prepared a remarkable meal of roast goose and dumplings in his honour, which they knew to be his favourite dish. There was an ample supply of the theoretically non-existent Schnapps and the only person not having a good time was a German Property

Control type, who must have felt rather impotent while all this was going on.

The status Diels was occupying in Nuremberg was so far outside any of the known categories – he was not a witness, not a prisoner, not a potential defendant, not a free man – that we had some trouble keeping him close at hand. He was, for the moment, living in the building set aside for German witnesses for the prosecution, however as he wasn't one of those, the officer in charge wanted him out. He could not be let loose into the community because the Germans would have arrested him. I could not put him up in my house in Nuremberg, as I had in Bad Oeynhausen, because my CO, Colonel Hugh Turrell, was a stickler for the rules and kept sniffing around our billets. He would have had a heart attack if he had found Diels in a 'billet, British officers, for the use of.'

Diels came up with the solution himself but an account of it will require some degree of camouflage of identities.

Many years earlier Diels had had a blistering love affair with a young lady, a gifted musician, who was hotly pursued by Dr Goebbels[4] (not in his capacity as patron of the arts). Diels had successfully protected the damsel, who was not German, from Goebbels' unwanted attention. This lady was now living somewhere outside Nuremberg, having married into a well-known Bavarian family. Diels felt that Marianne (as we shall call her) and her husband might put him up, as they had all been quite friendly in the past.

I made a call at the house where Marianne lived, some 25km from Nuremberg. She was indeed beautiful, charming and unusually intelligent. I had them investigated by the CIC before I called and found that the husband had had his problems with the Nazis and the Communists within his factory, who had denounced him to both the Americans and the German de-Nazification office as well.

My friend at the CIC and I cleaned up the mess and Marianne's husband, who looked quite terrified when I made my first call in British uniform, began to relax and, yes, of course, he would welcome Dr Diels as a guest to his house. Marianne had listened to it all with a Cheshire Cat's smile and refrained from making any comment.

So Diels was moved, promised not to run away, just as his host had promised not to let him, and there he remained, true to his word until I left Nuremberg in November 1947. (He was, in fact, still there two years later when I dropped in on them all. I noticed then, as I had before, how close the rapport between him and Marianne seemed to be, but that was, surely, no concern of mine. During my long stay in Nuremberg I spent many a happy weekend in that house and it is regrettable that, for reasons of tact and discretion, no more than that can be told).

The last time I saw Diels[5] was in June 1949 when I was collecting material for a series of articles that I wrote for the Paris edition of the *New York Herald Tribune*[6]. We went for a long walk while Marianne was preparing our meal. He told me of the long, uphill struggle he had had, trying to avoid a harsh verdict under the still functioning de-Nazification proceedings. Diels's farm near Hanover was, he told me, still being held by British Property Control[7].

## NOTES:

1. Marinus van der Lubbe (1909-1934), a Dutchman, was tried, convicted and executed for setting fire to the Reichstag building in Berlin on 27 February 1933, an event that became known as the Reichstag fire.

2. On 20 July 1944, Claus von Stauffenberg and others attempted to assassinate Adolf Hitler in his field headquarters near Rastenburg, East Prussia.

3. After the war the Allied Powers initiated a comprehensive 'de-Nazification' programme. Its purpose was to eradicate National Socialist thought from political, economic, intellectual and cultural life. Nazi laws were abolished and all signs and symbols of National Socialism were removed. The main focus of the programme was the systematic screening of all former members of the NSDAP – party membership was defined as the criteria for their dismissal from executive positions in industry and from public office.

4. Paul Joseph Goebbels (1897-1945) was Germany's Minister of Propaganda from 1933 to 1945 and one of Hitler's closest associates and most devoted followers. He advocated progressively harsher discrimination against the Jews, including extermination in the Holocaust. On 30 April 1945, Goebbels succeeded Hitler as Chancellor, the following day he and his wife committed suicide, after poisoning their six children with cyanide.

5. Rudolf Diels presented an affidavit for the prosecution at the Nuremberg Trials and was also summoned to testify in Goering's defence. After 1950 he served in the post-war government of Lower Saxony and then in the Ministry of the Interior. He died on 18 November 1957 when his rifle accidentally discharged while he was hunting.

6. Following the Nuremberg Trials Wolfe Frank risked his life again by going underground in both West and East Germany to write a series of articles for

the *New York Herald Tribune* (NYHT). During this period Diels was instrumental in bringing to Frank's attention the whereabouts of one of the highest ranked Nazi officers on the Allies most wanted list. Single-handedly Frank tracked him down, confronted him and turned him over to the authorities, not before however he had personally taken the Nazi's confession. The fascinating story of Frank's undercover operations for the *NYHT* are the subject of a separate volume entitled *The Undercover Nazi Hunter: Unmasking Evil in Post-war Germany* soon to be published by Frontline Books.

7. Many German-owned properties and estates were seized by the Property Control Division and handed over to reliable Germans or were held by the Board until the Control Council decided how to dispose of them in the interests of peace.

# FAMILY REUNIONS

BACK IN BAD OEYNHAUSEN IN 1945 my days in the compound were coming to a close with BWCE being rapidly brought up to full strength. We now had translators, clerks, drivers, a quartermaster and all the other paraphernalia that seems to be accumulated wherever an army unit is functioning. This included a number of lorries and Mercedes saloons for officers, one of which had been assigned to me. Within the unit we had three officers, six NCOs and some thirty ORs. Leslie Hill was still with us and we had been joined by Captain Emsley, who was also a linguist.

By the time we received our orders to set off for Nuremberg I had long made up my mind not to take the shortest and quickest route. There were two people I wanted to find first – my mother, from whom I had had no news for over two years, and, if at all possible, my ex-wife Maditta.

We had been instructed as to which route the unit was to take, and it was only after we had left the compound that I told my driver about the planned detour. There wasn't much he could do about it and, in any case, he didn't care a hoot.

We went from Bad Oeynhausen to the Allgau[1] where my mother had been living when I last had news from her (indirectly, of course) and I soon found the elderly woman who had once, during my childhood years, been our housekeeper. Yes, she knew where my mother was and I found her in less than an hour.

She was feeding chickens when I arrived. She had aged terribly and she looked much older than her sixty-seven years. We had not seen each other for seven years; seven years that had been a nightmare for her. She cried at first of course and then she told me of her ordeal. After our last meeting, in Switzerland in the spring of 1939, she had decided to leave Pasing, where we had lived together, and to move to the Allgau where a former governess of mine had promised to find a flat for her,

113

and this is where she was living when war broke out. For some time, nothing changed. There were blackouts and air-raid drills, and rationing was severe, however people were being decent to her.

Then one day in January 1941 an army officer called at her home, which was close to a tiny airfield. She was told I had joined the British Forces and might try to use her, for instance, to give signals for landings on that airstrip, and she would therefore have to leave at once. The local party organisation was taking over, following orders from the military.

That was when her misery began.

She was given just forty-eight hours to move out. No alternative accommodation was available. No, nobody was going to help her. She had, furthermore, been married to a suspicious man, possibly English, and possibly a Jew, and she was required to supply her '*Ariernachweis*' (proof of pure German race) immediately if she wanted to stay out of a concentration camp. My former governess provided a roof over her head and she spent endless hours, writing for documents, collecting birth certificates and resurrecting her pedigree. When it was done, she was told that she was under grave suspicion but would remain free. Her ration coupons, however, were withdrawn, she was not allowed to travel and her health insurance was annulled. Theoretically, she was condemned to death through starvation, or exposure, or illness, but our friends from the days long gone didn't let that happen. So, there she was, feeding their chickens and helping them where she was able, when I suddenly turned up, not as she was quick to say, in the least bit unexpectedly.

There had been one other nasty experience, which she hesitated to relate for fear that it might embarrass me. When the US Army had appeared, they had robbed her of every item of value she had saved and cleaned her out of all she had in the little room in which she was surviving – and they had not been the least bit gentle with her. So the side on which I was serving had stolen, from a helpless old lady, some of my childhood souvenirs. It was one of the injustices of war and it got under my skin.

Months later I was escorting General Curtis LeMay, the top American Commander, through the courthouse in Nuremberg when I interrupted his praise of my performance as an interpreter. 'General,' I said, 'I'm glad you were impressed. Now, could I ask you a favour?' I told him about his gallant men's conduct. He froze and handed me over to his adjutant – and that was the end of that, of course.

Mother had, however, succeeded in saving some pieces of antique furniture and a few pictures, by distributing them amongst some of her friends, and she had hidden a valuable china tea service; all of which she wanted me to take away with me. I could not do that of course, nor could I take mother with me. I was a British officer attached to the United States Army – so how could I turn up at Nuremberg with a German mother?

We had much to tell each other. This sort of reunion puts a great deal of emotional strain on two people who were very close and yet unable to be truly relaxed with each other. I had brought much suffering into her life through my flight from Germany and service for England and I couldn't do anything conclusive to make up for it. (When I was later in a position to offer her a comfortable flat close to me she preferred to remain in a home for the elderly, waiting to get well enough to move into a place of her own; which never happened).

When I had to leave mother with her chickens the following morning she was in excellent spirits. My driver and I headed for Munich and I was wondering whether I would be as successful in locating my former wife Maditta. I need not have worried. As my Mercedes was bouncing over potholes and rubble I spotted her walking along a street – which I had no business taking and where she had no cause to be. She was recognisable to me from 300 yards away by her slightly knock-kneed and very typical walk.

I pulled up alongside her and rolled the window down. She noticed the private, my driver, sitting next to me, and she said in her perfect English – and here I will quote her verbatim: 'Ah, there you are at last. I had expected you much earlier. Let's go to the Conti (the Hotel Continental, only half destroyed, and just around the corner from where we were) and have a chat.'

I told my driver to pick me up from there later and we descended the steps to the air-raid shelter of the Conti which was a cafe in the morning and afternoon, a restaurant for lunch and dinner and a nightclub after 23.00 hours. It was amazingly elegant. The owner, Max Billig, had unearthed some of his own antique furniture, someone had done wonders with wrought iron grills and the place had an atmosphere of luxury which was completely unbelievable to one who had just been picking his way through rubble, ruins and bomb craters and over mountains of bricks and lumps of concrete. Munich had been truly bombed to hell, totally destroyed – Rotterdamned, Hamburgered, to quote some of the ghastly expressions that had been used in the British Press during the war. Perhaps the picture had shaken me all the more because I had lived some of the best years of my life in Munich and was still emotionally attached to the city. (Now that Munich has been most effectively reconstructed I find myself happily aglow and sentimentally affected whenever I go back there. Munich is one of very few places where many things are 'as they used to be').

Having settled down with Maditta to coffee and *weinbrand* (German firewater replacing Cognac) we went about the difficult business of discovering a common denominator for our talk. We had spent a whole war on opposite sides and nine years had passed since we had parted, so hurriedly, when I was running for my life. Events, experiences, impressions and emotions of colossal dimensions had rolled over us. We certainly were two strangers that morning but, as we were groping for a breakthrough in that strange atmosphere, we knew we would find some common ground.

During the two hours we spent talking we could do no more than lay the groundwork for future meetings. We very wisely stayed clear of any suggestion that we pick up where we left off. We were going to see each other again. Years of mind-boggling events could not be catalogued in two hours.

Maditta came to Nuremberg several times thereafter and I saw her in Munich often. However too much had happened to us. No matter how clearly we understood that we had gone through it all on opposite sides of the lines without being opponents, our emotions and feelings for each other had been affected. We had both had many lovers during the intervening years. That didn't come between us; not in the least. What did matter, though, were the new gestures, the new expressions, the new actions and new behaviour that stemmed from those affairs – in other words the new and strange way of making love. None of this might have mattered without the impact of the war, we might have overcome its memories had we been able to go back to our emotional beginning. But it was too much and we finally admitted to it and parted the best of friends. Soon afterwards Maditta married a pre-war Canadian boy-friend and having been told, by German doctors, that she could never have children she presented him with no less than five. And they lived happily ever after.

How emotionally charged those two days had been, I reflected, as finally and irrevocably my driver and I resumed our journey. What, I wondered, was in store for me regarding my outrageous breach of discipline in leaving my assigned path to Nuremberg?

There were approving and disapproving looks when I eventually reported to the courthouse – The Palace of Justice – that afternoon. The approving ones came from those who knew of the mission to which I had assigned myself. The punishing glares came from the new faces that had arrived in Nuremberg together with my new CO, Colonel Hugh Turrell.

Amongst this new lot I discovered one Captain Wormser, a fat slob and a servile character I had known in the Pioneer Corps. He had tail-wagged his way into a promotion to major, which was due any day, and he was clearly miffed by the fact that there I was, promoted to a staff captain and in a fine regiment. Wormser took great pleasure in informing me that Colonel Turrell, who had gone to London for a few days, was only waiting to hear my story before court-martialling me.

Immediate action was called for. I did some asking around and discovered that the highest-ranking member of the British contingent at Nuremberg was Sir David Maxwell Fyfe[2]. I made straight for his office. I had heard nothing but the highest praise for him whenever his name was mentioned. Formally, there was no excuse for what I had done, but perhaps Sir David would listen to the human aspect of my story. He did, and although he thought the matter was serious, he could see why I broke the rules to see my mother. He couldn't and wouldn't say what disciplinary action I would have to face, but he would have a word with the colonel when he returned to see if my obvious linguistic contribution to the task on hand could be maintained.

Predictably, he succeeded. I got a dressing-down when Turrell returned which included the moot question of what would happen if everybody were to act like me, there being a war on. My in-born tact prevented me from enlightening the colonel to the fact that there wasn't a war, not anymore, except between him and me. Our mutual dislike for each other was blatant from the first moment we met and it survived until he went home to be de-mobbed. Hardly anybody liked Turrell. He was out of his depth among our lot. There were ex PoWs, including some real heroes, like Airey Neave[3], intelligence agents, historians, language teachers and writers and we were all very much through with 'soldiering' as Hugh Turrell knew it. (The situation is best summed up by his departure. He had given a party and, sadly, only a few of us had been able to attend. He walked up to me and another officer to bid us farewell. 'Goodbye, Sir,' I forced myself to say, successfully supressing the 'good luck' part of it. 'Goodbye, Sir,' said my companion, Captain Peter Fraser, 'it's nice to see you go').

I could see as I left Turrell's office after having been castigated that barring a miracle, my staff captain's rank was now safe forever – in other words, I didn't need to worry about promotion. I didn't try, and I didn't get it.

Turrell had no say regarding our assignments, our offices or our duty hours. The military nonsense was being performed by non-specialists among the officers and men, and the few occasions when we acted like soldiers involved the running of our billets – villas in a suburb of Nuremberg – drawing rations, being carried in Army vehicles, applying for leave and picking up the paycheque. The latter item was somewhat undersized compared to what our American hosts were hauling down. I discovered, for instance, that my pay including extras was considerably less than that of an American sergeant!

## NOTES:

1. The Allgau is a region in southern Germany that covers parts of the south of Bavaria and parts of Austria and stretches from the pre-alpine lands up to the Alps.

2. Sir David Maxwell Fyfe (1900-1967) was a Member of Parliament, lawyer and judge who variously held the offices of Solicitor General, Attorney General, Home Secretary and Lord High Chancellor. He later became the Earl of Kilmuir. At Nuremberg he was Britain's Deputy Chief Prosecutor and his cross-examination of Hermann Goering, which was translated by Wolfe Frank, is regarded as having been one of the most noted in history. At the time he was preparing to go underground in Soviet-occupied East Germany to write his 'Hangover After Hitler' series for the NYHT. Sir David wrote, 'From my knowledge and daily experience of your performance as a most efficient and capable interpreter during the trial of the major Nazi War Criminals at Nuremberg, I know that you have a profound knowledge of the Nazi Background in Germany, both from the historical and the personal point of view.'

3. Airey Middleton Neave (1916-1979) was the first British officer to successfully escape from the prisoner-of-war camp at Colditz Castle and later worked for MI9. A well-qualified lawyer, he spoke fluent German and at the IMT in Nuremberg he read the indictments to the Nazi war criminals on trial and was an investigator for the Krupp trial. He was elected MP for Abingdon in 1953 and was assassinated in March 1979 when an IRA bomb was exploded under his car as he drove out of the Palace of Westminster car park.

# THE NUREMBERG SCENE

ONCE AT NUREMBERG WE WERE HOUSED and fed by the US Army, on rations that made our British Army fare look like a starvation diet. We had our liquor allowance, which was substantial, we drank in the US officers' clubs for very little money, and we could not, of course, spend money on the German economy – firstly because this was strictly *'verboten'* and, secondly, because there was nothing to buy. There was however a lot to be traded and our American hosts, outside the trial staff, were deeply involved in these activities from the word go. Anyone involved in the trial was under such strict orders to keep away from the Germans that obedience was only one option, at least for a while.

The degree to which the rules were broken, as time went on, depended on the individual. As a rule of thumb, I would say that in the British contingent fat slob Wormser broke none and I broke the lot. We will come to that in due course.

I was assigned accommodation, a share in a batman and a desk in an office where Leslie Hill and I were to crank out translations. The Justizpalast (Palace of Justice) was buzzing with excitement, rumours and guesses as to when the trial would start. I obviously wanted to see the show. So did everybody else. Inevitably, it became apparent that only a miracle would get us into the courtroom that would have, we were told, only thirty to fifty seats for spectators. Clearly, we couldn't expect to see the show unless we were doing a job involving our presence in court – and translators were not involved. But for me the miracle happened. I owed it to the same voluminous personal history form that had made me the most successful machine-gun instructor in French, of my regiment, the Northumberland Fusiliers. Here is what occurred.

Enter full Colonel, United States Army, chest covered in impressive fruit salad (medals). Colonel casts approving glance upon virginal note pad on Frank's desk, winces at Hill's un-interrupted, frenzied activity. Obviously familiar with British badges of rank, he casts a glance at

Frank's three 'pips' and beckons him to follow. Outside office, he introduces himself:

'I am Colonel Dostert[1.]' This was said in English with a thick, French accent, 'and I am in charge of the language division here for the US Army. Come to my office weeese me, please.'

I hadn't a clue what this was all about. We pushed through a dense crowd of very busy people in an anteroom, some of them snapping to the American version of attention. I noticed that the office had a carpet. I was mixing with the haute-volee (VIPs), obviously – and then I saw it: Army Form (questionnaire) l7X49B/3l (94), dated sometime in 1940, truthfully completed by me. 'Wherever, Sir, did you get THAT?' I gasped. He then explained:

Dostert was President Eisenhower's English/French interpreter and a good friend. When 'Ike' had first become aware of the plans for bringing the top Nazis to trial he had tried to picture how the language problem could be solved. He had, understandably, had moments of irritation in the face of consecutive interpretations, in his activities as top commander.

'Surely, Leon,' the conversation between Ike and Dostert had run, 'this means if a guy says something in German, some other guy has to translate it into English?'

'Yes, General, and somebody else has to translate it into French, and somebody else into Russian … and if a guy says something in Russian that has to be translated into English, and into French, and into German.'

The Supreme Commander of Allied Forces was pacing the floor.

'Holy Mackerel, Leon,' he commanded 'You gotta do something.'

And simultaneous interpretation was born.

Dostert had taught languages at the University of New York. His mind had always been preoccupied with the subject of simultaneous interpretation. We will shortly hear what it involves. Heretofore in every sphere of life – diplomacy, industry, science and all other areas, interpretation had always been done consecutively. There had been attempts at the League of Nations, to accelerate these translations by doing them all at the same time via the required number of channels after the orator had finished, but nothing had come of it.

Leon Dostert had always wanted to create a system whereby the words of a speaker would be translated into another language as they were being spoken. However, the opportunity and the means were lacking – now, here it was. He had Ike's support, he would do it, and he did.

He sat in on the negotiations to set up the trial of the major war criminals. When the statesmen, the jurists, the historians and the military had had their say he raised his point as follows:

'If the trials were to hold water,' he said, 'it would be necessary that anything said in one language would have to be translated, verbatim, into the other languages used in the courtroom; English, French, Russian and German. This meant three repetitions, in three languages, of every sentence spoken during the trial. It meant that every written statement, every written exhibit, every written plea would have to be translated beforehand and read into the record, in court, in the other three languages. It meant also that every question addressed to a witness in direct or cross-examination would have to be translated first into his or her language, and then into the other two for the benefit of counsel, the tribunal and the defendants. Further,' he said, 'cross-examinations would lose their impact if questions were asked in a language which the witness understood, because he would have the right to hear the question in his mother tongue, a disastrous handicap for prosecution and defence alike. Every reaction in that courtroom would be delayed by a time factor of three times the original statement. It also meant that the trial would last three times as long, cost three times as much and that, to put it in simple terms, it would fall flat. There may also be many auxiliary effects, such as people dying, including defendants, or returning home (not including defendants) and many, many more.'

Dostert had put all this to the powers that be and the reaction had been something like, 'for heaven's sake, solve it,' and he did.

Simultaneous interpretation is now being used so widely that few people need information on it, but when the Nuremberg Trials started, no one knew about it. Thus, we read in the Press that: 'For simultaneous interpretation, an installation involving earphones, microphones and selector switches is required. The original statement, such as testimony before the court, is delivered into a microphone that is connected, by cable, to the earphones of an interpreter. As he listens to the speaker, the interpreter will deliver, simultaneously, a spoken translation into a microphone in his booth, or cabin. A cable connects his microphone as well as those of other interpreters, seated in other booths, to a selector switch, installed at every seat in the auditorium where a listener can dial that channel which carries the language he wishes to hear, such as, for instance, Channel 1 for English, Channel 2 for French, Channel 3 for Russian and Channel 4 for German'.

This was the system which Dostert was planning to install in the Nuremberg court room. He solved the problem of the installation easily, and Tom Watson, the head of IBM, agreed to have it built and shipped to Nuremberg before the trial began.

The second component of the scheme was not so easy to arrange; this was the interpreters, an indispensable item on the agenda, and they had to be found – if, indeed, they existed.

As far as Dostert was concerned, he needed truly bi-lingual people. They had to know, to all intents and purposes, every word they were going to hear during the trial in one language and know its counterpart in the language into which they were going to interpret. They had to know the psychology, the character, the intellect (or lack thereof), the history, and background, of the people whose mother tongue they were to interpret into their, the interpreter's language. In actual fact, they had to have lived in 'the other' country, or at least extensively among its people.

To achieve the total accuracy Dostert wanted for the trial, he would therefore need three interpreters for each booth – one for each of the languages from which the booth was working. For example: in the English booth he required one interpreter to work from French, one from German and one from Russian. This meant twelve interpreters were needed for the team, but one team could not have worked uninterrupted. Dostert decided, quite correctly, that he needed three teams, or thirty-six bi-linguists.

Having found a handful in the US, he ran out of candidates. He discovered a few more in Geneva and still didn't have enough. So he obtained carte blanche from a suitably high-ranking source to search all the personnel files anywhere in Germany that might lead to suitable candidates. His staff went to the US personnel office in Frankfurt and British Army Headquarters. Naturally, they researched personnel files in Nuremberg and that's how he discovered me.

During our first meeting Dostert grilled me for two hours about my background, education, topical subjects, hobbies, contacts, references and my Army career. When we finished, he requested (ordered would have been more accurate) my transfer from Turrell's minions to his own staff.

The CO was upset. Here was the worst officer he had, getting the best job. He even put up some resistance and got himself into everybody's bad books, but I bequeathed my stack of un-translated documents to Leslie Hill, pulled up stakes and departed towards the camp of the interpreting staff-to-be.

**NOTE:**

1. Colonel Leon Dostert (1904-1971) was a French born American scholar of languages who introduced Simultaneous Interpretation to the world at the Nuremberg Trials where he was Head of the US Language Division.

# INTERROGATIONS AND ASSISTING GOERING, ET AL.

THERE THEN FOLLOWED A FASCINATING PERIOD when, before the arrival of my colleagues and the equipment from IBM, I was assigned to pre-trial interrogations of the defendants-to-be and the innumerable witnesses whom teams of investigators had been rounding up on the orders of the prosecuting teams.

There were hundreds of these pre-trial interrogations and a series of small interrogation rooms had been constructed, most of them wired for sound recording, where the prosecution teams were busy piecing together the story of the Third Reich. Simultaneously, defence counsels were consulting with their clients; they, obviously, did not need interpreters.

The subject matter of these interrogations was often trivial such as the identification of a document or a minor clarification of a man's background, but there were also some enormously dramatic moments. An outstanding example was an interrogation of Field Marshall Wilhelm Keitel who was known as '*Lakeitel*' to the Germans, meaning 'The little lackey' because of his total subservience to the Fuehrer, in connection with the shooting of a number of British RAF officers. They had escaped from a PoW camp near Breslau. Most of them had been recaptured and, contrary to the rules, transferred into the custody of the Gestapo. Himmler reported the incident to Hitler who went into a rage. 'An example had to be made of the escape,' he declared. However, he refused to deprive Goering of the jurisdiction over these men, which he held since they were prisoners of the Luftwaffe. Hitler ordered that Goering appear at his estate in Berchtesgaden, however Goering heard of this before the order reached him and he went into hiding.

Keitel had to take Goering's place and Hitler ordered the execution of the RAF officers. Keitel's meek objections regarding the pertinent conventions were quashed by a screaming Fuehrer and the Field Marshal had to slink off to the nearest telephone to order the murders. He did so by contacting the top Gestapo man in Breslau, a man named Müller, who stood the victims against the wall and machine-gunned them to death. They had been in the hands of the Gestapo for nearly three days. Subsequently Ribbentrop, on Hitler's orders, concocted the official reply to an enquiry by the International Red Cross: 'The prisoners had been shot whilst trying to escape.'

When we, the interrogators, started unravelling the story, we were desperately short of facts. But Rudolf Diels reconstructed the channels of command for us and, working backwards from Müller's underlings (he was dead by now) we traced the events back to Keitel, mostly by conjecture. We now needed Keitel's admission of guilt for what had been one of the most incriminating deeds of his career. The interrogator was Colonel Williams of the US Army. He was brilliant. For three whole days he spun his net and finally Hitler's top officer was caught in it and admitted responsibility. He filled in the gaps in the record for us and claimed he was only obeying superior orders in mitigation. He was then left alone with me, and the two guards. I saw an excellent chance for an off-the-record chat.

'Herr Keitel,' (we weren't using ranks or titles) I said, 'you have had a long career as a German general officer. You must have known by heart every international convention on land warfare ever signed by Germany. You were obviously aware of the criminal aspect of this execution order when you handed it down. Am I right in thinking that you did so simply because you were still believing in a German victory and could not imagine, by any stretch of the imagination, that you could ever be held to account for this crime and the many others you have committed?' Keitel's face had turned purple whilst I was speaking. He rose from his chair and spoke past me, almost inaudibly, with his strong Saxon accent being very noticeable.

'I was with the Fuehrer when the bomb exploded in the *Bürgerbräukeller*[1]. I would give anything to have been killed by his side then.' With that, Germany's highest-ranking military figure clicked his heels and was marched off to his cell.

Shortly after I had my first encounter with Hermann Goering.

Intelligence reports had reached the security people in Nuremberg that all over Germany an unusual number of railway tickets were being purchased for Nuremberg. Unfounded rumours suggested that plans were afoot to kidnap Goering from jail. Security precautions in the courthouse had been dramatically increased and an order had been issued excluding him from the daily exercise period prisoners were allowed in the courtyard of the building. Goering could not, I was told, be brought to an interrogation room, so I would be taken to his cell to discuss with him his choice of counsel.

On that dark, rainy Sunday afternoon I came very close to making history – and I missed my chance! As the door of Goering's cell was noisily unlocked, the former Reichmarshall rose from his cot where he had, obviously, been napping. Feeling rather nervous, I told him why I was there.

'Ah,' he said '*sehr schoen*' (splendid). He offered me a seat on his cot and proceeded to apologise for the lack of hospitality. 'I have asked for some of my furniture from Carinhall[2] to be brought here,' he declared, poker-faced. 'It has still not arrived. I blame the management.'

Quite a sense of humour, I thought, looking at Goering for the first time, somewhat overawed by the occasion. I also noted that he was not using his dentures. He was lisping in the manner typical of the temporarily toothless. He had not bothered to put his trousers on either but had wrapped a blanket around his legs as he was sitting down next to me. He certainly looked very different from photographs I had seen. He was much slimmer and with a pasty complexion after several months in prison. He also had deep rings under his eyes, probably the effect of the drug withdrawal programme he had undergone[3], but his eyes themselves were very alert and his intelligence was obvious.

We turned to the matter at hand – the choice of a defence counsel. He looked at the list I presented to him and ran a well-kept finger down the forty-odd names. 'Thissh ish difficult,' he lisped. 'I don't know any of theesh people. In the past, when I had a legal problem, I changed the law.' But let me see ...' and he stopped at a name of Dr Otto Stahmer of Hamburg. 'Ah, that's a nice-sounding German name. I will have him' – and he did.

Stahmer arrived in Nuremberg a few days later, totally overawed by the thought of his client and the assignment. He needn't have been. Goering handled his own defence brilliantly as a strategist, tactician and performer par excellence. Stahmer was assigned his cues and, during Goering's performance in the witness box Stahmer's role was that of a prompter who asked hundreds of questions, all suitably arranged by his client in order to deliver a thirteen-hour speech in his, and the Third Reich's, defence. The questions had been dictated to a bewildered Stahmer whose own questions had been impatiently waved aside. He didn't really fathom the story line until he surfaced at the end of Goering's testimony.

Some time after Goering's suicide, I was relating the story of my Sunday visit to his cell to a friend, Tom Ready of Associated Press. Tom stared at me in amazement for a long time and then exploded 'You stupid …,' he screamed. 'Didn't you know Goering had perfect teeth?'

It took some time to sink in. If Goering had his own teeth, why was he talking like a toothless person? My God, I thought, because he was concealing something in his mouth … but more about that later.

A most memorable and bizarre duty came soon after my meeting with Goering. The peace of my duty-free Sunday was interrupted by a call from the courthouse. The authorities had finally completed the list of German lawyers who were considered eligible to defend the other top men in Hitler's Reich. As far as I could ascertain, they were lawyers who would not have to go before a German De-Nazification Court and could therefore be considered available. Presumably, they had been asked if they were prepared to go on the list from which the defendants could choose the counsel. They were living all over Germany and I had not heard of any of them. My orders on that Sunday were to present the list of lawyers to the future defendants and to have each of them settle on a counsel who was then to be contacted in order to obtain his consent.

The meetings were to be arranged in an interrogation room and I was to be accompanied by an officer of the tribunal.

My first customer on that Sunday in Nuremberg jail was Dr Robert Ley, Hitler's labour leader. He was brought to an interrogation room and I found him to be excessively nervous. In fact, he had difficulty in speaking. I put the list of lawyers before him but he began to talk, disjointedly, of the possibility of handling his own defence – he didn't however pursue this line for long. He looked at the list, absentmindedly, and then said: 'I have given much thought to being defended by a Hebrew lawyer, I mean, a Jew,' and he said something about it being a 'just turn of fate' if he were to be defended by such a person. I could not offer such a choice from the list for reasons that hardly require elucidation. He finally selected a name from the list but the services of this counsel were not required; Ley hanged himself in his cell soon afterwards.

Rudolf Hess was next. He looked terrible. His cheeks were deeply sunken, his burning eyes had an insane look to them, his mouth was only a slit and he remained defiant, if not belligerent, throughout our conversation. He had no intention of defending himself he declared at one moment and then announced that he would defend himself. I explained patiently that he would not know how to do this in the face of the unfamiliar rules of procedure.

'*Das ist mir gleichguelting* (I couldn't care less),' snarled Hess and that was his answer to any other argument I put forward. The interview ended inconclusively. Later, Hess was defended by Dr Alfred Seidl, one of the most intelligent, tenacious and vociferous lawyers before the

Tribunal, who put up an excellent fight for his client (and did so afterwards during Hess' imprisonment in Berlin).

Then a truly memorable discussion arose with Dr Ernst Kaltenbrunner, Head of the infamous Reichssicherheitshauptamt or RSHA – the Reich's security department – from which had come every one of the orders to detain citizens in the concentration camps. All the orders were signed 'Kaltenbrunner, Chief of Security Police'. Yet he claimed, during the trial, that this was done by means of a facsimile – a rubber stamp – and without his knowledge of its existence or function.

Kaltenbrunner looked very tall and monster-like when he entered the room late that evening. Only a desk lamp with a green glass shade was lighting the room and as he walked up to my desk, wearing heavy flying boots and a somewhat shapeless set of clothing, part Austrian costume, part uniform, the resemblance to Boris Karloff as Frankenstein was impressive.

He sat down and surprised me with a soft, cultured voice and he spoke with a pleasant Austrian accent. However, his eyes were small, watery and beady and I felt an intense wave of revulsion sweep over me. I knew nothing of his crimes or the role he had been playing at that time; the feeling was completely intuitive. (Some of Kaltenbrunner's stories, told in his defence when his turn came, were simply ridiculous. He was found guilty of the host of crimes with which he was charged, including executions which he ordered personally during a trip to the concentration camp at Mauthausen).

However, the Kaltenbrunner sitting opposite me that day was accusing his captors of considerable unkindness. He complained about the glaringly bright light shining into his cell at night, spoiling his sleep, and of the lack of notepaper and pencil on which to write his memoirs, or letters to his 'beloved wife and family from whom he had been separated for so long and who he was missing terribly'. (He had been captured in the house of his mistress who was now living with an American in Nuremberg and spilling the beans). I was totally dumbfounded when, in fact, he produced tears at that point of his monologue.

As far as a defence counsel was concerned, none of the names before him appealed to him. He wanted, so he explained, to be defended by a colleague from the days of his studies in Vienna, Dr Gustav von Scanzoni. This was a famous name. Scanzoni was an expert on international law who had been forced to leave Germany for political reasons when the Nazis came to power. He was known to be living in Zurich.

I aimed to give Dr Kaltenbrunner the perfect service and picked up the telephone.

Through an excellent performance by the US Signal Corps, Scanzoni was on the line within five minutes. It was against the rules to allow Kaltenbrunner to talk to him, so I conducted the conversation for him. I still vividly remember what was said:

'This is Captain Frank, British Army, speaking from Nuremberg, Dr von Scanzoni. I have been instructed by the International Military Tribunal to help the future defendants in selecting their defence counsel. May I ask whether you are familiar with the subject of the proposed trial?'

'*Natuerlich* (of course)' came the answer and the tone of his voice did not seem too friendly. I went on: 'I am now with Dr Ernst Kaltenbrunner, your former fellow student. He says you will certainly remember him. He wishes me to ask you if you are willing to handle his defence before the Tribunal.'

The lengthy answer was neither complimentary to Kaltenbrunner nor couched in terms as one would expect to hear from a man of such superior intellect. Nor was there any interrupting the outburst. In fact, before I had completed my piece of polite acknowledgement, the famous jurist had hung up on me.

Kaltenbrunner settled on somebody else. Before he was taken away to his cell I said something to him that was certainly a breach of the regulations: 'Kaltenbrunner, you have provided a most pleasant memory for me – I saw you cry!'

Nothing unusual occurred during my conversations with the other top Nazis when each of them picked their defence counsel from the names on the list.

**NOTES:**

1. The Bürgerbräukeller was a large beer hall in Munich where, on 8 November 1933, an assassination attempt was made on Hitler's life.

2. Carinhall, in the Schorfheide Forest north-east of Berlin, was Hermann Goering's country residence.

3. Goering was injured in the Beer Hall Putsch in 1923 and whilst receiving treatment for his injuries he developed an addiction to morphine, which persisted until the end of his life. Whilst awaiting trial at Nuremberg he was weaned off the drug and put on a strict diet, losing some 27k in weight, it has been said.

# REHEARSALS

A T THIS POINT WE MUST TRIFURCATE MY ACCOUNT because there are three aspects to this chapter in my life which deserve to be related: (a) the interpreting story; (b) the trial and the men involved; and (c) my own life in the middle of it all.

Having been an interpreter at the Nuremberg Trials of the Major War Criminals, Goering et al., is an unfailing conversation piece and as such seems to arouse as much interest as ever.

To have been labelled 'The Voice of Doom' in the international press after I announced to the defendants the verdicts – their actual sentences – entitles me to a minor degree of immortality, I suppose.

Towards the end of October 1945, all of Dostert's bilinguals had arrived, none of whom, including me, had ever interpreted simultaneously. We would all have welcomed the opportunity to practice the art. Could one really, we were wondering, listen to earphones and deliver speech into a microphone clearly, loudly and quickly enough to do the trick? We had to wait for the answer.

The IBM equipment had been duly shipped to Bremerhaven where a truck was to pick it up and deliver it to Nuremberg. However, perhaps predictably, the load went astray and ended up in Genoa, Italy, where some signal officer of the US Army was feeling at quite a loss as to what to do with it. Fortunately, he stumbled across a bill of loading from which he deduced the equipment's destination. Better still, he had heard about the trials and, knowing they were just about to start, sent a signal to his counterpart in Nuremberg, one Major Evans, whose technicians were waiting to install it all. The major roared off to Genoa and brought back the consignment.

Unfortunately, it was now late in the day: the trial would open on the 20 November 1945; the courtroom was being rebuilt; and when the equipment arrived it was time to install it. The technicians had a spare amplifier, a few microphones and a lot of earphones and they rigged it all up for us to practice in an attic. We had just five days (and nights) to turn ourselves into 'Simultaneous Interpreters' under Dostert's tutelage. Only one of us could practice at any one time since we had no booths, and these practice sessions covered every aspect of our brand new profession. (The institutes of learning nowadays allocate from one to four years for the teaching of the techniques necessary to achieve the required levels of competence). I shared the attic with an interesting collection of court interpreters-to-be.

There was Margo Bortlin, a tall, blonde American who was labelled the 'Passionate Haystack' so named partly because of the intricate structure of tresses piled on top of her head and partly because of some indiscreet rumours from the grapevine. Margot became a remarkably competent and accurate interpreter, only slightly handicapped by a voice that was unbelievably twangy and metallic, and a glass-hard American accent. She was as over-awed as the rest of us by the gadgetry before us and the first sentence she ever uttered into a microphone referred to a Nazi law as 'backfiring' (*rueckwirkend* in German), instead of being retroactive. I believe this was the only mistake Margot made at any time.

There was Tom Brown, Professor of Languages at the University of Florida. He was the most consistently successful poker player at Nuremberg. Tom achieved recognition – and as far as the long-suffering press corps was concerned, total approval – during testimony by a German who was asked if he had attended a high-level Gestapo meeting in Berlin. The German answer to this simple question ran like this: 'My Lord, it must of course be appreciated that this happened several years ago and I must endeavour to cast my mind back very far,' (There was no sound from Brown in the English booth) 'a difficult task, considering the momentous events which were taking place then and afterwards,' (still total silence from Brown), 'but I think I can recall that on the day in question I was attending the funeral of my brother-in-arms Schmitt in Munich. It would, therefore, be a safe and reasonable assumption and statement to say that I could not have attended the meeting in Berlin.' At which point we heard the translation from the English booth 'No, my Lord!' – it was greatly appreciated by all concerned.

There was Captain Harry Sperber of the US Army (see Plate 9). German by birth Harry became a successful cartoonist in New York. He had been one of German radio's most popular sports commentators and, as his speciality was boxing, he had been sent to the USA to cover the Max Schmeling[1]-Joe Louis fight. Whilst in New York, and having done some of the pre-fight broadcasts for German radio, the Nazi

Propaganda Ministry discovered Harry was Jewish. Goebbels was informed and had a cable sent to Sperber ordering him to withdraw from the assignment and, incredible as this may sound, to provide a suitable replacement. Sperber's reply appeared in every newspaper around the world, excluding Germany, and it read: 'Dr Goebbels. Goetz von Berlichingen. Sperber.' (Goetz von Berlichingen is the knight in Goethe's play of the same name who appears at the window of his beleaguered castle and shouts at the enemy: '*Leck mich am Arsch*' – 'Kiss my Arse' words which in polite German society one did not use.

There was a pretty girl from New York, Virginia von Schon, who had grown up in the sheltered atmosphere of a truly God-fearing, Catholic German-American family. She was an extremely literary young lady, with one serious gap in her education, she knew not one 'bad' word – not one. A German witness for the defence was on one occasion rendering an enthusiastic account of the 'holiday-like' atmosphere in a concentration camp, where, he asserted: 'They had schools, a university, library, a gymnasium, went for walks in the country and even had a ...' at which point Virginia had dried up. 'What did the witness say, they even had?' enquired Lord Justice Lawrence. This went back to the witness, via the German booth, and he reiterated his enthusiastic account of Himmler's, 'home away from home'. The third time round, the monitor, a much decorated American infantry captain, who was permanently seated outside our booths to cope with the unexpected, reached over and seized Virginia's microphone, 'A whorehouse, my Lord, a whorehouse,' he explained. 'And the Tribunal will look into the question of amending the record,' said his Lordship in closing the incident.

One other major correction off the record became necessary when another prim young lady interpreter, lacking profanity of language, did not know what to do with the German word '*Scheisskerle*' which means 'Dirty Shits' (plural). She searched her memory frantically for a dirty word and could only think of one – 'Fucking Fellows' she said, in impeccable King's English. The record was amended.

There was also a phenomenon among us, Prince George Vassiltchikov an American-born direct descendant of the late Tsar of Russia. I will always remember George for three outstanding qualities: (a) he had three unbelievably beautiful sisters; (b) he became the best Russian-English Interpreter at the United Nations; and (c) he suffered from an extremely bad stammer. This, for an interpreter, would appear to be an insurmountable handicap. But George's stammer disappeared the instant he faced a live microphone. It was an eerie thing to be listening to his linguistic stumblings one second and to hear them replaced by the smoothest possible delivery an instant later.

Back at the Palace of Justice our five days of rehearsals in the attic were soon over and the gadgets were whisked away to be installed in the courtroom. The opening of the Trial was only eleven days away. We kept reading to each other, practicing voice control, delivery, syntax, grammar, vocabulary, reading documents, hearing lectures by attorneys, and helping

Dostert set up the teams. He had wisely decided and decreed that a team could not work longer than an hour and a half at any one stretch. He had made up three teams; A, B and C. Team A would work the morning session, starting at 09.30 hours and continue until the morning recess at 11.00 hours. During that time, Team B would be sitting in an adjoining room – number 606, I remember – listening to the proceedings in the courtroom, thus ensuring complete continuity of terminology and awareness of what had been happening. Team C, on that day would be resting. On the following day, Team B would start, and C, as listeners, would pick up the vocabulary. Team A would be free, and so the rotation would continue. Each team had twelve interpreters, three per language, except for the Russians who ran their own show and never joined us in room 606, or anywhere else, for that matter.

This arrangement had the additional advantage of ensuring a three-day weekend for two out of three teams, one being off duty on Friday, the other on Monday, the third on the following weekend. Later, after we had overcome our initial stage fright and almost unbearable nervous tension, the working hours arranged by Dostert were the maximum of what we could do.[2]

**NOTES:**

1. Maximilian Schmeling (1905-2005) was a German former world heavy-weight boxing champion who fought American Joe Louis in New York in 1938 for the world title. Because of their national associations the fight became a worldwide cultural event. Louis won by knocking Schmeling out in the first round – an event that did not please Adolf Hitler or the Nazi Party.

2. At times 'Dostert broke his shift system to take advantage of Frank's outstanding qualities as an interpreter' (Ann and John Tusa, *The Nuremberg Trial*). It seems also that on occasions, and because he was the best, the BBC requested that the Tribunal use Frank for the more important broadcasts and in his memoirs Dostert makes it clear that Frank was the only interpreter who could be used in both the English and the German booths.

# DEBUT PERFORMANCE

THE DEGREE OF ACCURACY REQUIRED FROM US, the total concentration on the proceedings, even when one was not actually interpreting, and the tension emanating from the courtroom during the ten-month mental battle fought over the lives of the twenty-one defendants, put a tremendous strain on the nervous and mental stamina of the interpreters.

None of this was obvious to us when 20 November dawned after, for most of us, a sleepless night. I was to give my debut in the German booth and had been reading, and re-reading, the opening statements to be read by Justice Jackson and Sir Hartley Shawcross.[1] They were to be preceded by an opening statement by the President of the Tribunal, Sir Geoffrey Lawrence and the indictment would be read in open court. Translations of these documents had reached us a day earlier, so we had been able to prepare ourselves to the extent that we knew these texts. What terrified us most was the business of listening and talking simultaneously, and, of course, the prospect of impromptu statements that were certain to occur. I had met Karl Anders, a commentator of the BBC's German service a couple of days before and he had casually mentioned, 'About fifty million people will be listening to your German interpretation of the opening of the trial' – a prospect that did not exactly tranquilize my nerves. (That figure grew to several hundred million when I interpreted Goering's testimony four months later, but by then I was an old hand at the game).

Starting on that morning of 20 November 1945 we, the newly created 'Multi-Lingual Simultaneous Court Interpreters' set out on the seemingly endless task of voicing six million words – predominantly in English and German – that were spoken during the ten-month trial. On that first morning, seated in the German booth, my mouth was painfully dry and my hands were shaking. Never before, or since, have I known such nervous pressure or such a fear of the unexpected. It was comparable to those feelings I had had (in a previous life) at the start of those downhill ski races in which I had competed where one's fear is of having a bad tumble in full view of the spectators.

On opening day we had a full house, of course. The Press gallery was packed. The Defence and Prosecution teams were all in place. The lights were glaringly bright for the photographers (no film cameras). The glassed-in booths for radio commentators, above the room, were filled to capacity. Then the klieg lights[2] were turned off and the photographers withdrew. The Marshall of the court announced the entry of the Tribunal – and suddenly I was interpreting for the first time. I don't remember doing the few impromptu comments by the President, but I do remember having started reading the German translation of his opening remarks. I told myself to put more expression into my reading, to speak more clearly, to work on my voice control and to stop shaking. I managed all of that fairly quickly, but the jitters took weeks to disappear and the nervous tension never completely left me.

We were, after all, involved in the writing of history and our contribution was of the greatest importance. None of the judges understood German and everything said in that courtroom to them by the defendants and witnesses passed through the ears, brains and mouths of we interpreters.

It worked!

R.W. Cooper, the correspondent of *The Times* had this to say about our performance: 'It all worked splendidly, in spite of occasional delays through technical hitches and, in the beginning at least, translations that broke off in mid-air and made little sense. In such cases recourse could always be had to the recording of the original statement as a check to the shorthand record. Considering the limitless scope of the issues involved, technicalities of politics, military terms or the empty phrases of Nazi jargon, every credit is due to the international band of translators under Colonel Leon Dostert, a teacher of French literature in the United States.'

At this point Mr Cooper's comments become rather complimentary as far as I am concerned and modesty does not prevent me from quoting him further: 'And by common accord Captain Wolfe Frank, translating from German into English, who came to Nuremberg in British uniform and returned as a civilian, was the ace of them all.'

He did not, of course, listen to the German booth but writes: 'The translations into German, happily, were especially well done, as could be seen from the readiness with which the accused and their counsels followed the proceedings.'

Certainly, at no time during the entire trial was there a complaint, or even a challenge, directed at the interpreters. This implies an unqualified seal of approval for Dostert's daring experiment that, so a mathematically gifted observer pointed out, shortened the Nuremberg Trials by at least three years.

## NOTES:

1. Sir Hartley Shawcross KC, MP, HM Attorney-General was the Chief British Prosecutor at the IMT.

2. Klieg lights are powerful lights used in filming and photography.

# RETURN TO CIVVY STREET

BEFORE AND JUST AFTER THE BEGINNING OF THE TRIAL we were isolated from anything German, but as time passed by, I established good and sane relations with many Germans and I gradually worked out a way of living a normal life. Old friendships were resurrected, and new ones were made.

I had my contact, through Diels, with his friends who lived outside the town and for some time, my visits to them had to be kept secret.

There was no lack of diversionary activities. The US Army was doing a great deal more to entertain and pamper its men than we, in the British contingent, had ever known. The PX – the shop for the courthouse personnel – was well stocked with the kind of luxurious merchandise I hadn't seen since before the war. Food rations were generous and even our British Army cook could not ruin them completely. Most of the time I was eating in an American officers' mess, and the playground for all was the Grand Hotel, opposite the Nuremberg station, which served meals one could buy against 'scrip' – a military currency. The hotel boasted the Marble Room, a ballroom for dancing to German bands and a nightly floorshow. The bar was well stocked and Charley, the barman, was a first-class exponent of the art. There was hardly an evening when I did not adjourn to this 'home away from home'.

I did have a transportation problem. Colonel Turrell, who was in charge of transport, had introduced some absurd rule whereby senior ranks, major and above, were entitled to use staff cars with drivers whilst junior officers, including me, the eternal captain, had to ride in army trucks equipped with uncomfortable seats, and we were restricted to carefully planned communal outings. Such a truck would, for instance, depart from the Grand Hotel for my billet in Zirndorf five minutes after the official closing of the Marble Room, thus precluding any extracurricular activities, such as sex, unless one could stay overnight. This had to be corrected. I needed a car, but there was no way of getting one – officially. Barman Charley came to the rescue. He knew of a small Opel, tucked away in the garage of some widow or other, which could be obtained against some vital food and medical items the old lady needed but couldn't get on the German economy. Nor could she ever hope to get the car back on the road as she didn't rate any petrol under strict German rationing, and the car, furthermore, had no papers.

The deal was consummated, and I now owned an Opel Olympia that had no papers or number plates. Fortunately, Major Tom Hedges, the officer in charge of security in the Palace of Justice (who came through with all sorts of other gifts as time went by) produced some beautiful, self-reflecting plates from his garage. They were Swedish. He also introduced me to the sergeant in charge of the American motor pool – and I had fuel.

My undocumented Swedish plates were only challenged once. I was driving along the Autobahn towards Berchtesgaden, when I was flagged-down by an officer who had just overtaken me in a Mercedes. His car, to my horror, had Swedish plates. This could mean trouble. However, as the officer came walking up to me I saw that his uniform was that of the International Red Cross. Things were looking better. Then a flood of words in Swedish descended upon me. This was not so good. 'Sorry' I managed to interrupt, 'but I don't speak Swedish.'

How come, he wanted to know, was I driving a Swedish car? I concocted a totally insane and improbable story. I had, I told him, bought the car from a member of the British Embassy in Stockholm. My friend had gone back there and was sending me the papers and the car would then be registered with British plates. As this nonsense was pouring out, my tall and distinguished compatriot was beginning to grin. 'Ah,' he said, 'I see.' He introduced himself as Count Bernadotte, Head of the International Red Cross. He wished me good luck and departed with a friendly wave. He was a man who did not wish to make trouble for anyone. No other problem ever arose.

I was now, at last, enjoying complete freedom of movement, limited only by the 01.00 hours curfew for Allied personnel.

I set off for Munich and a visit to see my mother and I arranged for her to move into much better quarters. I had been sending her essential things and I found her looking much better and being pampered by people around her now that she was enjoying the protection of her British officer son.

I paid several visits to Maditta's home and we soon reached the conclusion that we were no longer right for each other. She had a visitor one evening when I called in to see her on my way to Garmisch for some skiing. I had seen him somewhere before and finally realised he was checking up on me. I started to ask questions, and he gave me all the answers. His name was Joe Warner, and he was with CIC. He had been assigned to investigate me. Somebody had become interested in my extracurricular excursions in my unlawful automobile. Having been found to be 'clean' I was left in peace and not a word reached my commanding officer. Joe Warner and I became firm friends and he was instrumental in getting the denunciations against Diels' hosts cleared up and he was able to protect them until he went back to the US. Joe also fell in love with Maditta, unsuccessfully, I'm afraid, but he cleared the way for her to depart for Canada and marriage long before Germans were able to travel overseas in the normal course of events.

Garmisch was the number one saving grace during my Nuremberg days. We used to travel up and down the mountain by means of a gondola, in which only a few Germans were allowed to ride – if there was any room for them. One day I was standing on the platform of the station, waiting for the gondola to swing in, and idly looking at the crowded German waiting area. There I saw, wedged into the tightly packed crowd, Lieutenant-Colonel Volchkov, alternate Russian member of the International Military Tribunal. Don't ask me how he had got in there and why. Possibly the German ticket collector had mistaken him for a displaced person. Certainly, nobody could have understood any protestations he or his side might have voiced, because if anyone had realised who he was they would have trembled in fear and bowed him aboard. Naturally, I went into action. I grabbed Hermann, the man in charge with whom I was on good terms, and told him that he had a guest of honour and who he was, and where. We dived in amongst the waiting Germans – 'There's a Russian General in there' shouted Hermann – and the crowd parted like the Red Sea and Hermann ushered the Colonel and his adjutant aboard the gondola.

As far as I was concerned, that's where the matter ended. But when I got off the cable car the next time, the adjutant was waiting for me. 'The Colonel is very grateful,' he said in passable English. 'He invites you to lunch at the Post Hotel at 13.00 hours please.' Who was I to decline such hospitality? Furthermore, the weather was closing-in, skiing wouldn't be good, anyway. I changed into uniform and made my way to the Post Hotel, one of Europe's famous resort hotels, situated in the centre of things and full of style and atmosphere. The owners, the Clausing family, had, I hoped, been taken to less elegant quarters, probably jail or internment, because of their devoted services rendered to the beloved Fuehrer. Many of the staff remained however and were now serving the

Hermann Goering (above) spent twelve hours in the witness box at the International Military Tribunal. Wolfe Frank (below, centre) spent nine of those hours interpreting what was being said. The US officer to the right in this photograph is Captain Harry Sperber who was monitoring this session. Prior to the war Sperber, a German sport's broadcaster, had, as the New York Times recorded, 'the distinction of having attracted Goebbels' personal protests against his anti-Nazi broadcasts from America.' (See Chapter 29 for further details of Sperber's personal response to Goebbels, that attracted world-wide publicity and turned him into a hero).

Plate 9

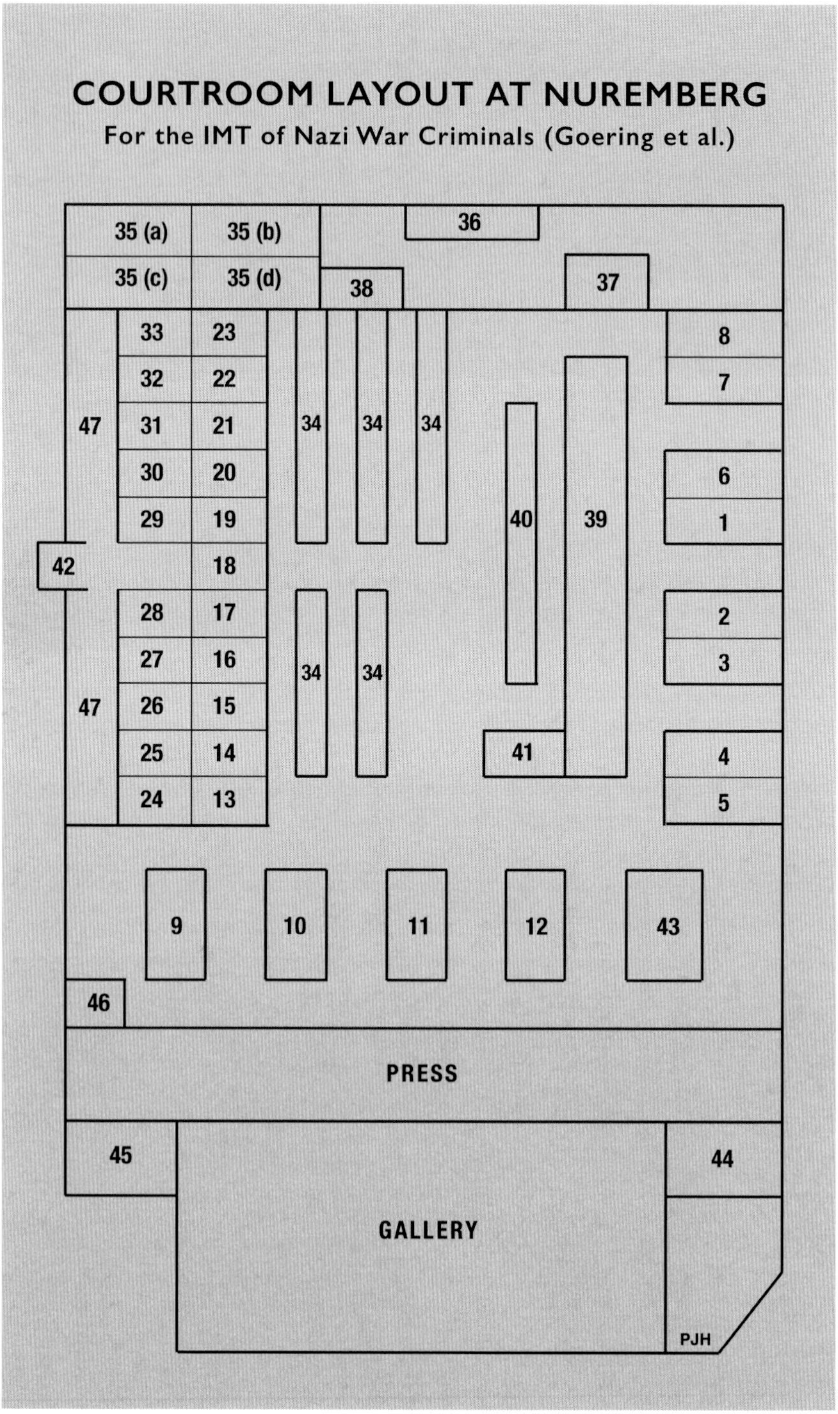

# COURTROOM LAYOUT AT NUREMBERG
## For the IMT of Nazi War Criminals (Goering et al.)

| | | | | | |
|---|---|---|---|---|---|
| 35 (a) | 35 (b) | 36 | | | |
| 35 (c) | 35 (d) | 38 | 37 | | |

33  23  34  34  34  8
32  22  7
47  31  21
30  20  6
29  19  40  39  1
42  18
28  17  2
27  16  34  34  3
47  26  15
25  14  41  4
24  13  5

9   10   11   12   43

46

PRESS

45   44

GALLERY

PJH

Plate 10

# KEY TO THE COURTROOM

## THE TRIBUNAL

1. Lord Justice Lawrence, *British Member, President*
2. Mr. Francis Biddle, *United States Member*
3. Judge John J. Parker, *United States Alternate Member*
4. Professor Donnedieu de Vabres, *French Member*
5. M. Robert Falco, *French Alternative Member*
6. Mr. Justice Birkett, *British Alternate Member*
7. Major General Iola T. Nikitchenko, *Russian Member*
8. Lt.-Col. Alexander F. Volchkov, *Russian Alternate Member*

## PROSECUTORS

9. France – *Led by:* M. Francois de Menthon
10. Russia – *Led by:* Lieutenant-General Roman A. Rudenko
11. United States – *Led by:* Mr. Justice Robert H. Jackson
12. British – *Led by:* Sir Hartley Shawcross, KC

## DEFENDANTS

13. Hermann Goering
14. Rudolf Hess
15. Joachim von Ribbentrop
16. Wilhelm Keitel
17. Ernst Kaltenbrunner
18. Alfred Rosenberg
19. Hans Frank
20. Wilhelm Frick
21. Julius Streicher
22. Walter Funk
23. Hjalmar Schacht
24. Karl Doenitz
25. Erich Raeder
26. Baldur von Schirach
27. Fritz Sauckel
28. Alfred Jodl
29. Franz Von Papen
30. Arthur Seyss-Inquart
31. Albert Speer
32. Constantin von Neurath
33. Hans Fritzsche

## MISCELLANEOUS

34. Defence Lawyers
35. Inerpreters
   (a) German Desk
   (b) French Desk
   (c) Russian Desk
   (d) British Desk
36. Film Screen
37. Witness Box
38. Marshall of the Court
39. Secretaries of the Court
40. Court Recorders
41. Prosecutors Stand
42. Lift from Prison
43. Secretary of the IMT
44. Official Sound Film
45. IBM Apparatus Control
46. US Army Doctor
47. Military Police

Plate 11

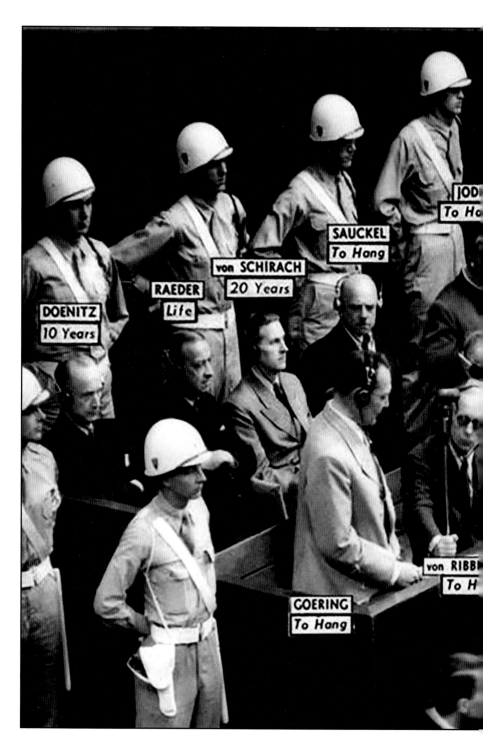

Plate 12

# THOSE ON TRIAL AT THE IMT

**Hermann Wilhelm Goering (or Göring) (1893-1946):** Reichsmarschall, Commander-in-Chief of the Luftwaffe and Hitler's designated deputy. Stole artwork and property from Jews. He was found guilty on all four counts and sentenced to death, however he committed suicide by ingesting cyanide.

**Rudolf Hess (1894-1987):** Deputy Fuehrer until 1941 and third most powerful man in Germany was found guilty on two counts and sentenced to life imprisonment. He committed suicide at the age of 92.

**Joachim von Ribbentrop (1893-1946):** Foreign Minister 1938-45 was convicted for his role in starting the Second world war and enabling the Holocaust. He was sentenced to death and was the first to be hanged.

**Wilhelm Keitel (1882-1946):** Field Marshal and Chief of The OKW. Found guilty on all counts. He was denied a request to be shot and was hanged.

**Ernst Kaltenbrunner (1903-1946):** Obergruppenfuehrer and Chief of Security Police. He was the highest-ranked member of the SS to be tried at the IMT. He was found guilty on two counts and executed.

**Alfred Rosenberg (1893-1946):** Minister of the Occupied Territories and ideologist of Nazism. He was found guilty on all four counts and executed.

**Hans Frank (1900-1946):** Governor-General of Poland where he instigated a reign of terror against the civilian population and was directly involved in the mass murder of Jews. Found guilty on two counts and executed.

**Wilhelm Frick (1877-1946):** Former Reich Minister of the Interior in Hitler's Cabinet. He was found guilty on three counts and executed.

**Julius Streicher (1885-1946):** Known as the 'The Jew Baiter' he founded and published the anti-Semetic newspaper *Der Sturmer* – a central element of Nazi propaganda. Found guilty of War Crimes against Humanity and was hanged.

**Walter Funk (1889-1960):** Minister of Economic Affairs and President of the Reichsbank he was found guily on three counts. Sentenced to life imprisonment he was released in 1957 because of ill health.

**Hjalmar Schacht (1877-1970):** As Minister of Economics he played a key role in implementing Hitler's policies. He was put on trial for conspiracy and crimes against peace but was acquitted.

Plate 13

**Karl Doenitz** (1891-1980): Commander-in-Chief of the German Navy he succeeded Hitler as Head of State and ordered Jodl to sign the instruments of surrender. He was convicted of War Crimes and sentenced to ten years imprisonment.

**Erich Raeder** (1876-1960): Commander-in-Chief of the German Navy 1928-43. He was sentenced to life imprisonment but was released early due to ill health.

**Baldur von Schirach** (1907-1974): Leader of Hitler Youth movement. He was found guilty of Crimes against Humanity and for his role in deporting Jews to concentration camps in Poland. He was imprisoned for twenty years.

**Fritz Sauckel** (1894-1946): Plenipotentiary General for Manpower. He was found guilty and executed for War Crimes and Crimes against Humanity by deliberately working people to death.

**Alfred Jodl** (1890-1946): Chief of Operations Staff of OKW. He was found guilty on all four counts and of ordering prisoners of war to be executed on capture. He was executed.

**Martin Bormann** (1900-1945): Deputy Leader after Hess he was found guilty *in absentia* of War Crimes and Crimes against Humanity and sentenced to death by hanging. However it was later established that he had died trying to flee the Allies after Hitler's suicide in May 1945.

**Franz von Papen** (1879-1969): A former Chancellor of Germany von Papen stood trial on two counts but was acquitted.

**Arthur Seyss-Inquart** (1892-1946): Austrian Minister and Reich Commissioner for Occupied Netherlands was found guilty on three counts and of crimes against the Jews. Sentenced to death by hanging he was the last to mount the scaffold.

**Berthold Albert Speer** (1905-1981): Minister of Armament and War Production, was also Hitler's Chief Architect. He was found guilty on two counts but was the only one of the accused to accept responsibility for the crimes and to say sorry. After much debate his life was spared and he was sentenced to twenty years imprisonment.

**Constantin von Neurath** (1873-1956): A former Minister of Foreign Affairs. Whilst he was found guilty on all four counts he was considered to be a minor adherent to the atrocities and was sentenced to fifteen years in Spandau Prison.

**Hans Fritzsche** (1900-1953): Head of Propaganda was charged on three counts and acquitted. However he was later charged by a deNazification Court and sentenced to 9 years imprisonment. He died soon after release.

Plate 14

# COUNTS, VERDICTS & SENTENCES

INDICTMENTS:  Count 1: Conspiracy to Commit Crimes

Count 2: Crimes Against Peace

Count 3: War Crimes

Count 4: Crimes against Humanity

| Defendant | Count 1 | Count 2 | Count 3 | Count 4 | Sentence |
|---|---|---|---|---|---|
| Hermann Goering | G | G | G | G | Hanging |
| Rudolf Hess | G | G | I | I | Life |
| Joachim von Ribbentrop | G | G | G | G | Hanging |
| Wilhelm Keitel | G | G | G | G | Hanging |
| Ernst Kaltenbrunner | I | – | G | G | Hanging |
| Alfred Rosenberg | G | G | G | G | Hanging |
| Hans Frank | I | – | G | G | Hanging |
| Wilhelm Frick | I | G | G | G | Hanging |
| Julius Streicher | I | – | – | G | Hanging |
| Walter Funk | I | G | G | G | Life |
| Hjalmar Schacht | I | I | – | – | Acquitted |
| Karl Doenitz | I | G | G | – | 10 years |
| Erich Raeder | G | G | G | – | Life |
| Baldur von Schirach | I | – | – | G | 20 years |
| Fritz Sauckel | I | I | G | G | Hanging |
| Alfred Jodl | G | G | G | G | Hanging |
| Martin Bormann* | I | – | G | G | Hanging |
| Franz von Papen | I | I | – | – | Acquitted |
| Arthur Seyss-Inquart | I | G | G | G | Hanging |
| Albert Speer | I | I | G | G | 20 years |
| Constantin von Neurath | G | G | G | G | 15 years |
| Hans Fritzsche | I | – | I | I | Acquitted |
| Robert Ley* | | | | | |
| Gustav Krupp* | | | | | |

Key: G: guilty; I: innocent; – (dash) defendant was not charged.

* Martin Bormann was tried and sentenced *in absentia*; Robert Ley committed suicide before the trial commenced; and the trial of Gustav Krupp was postponed indefinitely due to the onset of senile decay.

Plate 15

officers of the US Army, whose club the Post had become. I was assigned accommodation there on a later occasion and found myself occupying the owner's suite. Somehow, none of my American predecessors had applied the fine-tooth-comb treatment to the rooms and I discovered a hidden cupboard which I pried open. It contained such sought-after articles as SS 'Daggers of Honour' with the Clausing initials and several rather nice pistols and revolvers, which I felt compelled to impound.

I drank to excess on those occasions and am reminded of a drinking contest I organised between some fine, upstanding men. A friendly argument had arisen, in the library of the courthouse, between an American major, Sam Harris, Major Airey Neave of the British Army, a French colonel and a Russian major, over the question of who among those present in Nuremberg, was best able to hold their liquor – the French, the Russians, the British, or the Americans.

Anxious to ingratiate myself with my higher-ups, I ventured the innocent suggestion that the answer could be found later in the evening, at the Grand Hotel. Part of my thinking was based on patriotism. I had been out drinking with Airey Neave for one whole night earlier and at 07.30 hours the following morning he was standing up, admirably straight and seemingly sober in spite of the vast amounts of whisky we had absorbed. Such a man, I knew, would keep our flag flying. I was appointed referee and ordered not to drink, which was an undesirable development I had not foreseen. It goes without saying that at 21.00 hours that night, the Russian side appeared, armed with Vodka, France brought Cognac, Sam Harris was toting some bottles of Southern Comfort and Airey Neave was accompanied by man's best friend, John Haig, Black Label. Simple rules were to apply. I would fill the glasses with the chosen liquid, refill them when all four were empty, and he who stood up at the end would be declared the winner. The first white flag was raised by France.

Major Sam Harris, United States Army, retired next, to an arm-chair in the rear of the arena, where he fell into the sleep of the innocent. That left the Soviet Socialist Republic and the British Empire to settle the issue. We were in the early morning hours by now, and my seniors were finishing their second bottles. Then the Russian rose. He did not, as might be expected, lurch to his feet. He stood up straight 'Mister Neave,' he said, 'I will not go on. You win.' And he clinked glasses with Airey, sank back in his chair and passed out. Major Neave, the victor, cast a loving glance at the Black Label before him, sat down in the nearest chair and he too fell asleep.

At about that time I received the news that I was to be discharged from the British Army and my orders stated that I should report to an

Army depot at Guildford to be removed from His Majesty's payroll. The depot at Guildford was enormous; soldiers poured in at one end and somewhat odd-looking civilians in dreadful demob suits emerged from the other.

The paperwork came first, ending with the handing over of the wartime gratuity, a cash payment of, in my case, £166 in addition to one month's staff captain's pay. After five and-a-half-years of serving the cause of freedom faithfully I was now free myself – and rich.

I did a little stock taking. Did I regret the loss of those years? No, I didn't want to stay out of the war, I went through it, not as I had planned, but by doing the next best thing. Interment was a matter to be forgotten, though not forgiven. Did I enjoy some of it? Yes, the comradeship, the rivalry, the supreme physical fitness, the corners cut, the battles of wits – some of them won. Did I hate some of it? Yes. The time wasted in the Pioneers, the despicable types chosen as our superiors – the frustration, in other words. Did I profit from it all? And how! Self-discipline, tenacity, patience, self-control had been acquired and would remain constant assets. Was I a success? Emphatically no, as a soldier, but yes, in making a case for myself, and many more like me. I was now thirty-three years old, halfway, let's say, along the road of life. The order of the day was, clearly, to 'keep it up' for at least as long I am winning.

We are told that the unhappy frame of mind of a new soldier is called 'joining shock.' Nobody has ever mentioned 'demob shock' but it certainly exists – only it is over much more rapidly – to be replaced by utter euphoria!

On the morning after my metamorphosis I went to see my tailors in Maddox Street. They had not seen me since delivering a set of tails to me in September 1939, worn only once during an ill-feted theatrical appearance. I was greeted as if I had not been away. I was wearing my uniform, now an illegal thing to do, in order to save them the shock of seeing me in my gratuitous demob outfit. I ordered four suits, one to be delivered forthwith, the others to be sent to Nuremberg. As I was departing the elderly gentleman who always looked after me, took me aside. 'Would you mind, Sir,' he whispered, 'taking care of your last account, I mean the bill for the three suits we delivered to you in August and September 1939 – if it wouldn't inconvenience you too much, Sir.' They had never once sent me a reminder and I had completely forgotten that the account was unpaid. Those days have gone. But I am glad to say that I still have, and am still wearing, the suits.

# WOLFE FRANK OF THE F.O.

PROUDLY WEARING MY NEW SUIT, I returned to Nuremberg under the auspices, of all things, the British Foreign Office; Dostert had demanded that I return after coming out of the Army and things had been arranged accordingly. I was no longer subject to Army discipline and regretted that this had not occurred before my friend Hugh Turrell had left – we could have had such a happy, frank exchange of views.

My pay, now called salary, was better, of course, and I was assigned back my quarters at the Grand Hotel. I still had the Opel and was entitled to use all the US facilities available to Allied personnel involved in the trial.

My twenty-one 'clients' in the dock looked up with interest when I appeared in a new suit. There were even some barely concealed grins. Schacht, who sat nearest to the English booth, slowly nodded approval.

I went into the booth to interpret the testimony of Albert Speer, the man who has emerged as being the most remarkable of the top Nazis on trial; by virtue of the books he published after serving his twenty-year prison sentence and his rather dignified re-entry into human society.

As Hitler's Minister for Armament and War Production Speer had created a sensation when he was recalled to the witness box to give an account of his attempt to assassinate Hitler, at the very end of the war, by introducing poison gas into the vents of the Fuehrer's bunker in Berlin. This, and the considerable personal risk Speer had taken in sabotaging Hitler's earlier orders for the total destruction of production facilities in occupied territories and Germany, had been considered as being mitigating circumstances by the Tribunal and explains the comparatively mild sentence he received.

Later, before he was sent to Spandau to serve this sentence, Speer was called, as a witness for the defence, to testify in the trial of Field Marshal Milch of the Luftwaffe (this was one of the first trials under the

141

Subsequent Proceedings). I had once again gone into the English booth to interpret his testimony. When the mid-day recess was called, Speer asked permission to remain in the courtroom and expressed the hope that he would be allowed to talk to me if I were willing. Naturally, I was.

We sat down in a corner of the courtroom – much to the annoyance of the guards who had to go on hovering instead of playing cards somewhere – and Speer explained his somewhat unusual request for our cosy chat.

He had deduced from my strong tan that I was a skier. He was a keen skier himself, he said, and a mountaineer, and he had this need to talk to somebody about this hobby. It turned out that his forte was cross-country skiing in the mountains and he knew of many mountain huts in the Alps; we did, in fact, make some sort of an appointment to meet in such a refuge after his release, twenty years hence, during the first week of the following February. (As it turned out when he was freed from Spandau his eyesight had deteriorated so badly that he could not have kept our date).

We talked a lot about architecture, sports, travel, the theatre and many other subjects of that kind but not a word was said about the trial, his sentence, or that part of his life that had led to his imprisonment.

Albert Speer was the only one of all the guilty men I met before and during Nuremberg for whom I developed a liking; because here was an outstandingly intelligent man who conveyed, throughout our conversation, a very clear sense of guilt that he would carry with him for the rest of his life. There was none of the maudlin self-incrimination I had heard from the other Nazis – high ranking and low ranking – nor was an accusing finger pointed at the Fuehrer, or polemics put forward against the trial and the right of the victor to try the vanquished. It was clear that Speer had come to terms with the past, the present and the future – and himself.

'Can twenty years imprisonment be termed future?' I asked him.

'The twenty years will pass,' he replied wistfully, 'survival is so much a question of one's inner attitude, of willpower. Yes, I will survive that sentence, I am sure. I will write, and I will paint – I haven't had time to paint. Now I will – landscapes. It will serve a double purpose. I will be occupied, and I will train my imagination to visualise the things I won't be able to see – mountains, trees, the countryside, colours. Physically, I will be in a cell, but my mind won't be.'

I nodded, without comment. 'See you up there in that hut, in twenty years,' I said as I was leaving. But the story ends here; neither of us could keep the appointment.

Soon after my return to Nuremberg I wore another of the new suits on an illicit outing run by the US Army in Feldafing. I decided to go not as an ex-British officer but as a heavily disguised, strongly accented civilian of un-definable origin. I spent hours at a theatrical hairdresser's shop in Munich having a false beard constructed whisker by whisker and with added dark sunglasses I looked exactly like the Dr Morrison I professed to be.

I hadn't been at the party long when a slightly drunk lieutenant got hold of me and said. 'Some friends want to see you in the library – now!'

Three officers were waiting for me one of whom, a captain, was waving a service revolver in my face. He shoved me in a chair, rather brutally, and tore off my beard. These officers, so I was to discover, were attending the US Army Intelligence School. They were too sharp for words, had seen there was something sinister and were determined to unmask me. I was manhandled, and my credentials were declared to be forgeries. Fortunately, the colonel, who lived on the premises, knew me and came to my rescue. However, I was kicked out and told never to return by one Lieutenant Benny Schaefer, or Scheffer.

On my way back to Nuremberg I got my dander up. Yes, I had been out of line with my false beard and brand new suit, but the Americans involved were far more out of line: US officers on active duty fraternising with German girls; supporting a German ménage with US Army rations; providing US Army liquor for a German party; hobnobbing happily with a bunch of ex-Nazis I had seen in attendance; using threatening behaviour towards an only slightly disguised high ranking British civilian who was carrying proper identification. No, I will not stand for this, I thought.

The following morning, I attacked. I went to see Sir David Maxwell Fyfe, head of the British contingent, whom I knew well, and I told him all. He listened to me and managed a frown. I had, he said, been foolish and indiscreet.

'Be that as it may,' I said, 'however, the Americans had been guilty of appalling behaviour towards an Englishman. Towards, in fact, the British delegation at the trial.'

Sir David saw my point and said he would take it up with General Leroy Watson the US CO at Nuremberg. He too saw things our way and went straight into action by calling the CO at the Intelligence School and suggesting Benny Schaefer should be sent home forthwith. A couple of days later I was called in to Sir David's office. The small group assembled there included, in rank order: General Watson, a major, Lieutenant Benny boy, and an agitated US Congressman, whose eyes were red-rimmed from lack of sleep. He, it turned out, was Benny's dad and he had rushed across the Atlantic, at US taxpayers' expense, to get his offspring off the hook.

Apologies were delivered. Benny was allowed to stay in Europe and I got much more fun out of it than I had anticipated.

# TRANSLATING FOR GOERING

BACK AT THE TRIBUNAL I gave a marathon performance in the English booth when Goering took the stand. The BBC had wanted me to interpret as much of his testimony as I could manage since they preferred my voice and delivery to that of my colleagues.

My interpretation would be going out over every English-speaking network around the world – Great Britain, the USA, Canada, Australia, South Africa and the rest – amounting to several hundred million listeners. Dostert had given his blessing and the other two German-English interpreters had no objections.

I stayed on microphone for the whole of the first morning of Goering's direct examination by his counsel, Dr Stahmer, a total of three hours, worked for the first half of the afternoon and then continued on the following morning. In total I did nearly nine of the thirteen hours of Goering's testimony.

His performance was fascinating, indeed. The contents have been so thoroughly analysed, commented upon and criticised that I need not add to them here. However, the account, given to me by one of Dr Stahmer's colleagues, of how Goering set the scene, might be of interest.

It seems that the little lawyer from Hamburg was in a state of panic because twenty-four hours before Goering was to take the stand he had not yet consulted his counsel regarding the details of his testimony. Then, at the last moment, he sent for Stahmer. Cutting short any of the doctor's queries or suggestions, the former Reichsmarschall dictated several hundred questions, and ordered his despairing legal adviser to ask those questions, in that order, once he, Goering, had taken the stand. No ifs, no buts – this is an order. Stahmer tried in vain to discover the story line which would link them but time was too short and the subject too vast.

So he did as he had been told, and spun from question to question. There emerged the yarn of Goering's achievements during the Third

Reich, his vindication of the acts he had committed, his attempted justification of what he had done, and his message to the German people, and I quote: 'I did not want war, nor did I bring it about. I did everything to prevent it by negotiation. After it had broken out I did everything to assure victory. The only motive which guided me was my ardent love of my people, its fortunes, its freedoms, its life – and for this I call on the Almighty and my German people as witness.'

No easy stuff to interpret, this, and Goering's German was intricate and with full sentences so intertwined that many verbs failed to appear.

It is necessary to anticipate the verbs, which come at the end of the German sentence, when working into English. Most of the time, one gets away with it, particularly when one has tuned into a speaker, has got to know his mentality and can foresee what he wants to say. In the case of these 'entwined sentences' (*Schachtelsatz* is the German word) the interpreter has to supply the verb, as I did, many times during Goering's sojourn in the witness box. One day, I passed close to him on my way out of the courtroom. Nobody, I fancied, could hear me. 'You owe me 248 verbs,' I whispered to him, and was overheard, unfortunately, by a member of the Press.

'Goering owes interpreter 248 verbs,' was the headline I had to discover in an English daily on the following morning and there followed a conjectured but accurate account of the interpreter's trials and tribulations.

For this I was given a formal reprimand by an officer of the Tribunal and another one by Dostert, delivered with a broad grin; and I was still clutching the English microphone when defendant Goering left the witness stand!

There were two other memorable off-the-record chats with the accused that need to be recorded.

One concerned the Reichmarschall and my dog, Tiny, who accompanied me everywhere at Nuremberg – except in the courtroom of course.

I first met Tiny in the company of an American officer who was about to be 'zee-eyed', spelled ZI-ed, which was short for 'being returned to the Zone of the Interior,' or simply 'going home' to you and me. The major had purchased Tiny from a German kennel for a sizeable sum but had failed to obtain his pedigree. Without that document Tiny was of no value in the USA. He was a Harlequin Great Dane, was already fully-grown and required substantial amounts of food. He weighed some 70k and was eighteen months old (he was over 80 kilos when he left me eighteen months later). Tiny was the greatest Great Dane I had ever met and I fell for him instantly. The major was happy and relieved to find a sucker and Tiny trotted off with me happily, recognising me for the animal lover that I am. I was at the time in a third floor room of the Grand Hotel, overlooking the station square, not an ideal location for this huge dog.

A number of obstacles had to be removed before Tiny and I could settle into a reasonable routine. There was some limited opposition on the part of the hotel commandant (who later married the passionate haystack) but Tiny had an infallible way of wagging people over to his side. I then arranged for food supplies from the hotel kitchen (scraps against Lucky Strike cigarettes) and my driver Alois, known as Beethoven whom he resembled, brought off a deal at the slaughterhouse for a bucket of 'condemned' meat (unfit for human consumption) to be picked up twice weekly on a barter basis.

Next, I obtained a courthouse pass for Tiny from Major Tom Hodges who was in charge of security. Tom had some experience in such matters since, earlier on, he had tested the alertness of the guards at the entrance to the Palace of Justice by substituting the photograph of his German Shepherd dog for his own on his pass. It took three days before somebody stopped him and all the guards who had let him through were court martialled.

I made one attempt to leave Tiny alone in my hotel room. He howled the place down and was seen trying to commit suicide by jumping out of the window. So he accompanied me wherever I went and, in the process, was immortalised by Rebecca West, in an article on Nuremberg written for the *New Yorker* in September 1946 in which we read:

'The corridors of the Palace of Justice itself are paced by an image of Eros – a dog, marbled in black and white, its jowls quivering, as it follows its Master, a Viennese [*sic*] interpreter who carries off the situation with the gay complacency of a Schnitzler[1] here. When the interpreter has to go into a part of the building reserved for humanity, he opens the door of the nearest office and, to the surprise of anyone who may be present, throws in the dog. It is not in the heart of man to leave another man's dog alone, but, disregarding all the wooing, it looks around wildly. When it realises that the beloved has, indeed gone, it stretches out its front legs stiff on the floor and props its muzzle between them with a gesture of inconsolable widowhood, while its rear end, lowers itself slowly and funereally. So it remains, insensible to caresses, till the beloved returns. It shoots up with a whimper that informs him it thought he was dead, and lurches after him, out into the corridor, repeating with its ear and tail something out of Euripides beginning, "Oh, Love, Love, though that from thine eyes diffuses yearning and on the soul sweet grace inducest".'

147

The office into which Tiny was so frequently thrown was 606 (Plate 16) in which we sat and listened when not in court. Before and after the lunch break the room was very briefly cut off from the rest of the building because the defendants were served their lunch in a small dining room directly across from a door behind the dock. The short passage across the main corridor was roped off and heavily guarded by white-helmeted US soldiers for as long as it took the prisoners to cross over. Sometimes Tiny and I didn't make it out of 606 and away for our lunch before the ropes went up and there we stood, watching the defendants file by. Goering always made some approving sound or gesture when he saw Tiny.

Then one day, when I stood near him in the courtroom, I heard him say to me out of the corner of his mouth 'I wish you'd feed me to that dog of yours instead of hanging me,' and I just had time to whisper back 'It won't work – he's fussy about his food,' before a guard bore down on me to see if I had broken the rule and talked to an accused.

This palsy-walsy relationship between Hermann and me stemmed from another, somewhat unorthodox meeting I had had with him.

I was wooing a lovely member of His Majesty's Forces, Captain Clare McCririck, whenever I was in London on leave from Nuremberg. It seemed that fulfilment of my dream depended on something special I would have to add to dinners and flowers – so I offered her a trip to Nuremberg and the trial, something which, today, would rate on a par with, for instance, a Concorde flight with Prince Charles. I knew how it would be done. A very good friend in the US Army would provide travel orders for her, and the twice weekly British VIP flight would transport her there and back in something resembling an aeroplane and called an Anson.

All worked according to plan except the happy ending, because in Nuremberg she was assigned accommodation in 'Girls Town' (ladies only) and I could not smuggle her into the Grand Hotel. (This must have upset her terribly because she got married as soon as she returned to London).

Unfortunately, her arrival in Nuremberg coincided with a terribly dreary phase of the trial: the Russians were submitting documentary evidence for days on end and insisted on reading these documents into the record, voices without inflection droning on endlessly. It was also intolerably hot and Clare, when she emerged from the visitors-gallery, was not gracious and grateful but bored, hot and bothered. The Concorde had become an Anson, figuratively speaking. Something had to be done to create excitement.

'Would you like to meet Goering?' I asked over a terrible cafeteria lunch.

'You must be joking,' came the rather acid reply from the lovely Captain.

'You will tomorrow,' I announced nonchalantly, and went to work.

I produced an 'interrogation slip' – something to be completed by those with authority (not including interpreters) to question anyone in the jail, including the defendants, for legitimate reasons, not including wolfish projects. I filled in the details: Name: Defendant Goering. Purpose: document identification. Time: the next day; 17.30 hours (after the session's adjournment). I handed the slip to a friend in the right place, secured an 'Observer Pass' for Clare and, from the documentation centre, I obtained a copy of some totally unimportant letter from Goering's adjutant, General Koller, to the Reichsmarshall. I clipped an 'identification slip' to it.

At the proper moment, Clare and I were taken to an interrogation room, I sat down at the desk, looking mighty important, and she was shown to a chair, which stood at the side of the small room.

Goering was brought in punctually and I invited him to sit down.

'Herr Goering,' I said. 'I have here a letter purportedly signed by General Koller. Would you please identify the signature?' and I handed the two bits of paper to him. He glanced at them.

'But I have already identified the signature on this letter,' he announced.

'Have you really?' I said in utter faked amazement, 'then the slip must have got lost. Please sign again on this one.'

He nodded and signed with much authority.

'Thank you, that will be all,' I declared, and rose.

So did Goering, he nodded briefly and headed for the door, preceded and followed by the two MPs. When he was level with Clare's chair, he suddenly stopped and turned to face her. '*Gnaediges Fraulein,*' he said, 'no doubt I owe this little interlude to your presence in Nuremberg. I hope you have enjoyed it also.'

Then he bowed politely, turned and left for his cell. Clare had, indeed, met Goering and she had the interrogation slip with his autograph to prove it. He must have remembered this highly irregular performance of mine when he asked to be put on Tiny's menu.

**NOTE:**

1. Arthur Schnitzler (1862-1931) was an Austrian playwright and novelist known for his psychological dramas that dissect turn-of-the-century Viennese bourgeois life.

# PREPARING FOR JUDGEMENT DAY

IN SPITE OF THE SEVERAL REPRIMANDS I had received I was still on the microphone when, at the end of nine long months, the Tribunal adjourned to write its findings. A date was set for them to be read in court and we were given two weeks leave. When I returned from London we heard that the judges, closeted and heavily guarded, were reaching the end of their enormous task. They were, of course, running late. It was therefore no surprise when, about six days before the court was to reconvene, a team of translators, including the German-speaking interpreters, were rounded up and whisked away to carry out the marathon job of translating the judgement – which was being written in English – into German. Elsewhere, the French and Russians were preparing to do the same.

Extremely strict security precautions had been arranged for our (the German translators) team. There had been intelligence reports about growing opposition to the Trials in Germany and rumours included everything from planned abduction of the prisoners to armed attacks on the courthouse and the assassinations of key figures among the trial staff. Other measures involved total secrecy for the judgement – the findings – until it was read out in court. This, naturally, included sequestering the translators in a heavily guarded building, which was a schoolhouse some way from Nuremberg.

There were eight of us. We were loaded onto buses and driven off to our then unknown destination, heavily protected by armoured cars – machine-guns at the ready. Each translator was equipped with a typewriter.

When we arrived, there were four German typists, mountains of plain paper, but no judgement. The manuscripts began to arrive at 02.00 hours, a few pages at a time, and we set to work. The text had to be translated, translations corrected, the terminology compared and readjusted, the texts rewritten, reviewed, edited, finalised, assembled, typed, re-assembled and put onto stencils.

Since the original text kept arriving in dribs and drabs, we were either working frantically or twiddling our thumbs, but as always in cases of such extreme urgency, the job got done.

We returned to our billets at 04.30 hours on the morning of 30 September 1946 and the reading of the judgement was set for that afternoon. I would be on the German microphone. I knew the contents of the judgement – in other words, I knew who, amongst the defendants, had been found guilty and on which counts. I also knew that von Papen, Schacht and Fritzsche had been acquitted. I did not know, nor did anybody else except the judges, what the sentences were going to be. Nor did I know who would be interpreting them into German. There was a great deal of speculation everywhere, but particularly among the interpreters, about that sentence. Was it going to be hanging, the guillotine, shooting, prison or banishment? – No one knew!

# THE VOICE OF DOOM

HAVING RETURNED TO BILLET from the translating marathon, I caught some sleep, stood under lots of hot and cold showers and departed to the Palace of Justice for lunch. I went through numerous security checks, got my briefing from the monitor and descended to the cafeteria. It was unusually packed – everybody who had the right to be there was hanging around the courthouse and there was tremendous tension – an almost unreal anticipation of the sudden, it seemed, end to the toil of history-writing which in our respective capacities we had performed for nine long months. My nerves were taut. My colleagues were on edge. Most of us were dead tired after the sleepless nights of translating the judgement. We were constantly accosted by people trying to pump information out of us. It was an eerie, unpleasant, seemingly endless period of waiting for the great scene to come.

My brooding however was interrupted by the arrival, at my table, of some totally unexpected visitors in the form of four extremely pretty American girls dressed in a uniform I had not seen before. They turned out to be CATS. No not feline friends, but Civilian Actress Technicians.

I hauled myself out of my state of nervous tension by conversing with this most welcome group. I will need to go into the subsequent events in considerable detail at a later point. For the moment however, suffice to say, that after lunch, and on my way to the courtroom, I encountered our monitor, Captain Joe von Zastrow, to whom I said, 'I have just met the girl I am going to marry.'

'I bet you won't,' said Joe.

'How much?' said I.

'$500' (Joe was not the talkative type, which was why he was a monitor, not an interpreter).

He lost!

Having shaken hands on our bet, we went off to court and the long reading of the judgement began.

The four members of the Tribunal read it in turn. It was for me to read the German translation when it was Lord Justice Lawrence and Mr Francis Biddle's[1] turn, and I continued on the following morning when the judges dealt with their individual judgement on the accused Nazi leaders.

Then I was called out of the booth and told that in the afternoon I was to be the 'Voice of Doom' – translating to the defendants the sentences meted out by the International Military Tribunal.

I still did not know, and would not learn until their pronouncement, what those sentences were going to be. My nerves began their reverberations anew, in full rhythm, as had been the case on the very first day.

The scene of that afternoon has been the subject of so much coverage that I will confine myself to my own role in it. I was the only interpreter in the German booth, of course.

Punctually at 14.00 hours the tribunal entered the courtroom, to commence its last session. The sliding door at the back of the dock opened and Goering stepped out of the lift. He reached for his earphones and Lord Lawrence, looking at him fixedly, began:

'Defendant Hermann Wilhelm Goering, on the counts ...'

I began to interpret.

Goering shrugged his shoulders, pointed at his earphones and indicated that he had not heard!

It was incredible, unbelievable, but at that very moment of utmost tension, the installation had broken down! There was considerable activity around the amplifiers in the rear of the room. I went right on shaking. A technician made a sign towards me.

'I began to count, 'Eins, zwei, drei – koennen ie mich hoeren (can you hear me?)' and Goering smiled, yes he actually smiled, nodded in my direction[2], and Lawrence began anew:

'Defendant Hermann Wilhelm Goering, on the counts of the indictment on which you have been convicted the International Military Tribunal sentences you to death by hanging.'

This, then, was the formula of the sentence. And, as my eyes were riveted on Goering's face, totally expressionless but growing deadly white, I spoke as if hypnotised, into the microphone before me. 'Tod durch erhaengen (death by hanging),' instead of saying, 'Tod durch den Strang (death by the rope) – which is the accepted formula in German. When I realised my error Goering had already dropped his earphones, turned and was stepping back into the lift. Almost, but not quite noiselessly, the door slid shut. The first man to learn his punishment through me had gone from sight.

Within one hour, Lord Justice Lawrence spoke those words ten more times, ten more times did I repeat them, now correctly, to ten of those men who could never pay for their monstrous crimes.

Now, so long after that hour in the courtroom, the memories of the trial have faded. The faces of the condemned men have not – I memorised them too well while I spoke the fatal words to them. Let me quote from R.W. Cooper's[3] book once more:

'Death by the rope!' The words came to them in German through the headphones as each prisoner was brought up alone into the vast emptiness of the dock – the identical words pronounced by the Nazi People's Court upon the perpetrators of the July plot. They were uttered in translation by Captain Wolfe Frank, himself of German origin, who before departing from his country had watched the torchlight procession in Munich that hailed Hitler's coming to power. A strange turn of the wheel that he was now to utter the words that set the seal on Hitler's little day.'

The tensest hour of my life was over, an hour when history was indeed written indelibly, justly and rightfully. I remember the last, final adjournment of the Tribunal, the judges filing from the bench into their chamber, the departure of counsel, the press, the spectators and the last view of the empty courtroom, as I was making my way out of the booth – to which I did not, as it happens, ever return. I do not remember anything else about that day – the drama had been too powerful.

There was one last, very final chapter to come, of course: the executions.

**NOTES:**

1. Francis Biddle was the US Member of the IMT.

2. In conversations with linguists in later years Wolfe Frank went into a little more detail concerning the moment he translated the sentence, including Frances Calder who wrote:'Just as Wolfe was pronouncing sentence, Goering turned round towards him, and gave him the thumbs-up sign to indicate that he could now hear him. Wolfe said it was a moment of irony that he was never able to forget.'

3. *The Nuremberg Trial*, R.W. Cooper, Penguin Books.

# GOERING'S SUICIDE

THE CONDEMNED MEN WERE HANGED during the night of 16 October; all but Goering, the man with that incredible smile I saw at the moment of his sentencing.

Some comment is called for in connection with his remarkable feat of committing suicide, because I may have missed a clue to his scheme for escaping the noose the day I talked to him in his cell.

The non-hero of the story is Colonel Burton C. Andrus, Commandant of the Nuremberg prison. I had first seen him during a pre-trial press conference when he assured the members of the press that he had designed and organised a suicide-proof prison. Andrus was a fairly short, or short-seeming, man who looked every inch the professional, intellectually stunted officer. I remember him as being devoid of any sense of humour or imagination. His men, I was told, saw in him an intolerable disciplinarian. It is certainly true that he had them keep up their highly polished appearance all the way through the trial and they did their stuff persistently, standing behind the dock, wearing white gloves and white painted helmets, pouncing like trained seals upon a prisoner leaning forward in the dock to whisper to a colleague.

It was a pity that the Americans did not handpick these soldiers in order to avoid such incidents as, for instance, that of a guard addressing the President of the Court as, 'Hey, you,' when Sir Geoffrey Lawrence had slipped through some control point without showing his pass, but, most of all, so that Colonel Andrus's dream of a suicide-proof jail could come true. As it was, there was Dr Ley, committing suicide by hanging himself with a towel, torn into strips, on the water pipe of the WC in his cell. There was also a witness who managed to jump from an upper landing of the jail. Then, as the grand finale, there was Goering's dramatically timed suicide.

Could a professional jailer, a trained prison warden have prevented it? Probably, yes. At least, some members of the press corps at

Nuremberg must have thought so. Every year they sent a cable to Andrus on the anniversary of Goering's suicide 'fondly remembering' Andrus and his successful performance as Commandant of the Nuremberg War Crimes Jail.

How Goering had managed to kill himself has been the subject of conjecture and discussions ever since. It has not been resolved. I think Tom Ready, sometime afterwards, at the Press Camp at Schloss Stein[1,] supplied the first step of my own reasoning when, before the beginning of the trial, I called on Goering at his prison cell, I observed that he had failed to insert his dentures. However, as Ready quite rightly said, 'Goering didn't need to wear dentures and his slurred speech was a fake.' He was, it seems, concealing something in his mouth and because I had not seen his medical history sheet, I fell for the trick.

Two poison capsules had previously been found amongst Goering's possessions – one in the hollowed-out pages of a book and one in a tin of coffee. Such places of hiding were absurdly poor for a man of Goering's intelligence. Rather, I feel, he wanted those capsules found. To some extent, this would have dulled the minds of further searchers and it might produce the subconscious conclusion that 'two is all he could have had.'

Let us return to the somewhat simple-minded Colonel Andrus. He certainly instituted searches and controls of the prisoners. It went something like this: Every Monday: search blankets. Every Tuesday: look under the seats of the toilets in the cells. Wednesday: windowsills. Thursday: the prisoner's mouths. Friday: the rectum; and so on and so forth. The odds in favour of the brilliant mind of a Goering versus such military non-ingenuity must have been enormous. Goering had no other aim or purpose than to outwit his jailers. He succeeded. Whether he had the eventual capsule that killed him all the time or whether it was smuggled into the jail for him seems to me to be of secondary importance. It should have been found in either case, and the job was bungled. It certainly changed the record, but I don't think the history of the world was changed greatly.

**NOTE:**

1. During the Nuremberg Trials, reporters were housed in Castle Schloss Stein.

# THE EXECUTIONS

T HE EVENTS DURING THE NIGHT OF THE EXECUTIONS are a matter of record. I, myself, couldn't stay away. That the hangings would take place during that night was certain since the time between the sentencing and execution, set at fifteen days by the rules governing the trial, had elapsed. Midnight on 16 October 1946 was it.

The setting was exactly as a film director would have wanted – a little moonlight, clouds racing across the sky, a night almost without sound. The Press Corps was there, of course, in full strength and, as their papers were being checked by the Military Police, everybody it seemed was talking in a whisper.

Eleven lives were to be taken that night, as the result of a gigantic effort to examine a record of crime, of murder, of inhuman brutality that has no parallel in history. We had, all of us who were at the Palace of Justice in Nuremberg on that night, attended this examination and, I feel sure, we wanted to see that final act of justice carried out.

I cannot imagine that any one of us felt the tiniest spark of compassion for the men who were now to die for their crimes. However, I also felt that we all would be glad when at last this horrible chapter of history that we had helped to record was ended.

To cover the final act the authorities had ruled that two journalists from each of the Allied Powers were to be admitted to the hangings – one representative of the Press and one radio reporter.

The Americans had made clever use of this arrangement as they had somehow managed to obtain a ruling whereby those eight men – two Americans, two Brits, two Frenchmen and two Russians – were to be allowed out of the jail at 04.00 hours after the executions. This, of course, was early enough for the press in the United States but too late for Europe. It certainly wasn't cricket, but good American business sense.

Until 04.00 hours the prison was hermetically sealed off. At 01.00 hours I decided I had hung around the building long enough, and I headed for home. A US woman reporter, who shall remain nameless, was with me. At the exit she was stopped by an MP sergeant who obviously knew her well. 'Hey Jeannie,' he called as we walked by, 'Y'know what? Goering's just killed himself.'

'Ha, ha, funny joke,' Jeannie said, and walked on, heading for her couch and a nap. Had she taken the MP seriously and followed up his information she would have scooped the whole of the world's press by three or four hours, and she would have become world famous.

A second anecdote concerns Britain's most illustrious daily. It had two people on the spot that night, both of who were young, very ingenious and determined to give everybody else the slip. They hired a couple of Germans, equipped them with field glasses and had them climb to the top of a ruined building across the road from the Palace of Justice. By careful scouting they had discovered that from this lookout point their spies would be able to see the gangway, which had been constructed between the prison and the gymnasium, in the courtyard where the gallows had been erected. A gap had been left open at the top of the gangway, presumably to let in daylight.

Obviously, the condemned men would be walking to the gallows singly. Each would be preceded, and followed, by an MP wearing the white helmet of his uniform. The tops of these helmets ought to be visible to the two German lookouts, posted on top of the ruins across the road from the Courthouse – and, indeed, they were. First one helmet could be seen, glistening in the light of a naked light bulb or two in the gangway. Some ten feet behind, a second helmet could be discerned. This, clearly, was the procession of a death candidate being led to the gallows and a light signal, blinked to the two Englishman below, reported the passing of each such procession.

What the lofty observers could not, of course, have known was that the last of the eleven men was not walking, but was being carried on a stretcher, already dead. It was Hermann Goering who had just killed himself!

Thus, when eleven pairs of helmets, obviously with eleven death candidates between them, had passed, the story was filed with London, and there we read how Goering, the first man due for execution, had 'Walked, his head erect, face emotionless, to the gallows and his death.'

# THE SUBSEQUENT PROCEEDINGS

**Editor:** Following the International Military Tribunal (IMT) – the trial of the major Nazi war criminals (Goering, et al.) – other Germans were arrested and brought before the courts to face charges in a series of hearings that were officially entitled, 'The Trials of War Criminals before the Nuremberg Military Tribunals'. These trials are, however, usually referred to as being the 'Subsequent Proceedings (SP).'

Growing differences between the Allies (the US, the UK, France and Russia) had made it impossible to run further trials along the lines of the IMT. However, the Allied Control Council Rule 10[1] was a charter that allowed for a 'Uniform legal basis in Germany for the prosecution of war criminals and other similar offenders other than those dealt with by the IMT.'

After the conclusion of the IMT, and under this directive, the US held a series of twelve SP trials[2] within the Palace of Justice at Nuremberg, between December 1946 and April 1949, at which other Germans, including politicians, industrialists, high ranking military personnel, physicians and jurists, were charged with war crimes.

General Telford Taylor[3], who was one of the US assistant prosecutors under Mr Justice Jackson at the IMT, was appointed Chief Prosecutor and Wolfe Frank was appointed Chief Interpreter of the SP, and the courts were set up to, 'Try and punish persons charged with offences recognized as crimes in Article II of the Control Council Law No. 10.'

Since the IMT had already established the criminality of war crimes, aggressive war, and crimes against humanity, these trials were for the purpose of determining the guilt of lower-level Nazis accused of those crimes. In total the United States held twelve trials under SP and indicted 183 defendants. These resulted in twelve imposed death sentences, eight life sentences and seventy-seven terms of imprisonment. Other defendants were acquitted. The judges and prosecutors were all American and the proceedings were conducted in German and English only.

FOLLOWING A SHORT PERIOD OF READJUSTMENT after the IMT, I was persuaded to stay on in Nuremberg for three reasons.

Firstly, I was offered, and then accepted, the position of Chief Interpreter of the Subsequent Proceedings under General Telford Taylor.

Secondly, I had no specific job to go to back in England.

Thirdly, I had decided to ask the CATS entertainer I had met the night before my performance as the Voice of Doom, to marry me. She was touring Europe in a play called *My Sister Eileen* and needed yet to be told her fate.

Her name was Maxine Cooper[4]. Her father was a Chicago businessman and she had studied at the Pasadena Playhouse[5] and also under Joshua Logan in New York. That was the sum total of what I knew about her, plus what the eye had seen, which was that she was beautiful and radiated human warmth more than anyone I had ever met. It must be stated for the record that my $500 bet with Joe von Zastro did not enter into my considerations.

We met again and matters advanced, naturally and enchantingly, to the point where I popped the question and obtained consent. Maxine returned to Chicago in November to tell her family and to get ready for the wedding, which we set for February.

The Plans for the Subsequent Proceedings called for the trials of such men, or groups as Alfried Krupp, Friedrich Flick, the industrialist, a group of doctors who had carried out criminal medical experiments, members of the Administration of Concentration Camps, Otto Ohlendorf, mass murderer in eastern occupied territories and others not covered by the record written by the IMT.

Six trials were to run simultaneously, and the languages involved were, of course, only English and German. Following my appointment as Chief Interpreter, I had to find three teams of two interpreters for each trial, multiplied by six, that meant fifty-six such people, plus two spares were needed. They didn't exist, not where I was looking. Fortunately, the security services gave me the green light for hiring carefully vetted German nationals – indigenous personnel, as they were called – and this move produced some of the finest linguists I could hope to find for the German booth.

The English team was another kettle of goldfish (interpreters in their glass-containers were often called goldfish). I found a few amongst US personnel but we were hopelessly short of the necessary total. I went to London on a recruiting trip and called on the Air Ministry, the Admiralty and the War Office. I found no one. However, as luck would have it, I was having drinks with Tim Holland Bennett, who had covered the IMT for the *Radio Newsreel* programme of the BBC. I had done some serious drinking with him at 'Stalag Stein', as the Press camp, installed in the castle of Stein, had been labelled.

I had also found, as a souvenir for Tim, a pair of sheets from Hitler's large apartment in the Prizregentenstrasse in Munich. They were the genuine article with 'A-H' embroidered upon them. I had obtained them from an old pre-war friend who was now black-marketing everything from petrol to currency, booze to diamonds and coffee to automobiles. He had presented me with the sheets in exchange for a long-distance call to Teheran, that he made from my office telephone in Nuremberg in order to obtain urgently needed 'carpets, Persian, US Army personnel, for the use of', as army lingo would have put it.

Tim remembered my good offices in regard to his linen cupboard and offered to reciprocate. Having advanced to the position of Casting Director at BBC Television, he arranged for me to appear before the cameras on a programme called *Picture Page*, the forerunner of today's splendid BBC news coverage.

The interviewer would be Richard Dimbleby, a truly outstanding BBC commentator, and I was to appear, four days later, as the Nuremberg Interpreter who had become known as the 'Voice of Doom'.

A scriptwriter was assigned to me and we put the outline of the fifteen-minute interview on paper. It was scheduled to go out on a Thursday. However, on the Wednesday morning I received an agitated call from the BBC asking me to go on the air that same afternoon. I had had no time to learn the script but was asked to rush off to Alexandra Palace, where the BBC television studios were in those days.

I arrived at 14.00 hours. The programme was scheduled for 18.00 hours. Someone conducted me to an enormous, brightly-lit dressing room and, thoughtfully, stood a full bottle of Ballantine's whisky on the table before me. I felt lonely and rather nervous, and as the clock on the wall advanced, I was staring at the script and absentmindedly sipping the golden liquid. Unfortunately, I had not had time to eat lunch and when, finally, the producer called on me I had absorbed more whisky than script and felt no pain at all, or nerves.

Then I was on the air, after a run-through, where I was sitting down with Dimbleby. For the real thing, however, I was standing up and I am afraid I was swaying slightly, from front to rear, and the cameraman had quite a job keeping me in focus.

Having got the 'Voice of Doom' bit out of the way, Dimbleby asked me what I was doing in London. My commercial went something like this: 'I am recruiting interpreters for the trials of war criminals which the American Government is preparing at Nuremberg.'

Dimbleby: 'What sort of people are you looking for?'

Frank: 'Bi-lingual linguists – people who know English and German equally well.'

Dimbleby: 'How are you doing this?'

Frank: 'I have been loaned offices at Berkeley Square by the Air Ministry; a suite of rooms on the second floor. I am testing people thoroughly. If they pass they will be offered a job at Nuremberg with the Americans, on very advantageous terms. Good pay, you know, excellent accommodation and PX privileges, all that. And the job is fascinating.'

Dimbleby: 'Where, did you say, you're doing this?'

Frank: 'At Berkeley Square on the second floor.'

Dimbleby: 'Thank you, Mr Frank,' followed by 'that was Wolfe Frank the Voice of Doom and Chief Interpreter at the next Nuremberg trial. And now, ladies and gentlemen, we have with us the most amazing flea circus ever to come out of Liechtenstein.'

Over sixty applicants flooded the offices in Berkeley Square during the next three days. Seven or eight never got a word out – they simply dried up at the crucial moment. Some produced every twentieth or thirtieth word. Others gave a translation that had nothing to do with the original text. However, I did manage to sign up the best people and fill the required number and I had somehow got together a very fine group of people including a deputy, Sigi Rammler, Austrian by birth, who succeeded me when I departed Nuremberg in November 1947, before the SP were over.

In the meantime, I found ways of improving my finances by covering the trials for the BBC and a programme called *Radio Newsreel* and the recordings of my broadcasts are amongst my Nuremberg souvenirs.

## NOTES:

1. *Nuremberg Trials Final Report Appendix D: Control Council Law No. 10*, by Telford Taylor.

2. The Trials of War Criminals before the Nuremberg Military Tribunals (Subsequent Proceedings) were as follows:

| | Designation | Dates | Defendants |
|---|---|---|---|
| 1 | Doctors' Trial | 9/12/46 – 20/8/47 | 23 Nazi physicians |
| 2 | Milch Trial | 2/1/47 – 14/4/47 | Field Marshal Erhard Milch of the Luftwaffe |

| | Designation | Dates | Defendants |
|---|---|---|---|
| 3 | Judges' Trial | 5/3/47 – 4/12/47 | 16 Nazi German 'racial purity jurists |
| 4 | Pohl Trial | 8/4/47 – 3/11/47 | Oswald Pohl and 17 SS officers |
| 5 | Flick Trial | 19/4/47 – 22/12/47 | Friedrich Flick and 5 company directors |
| 6 | IG Farben Trial | 27/8/47 – 30/7/48 | Directors of IG Farben, maker of Zyklon B |
| 7 | Hostages Trial | 8/7/47 – 19/2/48 | 12 German generals of the Balkan Campaign |
| 8 | RuSHA Trial | 20/10/47 – 10/3/48 | 14 racial cleansing and resettlement officials |
| 9 | Einsatzgruppen Trial | 29/9/47 – 10/4/48 | 24 officials of the Einsatgruppen |
| 10 | Krupp Trial | 8/12/47 – 13/7/48 | 12 directors of the Krupp Group |
| 11 | Ministries Trial | 6/1/48 – 13/4/49 | 21 officials of the Reich ministries |
| 12 | High Command Trial | 30/12/47 – 28/10/48 | 14 High Command generals |

3. Telford Taylor (1908-1998) was an assistant to Chief Counsel Robert Jackson at the IMT. In October 1946 he was promoted to Brigadier General and appointed Chief Counsel for the Subsequent Proceedings.

4. Maxine Cooper (1924-2009) was born in Chicago and studied theatre arts at the Pasadena Playhouse. She travelled to Europe in 1946 to entertain US military troops, during which time she met and married Wolfe Frank. She stayed in Europe for five years working in the theatre and television and during this period, as her private letters attest, she and Wolfe were devoted to each other. The couple moved to the US in the early 1950s but divorced in 1952. Maxine continued to perform in the theatre and for US television and made her film debut in 1955 starring alongside Ralph Meeker in the film noir *Kiss Me, Deadly* (see photograph on Plate 19). She later appeared in another movie classic of the period, *Whatever Happened to Baby Jane?* In 1957 she married Sy Gomberg, a screenwriter and producer, and retired from the acting profession in the early 1960s to raise a family. The couple remained married until Sy Gomberg's death in 2001. Maxine became well known as a photographer and as a Hollywood activist standing up for minority groups in the theatre and human rights and against nuclear weapons and the Vietnam War. Maxine Cooper died, aged eighty-four, in 2009.

5. A school of theatre arts was established at the Pasadena Playhouse in California in the 1920s and it had become an accredited college by 1937. Amongst its most notable alumni and players the Playhouse lists such names as Raymond Burr, Victor Mature, Eleanor Parker, Tyrone Power, Robert Young, Charles Bronson, Gene Hackman, Dustin Hoffman and Maxine Cooper Gomberg.

# 'THE EVIL THAT MEN DO LIVES AFTER THEM[1]'

**M**Y ASSOCIATION WITH THE BBC was very beneficial indeed[2]. My broadcasts from the courtroom during the SP were not exactly overpaid. I did some work for NBC, New York, later on, and earned as much per minute as BBC paid me for an entire interview; but I had a press card, a sticker saying 'Press' for my car, which did its job for at least four years afterwards, and BBC friends helped me legalise my car. I also did some broadcasts for the German Service in London and my many contacts with Goering et al. produced a lot of interesting material for them.

The SP trials proceeded more or less according to plan, but the German lawyers increasingly began to slow things down. They were sensing the estrangement between East and West and deduced, quite accurately as we now know, that a wind of change was taking place – or as Dr Aschenauer put it (see Prologue) – 'A late verdict will mean a mild verdict.' The judges in Nuremberg were still meting out death sentences but the US was hanging the mass-murdering Nazis not with relish but with reluctance.

Many of the subjects of our interrogations contained mundane and trivial matters but, as had happened during the IMT, there were some enormously dramatic moments. For sheer horrific content, the interrogations of Otto Ohlendorf, Chief of the Special Action Group in the East, were amongst the worst.

I was called into an interrogation on a Sunday afternoon, unexpectedly and without even knowing who Ohlendorf was or what he had been doing – but I soon learned. The unit he commanded was charged with combatting the resistance fighters in German-occupied Eastern Territories and the extermination of Jews. Ohlendorf admitted to it all quite freely. He was very much at his ease when he was brought into the room. His appearance was neat, he was well turned out and he was quite good-1ooking – one would have invited him home without hesitation. He was intelligent, alright, and we all stared at him in utter disbelief when he avowed, without hesitation, that he had ordered the 'humane' killing of some 90,000 people.

His pride and joy, he told us, had been the mobile gas chambers, which he then described in great detail. They were vans, disguised as transport vehicles, which were driven to the scene of the murders. There, the victims were asked to board. Ohlendorf's claim to humanitarian fame, he felt, was his special system of loading and unloading these gas chambers in such a way that the victims never guessed what was awaiting them. Even more important, and this is where his listeners began to reel in horror, his staff were spared undue mental suffering. They had, so he explained, been very severely emotionally affected by the struggles and screams of the dying until he had designed his new solution for the 'Final Solution'[3]. Nervous pressure upon his brave henchmen, he continued, had created serious personnel problems that he had had to remedy.

Under his new system the victims, he asserted, did not know where the vans were taking them. The mechanism for locking the doors was so designed that the passengers did not know that the doors were being made air-, or gas-tight. The vans were soundproof and his staff could not hear the noise of death. They could not look into the vans because the windows were too high, and they did not need to see if the Jews were dead since the time for Zyklon B to be fatal was known. At the proper moment, large fans were switched on and only when the last trace of the gas was gone would the doors be opened and the corpses unloaded. Care was always taken, he assured us, that the next victims in line could not see this happen.

The staggering aspect of this testimony was not so much the ghastly story, which had already become terribly familiar, but the manner in which Ohlendorf told it. He was, without doubt, proud of his work. He talked quietly, with expressive gestures of well-shaped hands, smoking our cigarettes, of the attacks on German occupation troops by Polish freedom fighters and the unreasonable time and effort required to dispose of the Jews at the same time. It was here, he felt, that his talents as an organiser and his ingenuity had served the Fatherland so well, and surely, he deserved everybody's recognition – including ours?

Even now, over thirty years later, I remember vividly the frame of mind in which we, the listeners to his account, were leaving him late that evening.

165

None of us could ever have imagined, until that day, such utter total lack of moral, ethical or human standards as we had witnessed. The man was proud, self-satisfied and mentally at peace. Unlike all the other murderers, the henchmen, the executioners, the sadists, the monsters I had encountered, he was searching for no explanation, no excuse, no justification, because he saw it all in his outstanding services, rendered to the cause. He did so to the end of his trial quietly, accurately and steadfastly, and I am certain he remained thus as he was walking up the steps to the gallows.

There were days, such as that, when after my day in court I could not eat and I had to drown myself in alcohol before I could sleep; days when my reactions to anything or anyone German were not normal.

These were inevitable emotional reactions. What has remained is the realisation that a lifetime is too short for such horrors to be filed away in the annals of history as something destined to be forgotten. Forgiven, perhaps – forgotten – never. I flinch at the sickening sentimentality that demands the release of a Rudolf Hess, the application of the statutes of limitation.

**Editor:** Wolfe's interrogating of Otto Ohlendorf will have come during the Einsatzgruppen Trial, the ninth of the SP trials, which began on 29 September 1947 and tried Ohlendorf and twenty-three other officers of the Einsatzgruppen (SS Task Force), which was said, together with other units of the Security Police, to have murdered two million Jews.

Rudolf Aschenauer was Ohlendorf's counsel and it was following his suggestion that his delaying tactics might mean 'a mild verdict' for his client, together with the court handing out seemingly softer sentences – coupled, no doubt, with thoughts of the horrific interviewing of Ohlendorf (referred to within this chapter) – that Wolfe Frank decided to retire from his position as Chief Interpreter.

He had become involved in the Nuremberg Trials process as early as July 1945 (with the BWCE), had interpreted the opening addresses of the IMT and, after having delivered the lion's share of the English/German interpretations, he had closed those proceedings with his Voice of Death pronouncements. He continued to be involved with, and was responsible for all the interpreting at, the SP, right up until his resignation in November 1947. He had therefore, for twenty-eight continuous months, lived and breathed through, and been directly involved in – at the sharp end – the most harrowing interviewing, interrogating and translating processes the world had ever seen.

The coming together of Ohlendorf's testimony, Aschenauer's tactics and the US prosecutions softer-sentence policy will, no doubt, have been the deciding factors in Wolfe Frank's mind that day in November 1947 when he reached the point where he knew it was time for him to resign.

Alfred Steer, who took over from Leon Dostert as Head of the US Language Division in April 1946, described the lot of an interpreter at Nuremberg, his own resignation and how and why so many interpreters had left during the trials[4]: 'I shall never forget the words of one translator, working on the death-record book of one minor Nazi concentration camp. His voice shook as he realised with horror the full implications of what he was saying: "Those people died in alphabetical order!"[5].'

'There are other more pleasant places I could go, other more useful jobs I could do, without being forced all day every day to come face to face with such horrors. I give up! I quit! I'm going home!'[6]

Francesca Gaiba in her excellent book *The Origins of Simultaneous Interpretation*[6] makes similar points. Recording discussions and quoting exchanges of correspondence she had had with Alfred Steer, and speaking specifically about the interpreters at the IMT, she writes of: 'The psychological torture of being exposed every day to an unparalleled degradation of human beings and of witnessing the atrocities and depravation in the Nazi camps … The horror did not stop once interpreters left the courtroom. They were living in a city of intense misery and suffering, in houses whose owners had been thrown out, where Germans were hungry and indolent because of their poor diet … The whole atmosphere of degradation made people want to leave as soon as they had a chance, and the turnover rate for language personnel during the year of the trial [the IMT] exceeded 100 per cent.'

Given the level and intensity of Wolfe Frank's contributions over his twenty-eight-month involvement with the Nuremburg Trials the wonder is how this unique and remarkable man was ever able to continue for as long as he did – and to the standards that led Judge Michael Musmanno, the presiding judge during Wolfe's final performance, to send him a photograph of the two of them interrogating a senior Nazi officer, inscribed in the most glowing terms.[7]

## NOTES:

1. William Shakespeare, *Julius Caesar* (Act 3, scene 2).

2. Frank appeared twice-weekly on the *Dispatches* programme, *Newsreel* and on the German Service for the BBC and *World Report* for NBC.

3. The Nazi plan to exterminate the Jewish people.

4. Alfred G. Steer, *Interesting Times: Memoir of Service in U.S. Navy, 1941-47.*

5.  It is thought Steer was referring to a report that noted that on one day in March 1945: '203 people had died at regular intervals of heart attacks and in alphabetical order.' Ann and John Tusa *The Nuremberg Trial* Macmillan, 1983.

5.  Alfred G. Steer in a letter to Francesca Gaiba.

6.  Francesca Gaiba *The Origins of Simultaneous Interpretation*, University of Ottawa Press, 1998.

7.  Photograph with inscription from the Wolfe Frank records reproduced as Plate 2.

# FAREWELL TO NUREMBERG

I AM PROUDLY AWARE OF MY MINOR CLAIM TO FAME as the Voice of Doom, which Goering et al. heard when they learned their sentences.[1] I am a total believer in the Nuremberg Trials. I do not believe that any alternative solution existed. The fact that other similar crimes were committed, sometimes on the Allied side, does not mean that Nuremberg was morally, legally, ethically or historically wrong. No murderer would enjoy the mitigating argument that another murderer remains unpunished because the arm of the law does not reach him.

What other venue was there? German courts? – ludicrous. Neutral judges? – they were sought in Switzerland, Sweden and other countries, and refused on the basis that Germany might recover, therefore no copy-book must be blotted.

The Four-Power International Military Tribunal, which tried the twenty-one top men of the Third Reich, rendered an impeccable performance, in spite of the Soviet presence, and because of the total integrity of the British, American and French jurists. There were times when the French sided with the Russians over some issue that was in doubt. However, the tie-breaking vote was that of the President, Sir Geoffrey Lawrence, and he stood for judicially unassailable decisions. One case in point was Hjalmar Schacht, the former President of the Reich's Bank and known as Hitler's economic wizard. I later learned that the Russians and the French wanted Schacht hanged. Lawrence and Biddle (Britain and the US) however took the view that the prosecution had not adequately established his guilt. That was so. Certainly, Schacht deserved to hang, but under the Tribunal's rules of evidence – so the experts agreed – the IMT could not find him guilty. He was therefore acquitted against what seemed to have been extremely forceful protestations made by the Russians and the French.

Of course, the Russians only knew one verdict at the IMT – guilty. They also only knew one punishment – death by hanging. The

Subsequent Proceedings, with Telford Taylor in charge is a different story, into which I will not go, as I was not there at the end. Suffice to say I was glad when the time came for me to leave Nuremberg.

**Editor:** So concludes the extraordinary story of the first half of the life, times and involvements of Wolfe Frank, as he recorded them. He was surely one of the most charismatic characters of the twentieth century and he was still only thirty-four years of age when he left Nuremberg. Less than two years later he would embark upon another great adventure, details of which I will outline in the following chapter.

As has been mentioned earlier, the International Military Tribunal was described by Mr Justice Birkett, Britain's Alternate member at the Tribunal, as having been the 'The greatest trial in history.' Those who took part as translators and interpreters revolutionised the way trial and conference interpreting is conducted, and they made it what it is today. They were pioneers who introduced a system that is now used to great effect around the world at every level, but most notably at the world's great institutions such as the UN and the EU. Not only was the work of those interpreters carried out to the highest possible standards it is said they shortened the IMT by over three years.

The published trial records extend to over forty volumes and it is estimated that six million words were spoken and recorded. Yet, as Francesca Gaiba has pointed out, 'Not one word is said in this official, published record about the system of simultaneous interpretation that was created in order to permit the multi-lingual conduct of the trial.' (Ms Gaiba more than adequately sets the record straight in her book: *The Origins of Simultaneous Interpretation*).

So high a standard did the interpreters set that their work was entirely satisfactory to everyone involved. In Wolfe's own words, 'At no time during the entire trial was there a complaint, or even a challenge, directed at the interpreters.'

Without question the simultaneous interpretation system proved to be more successful than anyone had ever hoped. Those who made it possible were a credit to their countries, the justice system, their profession and themselves. Quite simply they were a major contributing factor to the success of that 'greatest trial in history,' and from amongst all those capable linguists from the four great nations running the IMT, one name stands out as being the 'Ace Interpreter at the Nuremberg International War Crimes Trials'. That man was Wolfe Frank and it is fitting that I should leave the concluding words praising his performances to those who, at every level and from every angle, witnessed him in action and/or those historians who have spent years studying the Nuremberg Trials:

## HIS ULTIMATE SUPERIOR'S VIEW
'Wolfe Frank's performance was most excellent and, indeed, may be described as brilliant … he is an outstanding expert in not only simultaneous

Above: Wolfe Frank and other interpreters following proceedings whilst awaiting their turn in the interpreting booths (probably in room 606).

Below: Defendants von Papen, Schacht and Fritzsche hold a press conference in the courtroom immediately after Wolfe Frank has announced their acquittal.

Plate 16

Plate 17

Above: The rather spartan
backroom conditions that the
translators and interpreters
were working in at Nuremberg
– all situated within an armed
compound.

Right: A rare moment of
relaxation for Wolfe as he awaits
further instructions between
translating and/or interptreting
sessions.

Left (Plate 17): Drowning in
paper and hardly able to cope
with the volume. Handwritten
translations had to be proofread,
typed, changed and then
translated into all four languages.

Plate 18

Above: Wolfe's second marriage to a rather nervous looking Maxine Cooper at Nuremberg in February 1946.

Right: A rather more confident Maxine in the arms of Ralph Meeker during the filming of *Kiss Me, Deadly* in 1955. Based on the novel by Mickey Spillane and directed by Robert Aldrich *Kiss Me, Deadly*, which is considered to be a film noir, marked Maxine's debut on the 'big screen' (for further details of her career see information included in this book's Epilogue).

Plate 19

Above: Wolfe's fourth marriage in November 1960 – to Susi Alberti – at Davos.

Although the marriage was at times turbulent it lasted for fifteen years, and Susi continued to visit Wolfe after their divorce and into his declining years.

The couple were the proprietors of several restaurants in Spain and Andorra and the photograph left shows *La Reja* the one they opened in the early 1970s at Mijas in the Malaga region (see Epilogue for further details).

Plate 20

Wolfe and Maxine at Davos in c.1946

Plate 21

Captain Wolfe Frank of The Royal
Northumberland Fusiliers.

Patricia Leonard was one of Wolfe's
great pre-war loves (see Chapter 14).

'A British reporter buttonholed the star interpreter, Wolfe Frank.
Would Frank be handling the afternoon session [the announcement of
the sentences]? the reporter asked. 'Yes' Frank answered. 'I've been
practicing my "Tod durch den Strang" (death by the rope) for days'.

Joseph E. Persico, *Nuremberg – Infamy on Trial*

Plate 22

Right: Wolfe Frank c.1985.

Below: The *Old Ship Hotel* at Mere in Wiltshire and adjoining it to the left *The Malt House* – Wolfe's former home.

It was from the *Old Ship* that Wolfe Frank departed on his last fateful journey after having treated himself to a rather splendid meal and a bottle of vintage champagne (see Epilogue for further details).

Plate 23

interpretation, but in the selection and training of interpreters for this very difficult work.'
*Brigadier General Telford Taylor, US Chief of Counsel for War Crimes (in a testimonial).*

## A JUDGE'S VIEW
'Wolfe Frank, Ace Interpreter at the Nuremberg International War Crimes Trials, and so far as I am concerned the whole world round.'
*Judge Michael Musmanno, one of the Presiding Judges at Nuremberg (inscription on a photograph, see Plate 2).*

## A PROSECUTOR'S VIEW
'Frank's translations were delicious. He had a great command of the English Language. I used to go to the courtroom sometimes in the afternoon just to listen to him.'
*Henry T. King Jr., one of the US prosecutors at Nuremberg:* The Nuremberg Context Through the Eyes of the Participant – Military Law Review, *1995.*

## A DEFENDANT'S VIEW
'Of course I want counsel. But it is even more important to have a good interpreter.'
*Hermann Goering, "Germany: The Defendant"* Time Magazine *29 October 1945. At the time he was most involved with Wolfe Frank.*

## A COLLEAGUE'S VIEW
'Frank was the best. He could interpret just as deftly from German to English as the other way around, and was able to keep up with any speaker, no matter how fast.'
*Lieutenant Colonel Peter Uiberall (Chief German Translator at Nuremberg)* The Origins of Simultaneous Interpretation.

## A NEWSPAPER'S VIEW
Wolfe Frank, ex-German and ex-British officer, as chief interpreter for two years at the Nuremberg trials materially contributed to the practical success of those enormously difficult procedures. He won the unreserved tributes of the American and British jurists.'
*New York Herald Tribune*

## A REPORTER'S VIEW
'By common accord Captain Wolfe Frank, translating from German into English, who came to Nuremberg in British uniform and returned as a civilian, was the ace of them all.'
*R.W. Cooper, correspondent of* The Times *and author of* The Nuremberg Trial *(1947).*

## A HISTORIAN'S VIEW

'The unanimous judgement on the simultaneous translation system was that it was a miracle like Pentecost. No one was ever unreasonable enough to expect all the translators to reach the standard of the ace of them all – Wolfe Frank … his use of German and English was noticeably better than that of most native speakers. His voice and manner, the nuances of his vocabulary, the ability to convey the character of the person for whom he was translating were all outstanding.'

*John and Ann Tusa,* The Nuremberg Trial *(2010).*

Finally, a few further comments from the incomparable Wolfe Frank himself:

'Even Goering thought they [the trials] were fair. I talked to him many times off the record. As far as the principle went, he refused to recognize our right to try him, the victory [*sic*] trying the vanquished. But even he agreed the court was incredibly fair.' (Wolfe Frank in a 1970 interview he gave to *The Oregonian* a daily newspaper based in Portland, Oregon, USA).

'None of the judges understood German and everything said in that courtroom to them by the defendants and witnesses passed through the ears, brains and mouths of we interpreters'.

'I had been involved in the writing of a chapter of human history that would be read, talked about and remembered forever. I had been more totally and decisively immersed in recording the horrors of the war than most of the millions who had fought in it. It had changed me'.

'A lifetime is too short for such horrors to be filed away in the annals of history as something destined to be forgotten. As long as there are orphans who remember the extermination of their families, as long as there are men and women mentally or physically crippled by the faithful servants of Hitler's Third Reich, we should not afford ourselves the luxury of burying such ghastly memories'.

## NOTE:

1. Wolf Frank, as the Voice of Doom, can be heard delivering those sentences to Goering et al. by going to YouTube and clicking on the following link: www.youtube.com/watch?v=19C2JhKdxIU

# HANGOVER AFTER HITLER

**Editor: The Wolfe Frank Story, 1946-1950.**

Maxine Cooper returned to Nuremberg in early 1946. As Wolfe was not American, he could not be joined within the security complex by dependants. He got over the problem by arranging for Maxine to be employed on the base, at US Government expense, as a filing clerk – a job at which he says, 'She was not an outstanding success … apart from that she was a sheer delight.'

Wolfe and Maxine were married on 15 February at the Villa Shickedanz in Nuremberg (see Plates 19 and 21). It was a 'splendid affair' attended by 'all the nobles in General Telford Taylor's court.' Following the ceremony, the couple drove to Davos for their honeymoon in the brand-new Ford convertible Maxine's wealthy father had sent over as a wedding present. (Davos was Wolfe's favourite place, to which he returned often during his life, where he lived on several occasions and where he hoped, eventually, his ashes would be scattered). Having 'tied the knot' Wolfe also collected the $500 bet he had waged with Joe von Zastrow on the eve of his performance as the Voice of Doom.

Assigned a villa and a Bohemian couple as housekeepers, the Franks led an idyllic private life and mixed socially with those of wealth and position within local society, as well as those involved in the theatre and local arts scene, and black marketeers!

The life Wolfe enjoyed away from the horrors he relentlessly encountered within the Palace of Justice, coupled with his happy and more settled domestic situation were, no doubt, also very much in his thinking as he pondered his future during the Einsatzgruppen Trial. He then decided that after twenty-eight months of constant listening to, and speaking about, the most monstrous crimes the world had ever seen, the time had come for him to bid farewell to Nuremberg – in his own words: 'I had heard enough about atrocities, mass murder, war crimes, extermination camps and genocide. It was time for me to quit'.

He did not arrive at that decision lightly and it was a profound moment for him as he records in his memoirs:

'That was the end of a very, very important part of my life. We interpreters had, after all, been involved in the writing of history and our contributions were of the greatest importance'.

True to form however, the weeks leading up to the Frank's departure from Nuremberg were not without incident, intrigue and adventure, and the following examples are further evidence of how closely, at times, he sailed to the wind, and how he was never slow to take advantage of each and every opportunity that presented itself.

The first of those incidents concerned Wolfe's Opal car. The US Army had suddenly declared that all motor vehicles captured during hostilities would have to be registered under newly created occupation plates, and proof would be required to show where and when the vehicle had been captured. To get over this little problem Wolfe persuaded a departing BBC executive to provide a letter stating that he had captured the vehicle near Tobruk and had sold it to Frank. The necessary endorsement, exit permit and fuel allowances were then provided by a departing US major who told Frank as he was going home tomorrow he was prepared 'to sign anything put in front of him.'

At about the same time Wolfe's driver knocked down and killed an elderly German. In an off-the-record discussion – that seems astonishing but was perhaps indicative of the awful times the Germans were living through – the representative of the insurance company handling the case said to Frank: 'The family were really rather glad to get rid of the old man who was eating and not producing. They would sign a total release for twenty cartons of cigarettes. He could not do it on behalf of his company, but – would you?' Wolfe then records, 'I did. Twenty cartons of cigarettes cost me roughly $18 at the PX. Not much to compensate for the loss of a life.'

The third incident involved Wolfe and two friends, Fredy Stoll[1], the former German ski-jumping champion and Fritz Haegele, Goering's valet, who was being employed by the US as caretaker of the 'Eagles Nest', Hitler's famous mountain retreat near Berchtesgaden, where Wolfe and others would often retreat themselves to cook meals on 'Hitler's stove.' The three had been stripping the Nest of certain items – in particular three large bathtubs – when Stoll was arrested by the CIC, who had been tapping Haegele's phone. They suspected Stoll of looting much more than bathtubs, namely the art treasures and jewels that Goering had stolen from the Jews and hidden away. When they heard Haegele tell Stoll 'The stuff's ready' they swooped believing they had hit the jackpot. The CIC officers were not happy when all that could be found in Stoll's van was a bathtub and, following a Frank intervention, Stoll was released without charge and allowed to keep Hitler's bathtub; about which Wolfe comments: 'I have often soaked in it, and it was sheer luxury.'

In late 1947 Wolfe and Maxine departed Nuremberg under the cover of darkness, in their two cars and a trailer which bore a variety of false number plates and were covered by forged documents, to spend the winter in Davos before moving on, in May 1948, to Paris where Wolfe became a script writer for the radio section of the Marshall Plan[2]. They moved on to London in July, where they were joined by Maxine's 'incurable alcoholic and divorced mother Gladys'. Although fifty-four years of age (and in Maxine's absence) Gladys stripped off and invited Wolfe to put her bra on – an invitation he turned down. He later informed Maxine of what had taken place. The whole episode was to later have disastrous repercussions on the Frank marriage, as Wolfe says: 'The words Gladys uttered at the time were ominous: "I'll get you for this you son-of-a-bitch" – she sure as hell did'.

By 1948 Wolfe was a partner in Fellowes & Frank, an import-export company and an adviser to a firm of aircraft brokers. However, business was not good, and Wolfe had become seriously concerned about the way Germany appeared to be hoodwinking the rest of the world with the information it was providing through the media. This led to another great episode in the Wolfe Frank story that was to once again put his life at risk and led to him going under cover on false papers into the occupied East and West sectors of Germany, to gather evidence for what became an acclaimed series of articles for the *New York Herald Tribune* (*NYHT*) entitled *'Hangover After Hitler'*. During the covert operation, he single-handedly discovered, unbelievably working in a position of trust for the British Property Control Board[3] under an assumed name, the SS officer who was 'fourth' on the Allies most wanted list of war criminals. Wolfe eventually turned the former Nazi general over to the appropriate authorities but not before he had taken his signed 'Confession'. Of the two copies produced one was handed in as evidence (along with the SS officer) whilst the other signed copy remains in the Wolfe Frank archive along with his memoirs and other documents of importance.

The astonishing story of Frank's clandestine undercover operation, the articles he wrote, his apprehending of the Nazi general and, for the first time, a translation and reproduction of the entire Confession are to be the subject of a separate book entitled *The Undercover Nazi Hunter: Unmasking Evil in Post-war Germany*, which is to be published by Frontline Books. (A copy of the *NYHT* flyer announcing the *Hangover After Hitler* series can be seen on page 194).

## NOTES:

1. Alfred 'Fredy' Stoll was a ski jumper born in Berchtesgaden who became the German champion in 1934. On that occasion he was awarded an engraved cup by Hermann Goering as a special prize for the furthest jump of the day. He was described as being 'a daredevil without fear, who not only jumps

further than anybody else, but, by testimony of a friend, would also make a good race car driver and motorbike racer.'

2. The Marshall Plan (officially the European Recovery Programme) was an American initiative. Named after US Secretary of State George Marshall, the Plan gave $13 billion in aid to help rebuild Western European economies after the Second World War.

3. Following the war many German owned properties and estates were seized by the British Property Control Board and handed over to reliable Germans or were held by the Board until the Control Council decided how to dispose of them in the interests of peace.

# EPILOGUE

Any follower of the Wolfe Frank story thus far would be forgiven for thinking that such a man might consider his involvements at Nuremberg, and his post-war undercover assignment and single-handed apprehension of one of the 'most wanted' Nazi war criminals, to have been something extraordinary, and that the rest of his life might prove to be something of an anti-climax. Certainly, in today's world, such service to one's country would be more appropriately recognized, and the accompanying media coverage would guarantee that those achievements were more publicly acknowledged and rewarded. Together with his striking good looks, his personality, his charisma, his ability and his intelligence, these qualities would make a modern-day Wolfe Frank a PR management company's dream client – and would, no doubt, lead to him being considered a 'hot property' with the potential of having his profile raised to the kind of 'superstar' status many less able and less talented 'personalities' enjoy today.

However, whilst those events were undoubtedly two of the highlights in a quite extraordinary life, Wolfe viewed them as being no more than transitory events from which, once over, he quickly moved on – without much more than the occasional backward glance. To him they were simply two of the challenges destiny had set him during a lifetime in which he more than fulfilled Rudyard Kipling's counsel to 'fill every unforgiving minute with sixty seconds worth of distance run'.

In fact Wolfe Frank seems to have been the embodiment of the character described in *IF* – the kind of man Kipling hopes his son will eventually become.

Certainly Wolfe, in spite of his hedonistic, maverick and cavalier tendencies, could, whenever necessary, be relied upon to keep a cool head in difficult and dangerous situations and to carry out whatever was asked of him – to the highest standards and with the greatest integrity and professionalism. He could be a patient, trusting and forgiving, yet determined man, as he demonstrated during and after his period of internment and throughout his successful campaign (and twenty-three applications) to be allowed to join a fighting unit of the British Army. He proved himself to be equally at ease with the lower ranks and the hoi polloi as he was amongst the officers, the nobles, the gentry and actors in whose company he would so often be found. He was also an optimist, a dreamer and a chancer who took risks, financially and romantically, which sometimes left him bereft of money or love – situations from which he always recovered to fight another day – often to his greater advantage. 'Triumph and Disaster'? – Wolfe Frank really did 'treat those two imposters just the same'.

Irresistible to women Wolfe was married five times and had countless affairs, casual relationships and one-night stands. It is true to say that throughout his adult life he was never without a love interest; apart from the months he was interned as an 'enemy alien', and even then he was preparing for a liaison with a new conquest at the very moment of his arrest and, within 'five minutes' of being released (and looking more like a vagrant than the Army captain he was to become), he was once again invited to share the bed of a an admiring stranger.

Many men also held Wolfe in high esteem and sought his company and friendship. They admired his abilities and his free-spirited approach to life, they envied the ease with which he captured the hearts of the fairer sex, they marvelled at his linguistic skills and his eloquence and they thoroughly enjoyed his bonhomie, his bon viveur and his devil-may-care attitude – especially in those situations where so many would err on the side of caution.

In short Wolfe Frank seems to have been a mixture of Casanova, with whom he had much in common, Cary Grant, the Scarlet Pimpernel, James Bond and Oliver Reed; and he had that rare ability to be a man's man – a worldly-wise, educated gentleman who possesses class and admits his faults – as well as being a ladies' man.

Wolfe structured his memoirs around his five marriages and it seems right that I should adopt that format to conclude the Frank (and his remarkably frank) story with some brief biographical details surrounding those five phases of his life, as well as some of the other relationships and involvements he enjoyed, or experienced, in between – or simultaneously!

His short-lived marriage to, and his later relationship with, Baroness Maditta von Skrbensky (1936-37) has been covered by Wolfe within the autobiographical section of this book, save to say that in December 1947 Maditta moved to Canada to marry Colin R. Watson at St Andrew's Presbyterian Church in Toronto.

Wolfe has likewise explained the wedding ceremony and the early years of his marriage to his second wife, American actress Maxine Cooper (1945-1952) – details of which I have expanded upon in the last chapter – up until the time of his clandestine reporting assignment in 1949 (see also Chapter 38, Note 4).

Following the completion of the project with the *NYHT* Wolfe and Maxine moved to Paris where he became a scriptwriter. 'I wrote the odd line here and there for an incredible array of talent – Ella Fitzgerald, Bing Crosby, Frank Sinatra,' he recalls casually, 'and there were Canasta lessons by Mary Hemmingway – the great man's widow.'

In October 1950, the Franks returned to Davos for the winter during which period Wolfe took part in the famous Parsenn Derby downhill ski race, one of the most important events on the international racing scene. Unfortunately, in the middle section of the run, and in full public view, he skidded off the track and badly fractured his leg in two places. Wolfe's cast was signed by many of the friends who came to visit him including 'Irwin Shaw, Joshua Logan, Deborah Kerr and many top skiers'. In the months that followed Wolfe supplemented his script writing activities by becoming more involved in his import/export business within the aircraft industry and Maxine returned to her stage career, still using her maiden name.

In September 1951, having discovered Maxine was pregnant, the Franks set sail on the *Queen Mary*, tickets paid for by Maxine's father, bound for the USA. They stayed for ten days in a hotel on Central Park and took delivery of a new Ford station wagon, also paid for by Mr Cooper, before travelling down to their new home in Hollywood. Here Wolfe was introduced to many of Maxine's friends including Ronald and Nancy Regan, Hedy Lamarr, Charles Boyer and Rock Hudson (clearly during his heterosexual phase) an event Wolfe records as follows: 'The former truck driver cum star addressed Maxine, whom he had just met as my wife: "Whaddaya doin' fa dinner tammarragh" was the tactful and beautifully spoken enquiry. Her negative reaction produced a shrug of padded shoulders and the ogre flounced off into the night.'

Wolfe invested all his time, energy and money into trying to set up a Davos style ski resort amongst the mountains of Mineral King in California and Maxine gave birth to a son in January. Soon after, however, there were two events that led to the breakdown of their marriage. Driving back from Mineral King one day a horse collided with the Frank's car and Maxine sustained injuries, including a fractured jaw, for which she was later awarded over $100,000 ($1 million today). This led to Maxine's mother, Gladys, taking charge of her daughter's and her grandson's welfare and to Wolfe being served with divorce papers. Remembering Gladys' earlier proclamation of, 'I'll get you for this you son-of-a-bitch' following his spurning of her advances, Wolfe believed his mother-in-law had poisoned his wife against him. That may be so, or perhaps his belief that, 'the occasional fling in the horizontal had long been forgiven (and legally condoned) by Maxine' was a less than accurate reading of his situation.

Frank left the ensuing court hearing 'with a car, a few possessions and $12.48 in cash' – his dreams of opening the ski resort at Mineral King were over.

(In 1957 Maxine married Sy Gomberg, a screenwriter and producer, and retired from the acting profession in the early 1960s to raise a family. The couple remained married until Sy Gomberg's death in 2001. Maxine became well known as a photographer and as a Hollywood activist standing up for minority groups in the theatre and human rights and against nuclear weapons and the Vietnam War. She died, aged eighty-four, in 2009).

Forced to find work following his divorce Wolfe joined a firm of garment manufacturers and sold their products door-to-door. It turned out to be 'The most incredible, ridiculous and sometimes sordid expedition of my life.' It is easy to see why Wolfe would think this. Most of his customers were women, left on their own, who were more interested in Wolfe than his wares – and his best customers were those who lived and worked in 'whorehouses situated on the wrong side of the tracks.'

Wearied and sickened by his fall from grace and the kind of work he had been reduced to carrying out Wolfe secured a position with a local NBC radio station in Las Vegas interviewing visitors in their own languages and translating their replies over the airways for the locals. The series seemed to be going well for both Wolfe and the radio company until the day he received a visit from the Mafia who spoke to him thus: 'Okay Frank, you don't wanna do no radio show around here, no more than you wanna hole in ya head. You're gettin outa town, like today, see? The Mafia feared that one of my interviewees might say something detrimental about Vegas or the casinos.' Wolfe wisely left town the same evening and, as his visitors had predicted, NBC had no difficulty in releasing him from his contract!

Wolfe moved on to San Francisco and over lunch with an old friend was offered a job in the UK with an electronics company called Ampex. He would be given four months training before he departed, and he was loaned a luxury flat. At a house-warming party he held in the flat he was propositioned by three young ladies – which led to him seeing them, on a rota basis, for the period he remained in San Francisco, as he records: 'The order of appearance had also been settled during a prolonged visit to my bathroom (actually, the apartment was so elegant, it was a powder room) – Tuesday: Lois, dark hair, Hedy Lamarr type, schoolteacher, twenty-two years old, from Houston, Texas. Thursday: Martine, short-cropped hair, tiny, highly intelligent, interviewer at an employment agency, age not announced. Saturday: Jean. Very tall, not at all pretty but with a tremendous sense of humour, Swedish descent – the best teller of dirty stories with a Swedish accent I ever knew.'

Arriving in London in 1954, as a newly trained electronics engineer, Wolfe was assigned to man the Ampex stand at the Vienna Trade Fair where his companions were 'seven beautiful Viennese model hostesses.' Wolfe's own words describe what happened next:

'When the Fair finished I packed my gadgets into the station wagon and was all set to leave. Only, when I got into the car I found I had a passenger: Vilma [one of the hostesses], lovely, stacked and determined, at seventeen, to get away from home. Her arguments were sound and she even had a letter from her mother, stating that she had permission to go to England to learn the language.

'Vilma explained that her one and only desire was to look after me, my household and my needs, which, she thought, we might usefully and jointly satisfy. I was then at an age where one does not necessarily recognize the attraction of so young a playmate. I preferred experience and sophistication. Vilma, I hasten to say, soon put me straight. She was of Czechoslovakian descent and she had inexhaustible physical and mental reserves that later made her the owner of a successful import-export business in Vienna, a souped-up Porsche and a staggering collection of fur coats. I know she did it all herself, and out of bed.

'I had a small cottage in London and Vilma took over as mistress, hostess and language student. In bed, she was insatiable. She would turn into a wild animal at the critical moment, baring her teeth, eyes turned back and her body shaking with orgasm after orgasm'.

Wolfe and Vilma stayed together for some time until one day he was 'unforgivably destructive' in a comment he made about her cooking. 'She left the next day and it was only when she had gone that I realized what I had lost, or thrown away'.

Perhaps on the rebound, and with his defences down, Wolfe was soon to meet and fall in love with a woman 'of Eastern European origin' who was to become his third wife – Galina Verbeek (or Halpern, or Harden). She was in her twenties, claimed to be a model, and was 'as beautiful without make-up as any woman could be.'

Wolfe became 'mesmerized and love-stricken' and against the advice of many friends he married Galina at Caxton Hall in the autumn of 1955. 'Immediately the knot had been tied however, her whole attitude changed from that of a demure young damsel into a fiery sex symbol and she became a snarling, hostile, argumentative, hellcat. Then mail started to arrive from the wrong side of the Iron Curtain, there were telephone conversations in a strange tongue and finally applications for British citizenship'.

Realizing he had been taken for a ride, Wolfe refused to sign her documents. 'With fluttering eyelids' however 'she persuaded a doctor, a banker and a local clergyman to sign the necessary forms with each declaring they had known her for over five years and could vouch for her in every way.'

The relationship turned physically violent with both parties sustaining bruising, following which Galina visited Wolfe's boss to show him hers. This led to Wolfe being dismissed from Ampex and to him willingly paying for Galina's one-way ticket out of the UK – and his life. He immediately started divorce proceedings, however it would be many years before he could catch up with her to serve the papers. Soon after her departure Wolfe was pulled in by Scotland Yard and was questioned at length by the intelligence services about how he brought the woman into the country, her phone calls, her letters, her movements, who she had met, where she'd been. Frank's own background was investigated and although he was eventually cleared it was apparent the intelligence services believed Galina, who was known under a number of aliases, was a Russian spy and that Wolfe had been used merely to allow her into the country and to enable her to claim UK citizenship.

Wolfe was not alone and out of work for long. He took on translation and interpreting commissions and after a number of casual affairs met and set up home with a German lady, Helma Scheidt: 'Who occupies the uncontested first place on the list of women I ought to have married.' Helma was from one of the wealthiest families in Germany and this led to Wolfe being offered a position selling products for the Controls Company of America.

Wolfe and Helma stayed together for three years and they had a house built for them in Davos, which they moved into on Frank's forty-fifth birthday in 1958. This turned out to be a mistake. Many of Helma's circle of friends were wealthy Nazi sympathizers and now, living close to the German border, they visited frequently and expected Frank to adopt their ways and their beliefs. Remembering so many of his own friends, his half-sister and her mother (his father's first wife) who had perished in concentration camps and his years of involvement at Nuremberg, he found it impossible to change in order to be accepted by Helma's friends, and 'a Teutonic cloud had begun to darken our relationship.' Once again he moved on, even though that meant leaving the dream home situated in his favourite location.

By the early 1960s Wolfe had moved to Dusseldorf, where he rented a penthouse and he had become a very successful businessman earning in excess of $80,000 per year (then about £32,000).

This brought him into contact with an old friend who headhunted him for a company called Investors Overseas Services (IOS), which was involved in the Mutual Fund Industry (MFI) – companies that pool money from many investors to purchase securities. IOS was run by Bernard Cornfeld, a flamboyant financier, and Frank was hired to head up the German operation. This proved to be both an uplifting (initially) and then a traumatic (eventually) experience for Frank and was another major watershed in his life. Over the coming few years he helped build IOS into a company that at its peak raised US$2.5 billion and employed 25,000 salesmen who sold MFI products door-to-door, especially in Germany, to small investors. After years of success the company overtraded, made a public share offering, diversified too widely and created a cash shortage. The company was eventually put into liquidation leaving millions of small investors out of pocket. Fraud charges were brought against Cornfeld and he spent almost a year in a Swiss jail awaiting trial. However, when the case did eventually come before the courts he was acquitted.

None of this was apparent of course to Wolfe at the time he joined the business and when he did realize what was going on he was one of the first to depart. Of his association with IOS Wolfe comments: 'If there is anything Cornfeld and his fellow freaks deserve, then it is to be forgotten, except for the fact that they, with their total lack of honesty and morality have been responsible for much misery, even death, for those they hoodwinked.'

Entering a new decade Wolfe started a new relationship with the bisexual wife of a friend. Her name was Susi Alberti and she became the fourth Mrs Frank (1960-1975). They were married at Davos on 12 November 1960 (see Plate 20), 'and thus started,' records Wolfe, 'a battle that would last for fifteen years and included every conceivable type of row, parting and reunion in the book – and it left very little time for interludes of happiness or passages of time that were not stormy.'

Wolfe joined a small Swiss electronics company and was sent to the Orient on business. As he departed his new wife gave him permission to sleep with local women if he felt he needed to. 'I resolved to obey orders,' he recalls, 'it was easy in Bangkok because there is a temple of sex where gorgeous long haired beauties were competing for the attention of the stray male in exchange for a minute contribution to their cash resources.' He records similar experiences in Hong Kong and Tokyo where he was invited by a surgeon friend to sit in and watch him carry out breast implant operations.

On his return Wolfe was tracked down by Cornfeld and asked to deal with the French and Swiss authorities in matters that were being investigated. Without becoming involved in the business, Frank accepted, in return for $300,000 per annum, a generous expense allowance and accommodation in Geneva. Susie split her time between the Geneva penthouse and their other home in Davos whilst Frank handled some delicate matters with French government ministers and officials and Swiss financiers. Unlike most of the others associated with IOS, he was greatly respected in both countries and when he was shown irrefutable evidence that ISO had been trading illegally he quit immediately and moved to New York to resurrect the financial skills he had acquired in the MFI. This led him back to Germany and Switzerland.

As Wolfe moved into a new decade he took stock of his situation:
'The year was 1970. I was fifty-seven years old. A computer read-out might have looked something like this:

Marriages: four (three divorces, one on the rocks, like a dry martini).
Children: one son (official) one daughter (unofficial).
Assets: one house, three cars, $20,000 cash and securities.
Health: outstanding.
Spirit: undaunted.
Future: nebulous.
Past: extremely varied, mostly satisfying.
Its components: politically praiseworthy, morally open to argument, professionally successful if only in sales.

'With all this in mind there was only one thing anyone could do – open a restaurant!'

That is exactly what he did, and he did it on his own, Susi having left him 'for the nth time.' (Wolfe and Susi had a very 'open' relationship. They each had extramarital affairs, there were many bitter arguments and they parted often, sometimes for lengthy periods, during what was clearly a stormy time together. Yet there were also many periods of contentment and it was a union that lasted fifteen years, the longest of any of his marriages).

Throughout his adult life Wolfe's culinary skills had been much admired and he decided to put them to good use by opening a restaurant called *La Reja* (meaning iron grill outside a window) which was, 'located in a famous tourist spot amongst the snow white houses of Mijas', a coastal village in the Spanish region of Malaga (see Plate 20).

The venture proved to be less than successful. Staff, customers and suppliers all took advantage of Frank's lack of knowledge and naivety and his trusting nature. There was a temporary respite to the losses Wolfe was incurring when Susi arrived some months later. She kicked out Wolfe's then current mistress and took charge of the management of *La Reja*. Soon they were at each other's throats again and Wolfe records, 'this time it knew no pause and went on to the end, but it raged for nearly five more years'.

As a diversion, 'to fill an emotional vacuum Susi had created' and appalled at the Spaniards widespread cruelty to animals – about which he is scathing – Wolfe set up his own unofficial animal refuge.

Things reached the lowest ebb over one Christmas period. After a heavy drinking session, and a particularly hurtful outburst by Susi, Wolfe attempted to take his own life (this was the second time he had tried to end it all). He records in his memoirs:

'These lines would obviously not have been written if I had done things properly. Would-be-suicides please note that you must make sure you take the right dose. I took too much, namely: thirty sleeping tablets, thirty-six tranquilizers and twenty suppositories, plus a few odds and ends.'

Believing him to be suffering from a hangover, and even though a cat died after having licked the saliva trickling from his mouth, Susi left Wolfe to sleep it off – for thirty hours! It was eventually the maid who raised the alarm and, close to death, he was rushed to a private clinic in Malaga, where he eventually came round some fifty hours later and was released after five days. Following this Wolfe comments: 'We never again returned to anything resembling the old-fashioned concept of marriage. We had sex occasionally, "to release glandular pressure," as I was fond of saying.'

Soon after this incident things got even worse for Wolfe. He was arrested for a motoring offence he had committed some years earlier in Ibiza, and was chained to other prisoners 'in full view of gaping tourists' and marched through the busy streets of Malaga to be incarcerated in the local jail. There he spent a week 'scared witless' alongside some 500 inmates, including murderers, rapists, bank-robbers, drug dealers, addicts, drunks and embezzlers, until Susi was able to get him bail. 'I had been in jail for seven days, four hours, and thirty-nine minutes,' said a relieved Frank. On his return some months later for the court case Wolfe, after having been submitted to what he considered to be a doubtful hearing, was convicted of dangerous driving, given a six months suspended prison sentence and ordered to hand in his driving licence: 'I sent them the licence they had recorded during the trial and went on driving using one of my other licences, being careful not to be caught, and I stayed away from trouble during my "parole". I also decided that I had had enough of Spain and resolved to get out very rapidly.'

'Under the weight of intolerable and unresolved conflagration between Susi and me,' Wolfe departed for Andorra in the company of 'an American enchantress named Caroline', where his old friend Hermann Hemmeter (the Garden Dwarf) had settled. After further periods in Davos – to settle his affairs there – and Paris to take part in a number of orgies (graphically described) Wolfe's notes tell us that he purchased some land in Andorra, sold his business in Spain and moved with his 'sixteen cats and six dogs' to a mountain retreat of Soldeu in Andorra where, on 4 February 1974, he opened a new restaurant, bar and disco complex called *El Duc* (the owl).

For two winters the business was a success. However, 'thereafter the decline was staggering and summer number two was a disaster– simply tourism in Andorra was down, in fact, almost out.' *El Duc* also suffered from 'freezing pipes, collapsing power cable supports, landslides, cracking walls, moving floors and a disintegrating roof.' There was also the old problem of untrustworthy staff and suppliers as well as problems with bankers and local authorities.

Wolfe had one other major problem. Susi was back on the scene and had pointed out to him her vulnerability should he die (he was then approaching sixty-five years of age). She explained: 'No Andorran court would assume jurisdiction for a will, left by a British subject, married in Switzerland to a, then, German, and now British subject, both of whom held no more than a temporary permit to reside in Andorra.' Subsequent to this the restaurant, land and other buildings were registered in Susi's name. This in turn led to the rather sad final breakdown of the marriage and perhaps explains how in the final chapter of Wolfe's story life was to become such a struggle for him. Without bitterness, however, he records:

'This made it relatively simple for me to, finally, walk out on her: she now had everything I owned –and owed. (Over a number of years, she divested herself of it all, asserting that debts exceeded assets by far and that she had been terribly wronged. She never attempted to run the business, being a firm subscriber to the theory that men had a duty to look after her, and work was not her beer – surely the wrong philosophy for a lady restaurateur). So I departed, fortunately with somewhere to go – the Common Market, also known as the European Economic Community (EEC), in Brussels as an interpreter.'

Wolfe is scathing about the way the EEC was wasting money in general and about the way the translation and interpretation services were being run in particular. What follows is just one example he gives:

'Each participant who has something to say will begin, "Thank you Mr Chairman for giving me the floor." This then has to be simultaneously interpreted into all the other languages spoken, which at the time of writing, [c.1976] are: English, French, German, Dutch, Italian Danish and Greek. Therefore with this meaningless and superfluous bit of dogmatic drivel being repeated literally thousands of times every day, and based on the expenses needed to run the meeting (remuneration to delegates, interpreters, technicians, backroom and back up staff, room rent, electricity, etc.) it can safely be said that every year £1,367,000 (approximately) are used up by saying "thank you Mr Chairman etc" – I defy the critical reader to prove me wrong.'

Wolfe gives many other examples of EEC profligacy and accepts that he is, 'biting the hand that fed him' before he concludes his observations by explaining the terms under which he was employed: 'My arrangement with the Commission was quite lucrative: they employed me for the maximum permitted twelve days per month and credited me with a first class rail ticket to Toulouse, which was now my professional domicile. I would work say Monday to Friday during two consecutive weeks (ten days) and then Monday/Tuesday in week three, or start on a Thursday plus Friday plus two five-day stints during the next two weeks. I did not, normally, go home for the in-between weekends.'

Working at the EEC brought Wolfe into contact with the final woman of importance in his life about whom he says she 'entered my life under the somewhat constraining conditions of an interpreting booth.' Her name was Ursula Weissenbock, an Austrian interpreter, and in September 1981 she became the fifth Mrs Frank.

Wolfe did not wish to include in his memoirs, which he clearly hoped would be published after his demise, details of his years with Ursula other than to observe that he thought they were generally happy ones during which, 'they travelled a lot, ate the best food, drank the finest wines, heard the best music, saw the best plays – and drifted apart.'

Out of respect for Wolfe's clear wishes I will add nothing about his relationship with Ursula other than to say that their marriage had ended sometime before January 1984 when Ursula remarried.

Wolfe had for a time prior to this period resumed his career as a financial adviser and had clearly had one last period of success. However, in addition to the break-up of his fifth marriage it seems that his resurrected business career had also floundered. Yet whilst this was undoubtedly another low point in his life he remained, as ever, optimistic – as the final paragraph of his epic 500-page manuscript, completed at the age of seventy in the autumn of 1983, clearly indicates: 'Until a few months ago I was tycooning [sic] in the field of world-wide investments and I wrote over $800,000 dollars-worth of sales in three months – I hadn't lost my touch. Maybe I still haven't.'

In trying to sum up Wolfe Frank I would say he was a quite unique character of extreme contrasts. On the one hand he had spent a lifetime in the fast lane thoroughly enjoying himself – even during the most difficult of times. It cannot be denied that he was a lothario, a playboy, a risk taker, a serial adulterer, a heavy drinker, a participant in (sometimes an organizer of) orgies and he was an opportunist who liked nothing more than a challenge – even if that meant him risking his life. For most of his adult years he stayed on just the right side of whatever laws, rules and regulations were applicable, or he managed to avoid getting caught or severely punished if he ever broke them.

His other side showed him to be a man of immense courage, charm, good manners, honour and ability. He was highly intelligent, a gifted linguist and raconteur and one who, at times, moved in the highest circles of society and the theatre. His handling of the translations and interpretations at Nuremberg sets him apart from all other interpreters of his time, perhaps of all time. He was asked to undertake the toughest of assignments imaginable and he was perhaps the only man in the world who could have so satisfied all concerned. Wolfe not only rose to that challenge he surpassed all expectations and he was a major contributing factor in seeing justice prevail in less than one year when it could have taken four.

Following his finest hour, it seems Wolfe was not given the level of recognition he deserved – perhaps a too colourful private life and his less than total commitment to establishment rules and conventions denied him the honour his efforts so clearly merited. Although he rose again to a lesser extent during the 'Subsequent Proceedings' and then with his 'Hangover after Hitler' project, his life was never the same and he never capitalized on his achievements or used the celebrity status he could have adopted in the way so many lesser men do these days. Consequently, as he aged, public awareness of his outstanding contributions faded from memory.

Wolfe's two great passions were enjoying life to the full, in whatever circumstances prevailed, and making love as often as he could to as many women as possible. As a strikingly handsome man with a personality to match he was irresistible to the fairer sex right up until his final days – yet was he ever really satisfied with his love life or happy with the 'gift' that had been bestowed upon him? Included in his memoirs, and written during the final days of his last marriage, is the following passage:

'"Woman" to me is what makes the world go round. She is a being to be loved and adored, but I don't like women. I have trusted women because I loved them, or was in love with them, and I knew during every minute of such a relationship that it is madness to trust any woman in every way – and the disappointments which ensued have proved me right.

'It goes without saying, but should be said, that I have disappointed them every bit as much.

'In retrospect, every relationship that went from love to disappointment, or from being in love to being indifferent, has been worth every moment it lasted.

'There were four marriages and now there is a fifth. Each of these marriages was an outstanding factor during a particular phase of my life, a dominating factor, to be precise, and for that reason my life is "A Tale of Five Wives" whom I have loved and the memories of whom become more golden as time goes by.

'It is doubtful that such feelings are being reciprocated. It has always been my decision to write things off, or not to resurrect something that looked hopeless.

'Only, the ladies looked at such development with disfavour, all of them.'

Early in Wolfe's memoirs he tells us how hurt he and his mother were by his father's infidelities, yet he behaved in the same way. He was unfaithful to all his five wives as well as countless lovers, mistresses and lesser and casual conquests, many of who seemed to view him as a being a loveable rascal so often deserving of another chance.

In the early 1980s, Wolfe's fifth marriage irrevocably broke down and a project in which he had invested was a financial disaster. Bereft of savings, Wolfe moved, quite by chance it seems, into private rented accommodation – *The Malt House* in the delightful village of Mere, which is situated on the Wiltshire/Dorset border (see Plate 23). There he became rather reclusive and, it seems, lived a somewhat lonely life. He was befriended by Mike Dilliway, the proprietor of a vehicle and bodywork repair business, which was a facility Wolfe needed to visit often because of the number of minor motoring accidents in which he was involved. To earn a living Wolfe had resumed his interpreting work at the EEC, but with failing health – he was suffering from Parkinson's Disease and Glaucoma – and, not wanting to see a less than reliable car on the road being driven by a less than reliable driver, Mike persuaded Wolfe to allow him to drive him to and collect him from Heathrow Airport for his EEC trips.

Mike also found time to visit Wolfe at home. 'He was a superb cook, great company and a wonderful raconteur. The stories of his early life, his escape from Nazi Germany, Nuremberg and his undercover operation never ceased to enthral me,' said Mike when I interviewed him, 'and the other things that impressed me and left a lasting impression were his intelligence, his immaculate appearance on all occasions, his bearing, his good manners, his fellowship, his charm and his sincerity. He was a dear friend whom to this day I miss very much'.

On one of his last visits to Brussels Wolfe must have mentioned his illness and his changed circumstances to others, for amongst his papers was found the kind of letter few men will ever be fortunate enough to receive:

'It doesn't matter whether or not you remember who I am,' wrote the admirer (or former lover?) 'this is not fan mail. I am only telling you something many other people have thought … you are still totally recognizable as one of the most attractive men I have ever seen. When I first met you, some ten years ago, I was struck by your very special air, that of an exceptionally charming man. What you had then you still have now, and I daresay you will keep it about you through whatever illness and age do to you. I hope you enjoy it even half as much as those who meet you do'.

Back in Mere Wolfe's finances and health continued to decline and he was forced to vacate *The Malt House* where he had been living for several years. With nowhere else to go he was obliged to seek accommodation from a very sympathetic and helpful Salisbury District Council who, acknowledging he was on the point of being made homeless, provided him with a bungalow in Mere and further helped him by paying utility charges, providing second-hand furniture and arranging other social benefits.

Wolfe's illnesses eventually made it impossible for him to continue travelling to Belgium and he was forced to accept even more State benefits. He said one day to Mike Dilliway, 'I can live with Mr Parkinson, but I can't live with going blind.'

A few days later, on 10 March 1988, reflecting on his situation, upon what he had once had and (in spite of what his admirer suggests in her letter) knowing what he had lost for ever, this proud man visited his friend Mike Dilliway at his repair shop and asked if he could borrow a roll of masking tape. When Mike asked him what he wanted it for Wolfe simply replied: 'If anyone asks I'm going to be doing some decorating.' It was the last thing said between the two friends.

Wolfe returned to his home, prepared himself to look his immaculate best, dressed himself in his finest clothes and went to his favourite local restaurant, *The Old Ship Inn* at Mere (see Plate 23) – which abutted his former Malt House home – and he indulged himself in their finest cuisine which he washed down with a bottle of vintage champagne before getting into his car and driving off into the night.

The following day Mike Dilliway was visited by Wiltshire Police and, as the local recovery service, he was asked to go to a farm track just off the Mere By-pass and remove a car in which the body of a man had been discovered. The driver had died, Mike was told, from carbon monoxide fumes he had inhaled whilst in a vehicle that had a hose pipe attached and its windows sealed with masking tape. Mike did not need to ask the number of the vehicle or the name of the deceased.

Some days later the Police returned and handed Mike a copy of a document, released by the Wiltshire Coroner's office – it had been discovered on the passenger seat of the car. It was a last will and testament and simply stated Mike Dilliway was to be the sole beneficiary of the Wolfe Frank estate, which consisted of a few less than valuable chattels and his memoirs. Mike, not realizing their importance, promptly placed the documents in his loft where they remained uninvestigated for over 25 years.

There was not enough money left in the Frank estate to cover his funeral expenses and it was Mike who ensured his friend did not suffer the indignity of a pauper's burial and it was he who also settled Wolfe's other outstanding debts.

Wolfe, with his privileged background and his mother persuading whoever delivered him to record his birth as having occurred on St Valentine's Day, came into the world in style. He lived every moment of that life in style and he died with style in his own way, in his own time and by his own hand.

Following the release of his body there was yet one final terribly sad twist to the Wolfe Frank story. After a lifetime of being surrounded by more friends and acquaintances than any man has a right to expect – and having once been listened to by an estimated world-wide audience of four hundred million – just five people were in attendance at Wolfe's funeral service which was held at Salisbury Crematorium.

Wolfe's few possessions went to charity and his ashes were, eventually, collected from Mike by a lady – probably one of his ex-wives or past loves – and they were hopefully scattered, as he had wished, on the snow covered slopes of his beloved Davos.

All Mike was left with was his memories and the several boxes of documents he had placed in his attic. A quarter of a century later Mike asked me to take a look at those documents … the rest, as they say, is history … this printed history of a man whose life, involvements and achievements, together with the important historical information contained therein, deserve to be recorded for posterity.

I only hope I have done him justice and that I have told the Wolfe Frank story the way Wolfe Frank would have wanted it to be presented – warts and all. I hope too that historians, romantics and casual readers alike will see what I see – that once there was a man whose 'superlative scholarship, administration, intellect and integrity' won him the unreserved praise of all who were fortunate enough to witness his performances on a world stage, and that he was a major contributing factor in the success of the 'greatest trial in history!'

# ACKNOWLEDGEMENTS

The mine of information contained in Wolfe Frank's memoirs and the other records he entrusted to his friend Mike Dilliway have made this book possible. I would therefore like to put on record my gratitude to Wolfe for the vast amount of time, care and effort he put into recording his life's history and involvements – especially those concerning the events leading up to and including the Nuremberg trials and the pioneering work he was involved in that brought about Simultaneous Interpretation. I am also grateful to Mike Dilliway for entrusting me with the task of editing Wolfe's work and putting together this record, and Martin Mace and Frontline Books for encouraging me to bring this, what I consider to be important information, to the attention of a wider audience.

I also thank my son Simon Hooley for his considerable help with some of the graphics included in this book and my wife Helen for her proof reading skills, and for her understanding of the months that I spent two floors above her in my man cave sorting, researching and producing this work.

Henry and Peter Goyert, the son and grandson respectively of Wolfe's half sister Olly, were able to provide me with valuable information and photographs that helped enormously to fill in parts of the Frank family life from the late 19th century up until the time of the Holocaust which took the lives of Olly's mother and sister.

Others whose help I gratefully acknowledge include: Wolfe's housekeeper Gillian White and his neighbour Valerie Hill; Paul Brown and the US National Archives; Holly Reed of the US National Archives & Records Administration; Allan Bishop and Connor Drewitt of Gillingham Press; Ann Corcoran and the Wiltshire & Swindon Coroner's Office; Melanie Loveland and translator Frank Mercer.

I also take this opportunity to pay tribute to Sir Tim Berners-Lee and his colleagues for inventing the World Wide Web and for making the 'Internet' available to all free of charge – an act of monumental generosity that has benefitted mankind in general and every computer user in particular, especially historians and researchers at every level. Credit must also be given to the countless experts and amateur enthusiasts who so willingly share their knowledge

# ACKNOWLEDGEMENTS

via the information super-highway. Without this technology and the wealth of resources it has made available to us all, books such as *Nuremberg's Voice of Doom* would have been more difficult to produce and would be far less substantial in content. Whilst there are far too many to name individually, and many anonymous sources who fall into this category – I am grateful to them all. I do however make special mention of Wikipedia and its contributors for the direct service provided and for the invaluable other reliable sources, links and references they gather together for the benefit of the millions of daily users of this wonderful innovation.

Finally, I apologize unreservedly for any names I have inadvertently omitted from these acknowledgements or for not giving proper credit in any instances where it has not been possible to verify authorship or ownership – if any such instances are found and brought to my attention I will ensure appropriate permissions are sought and that any future editions of this book are amended accordingly.

*Paul Hooley.*

# BIBLIOGRAPHY

Wolfe Frank manuscript and records

Cooper, R.W., *The Nuremberg Trial* (London 1947)

Gaiba, Francesca, *The Origins of Simultaneous Interpretation* (University of Ottawa Press, 1998)

Gomberg, Maxine (née Cooper and formerly Frank) various biographical notes

Goyert family records

Jackson, Sophie, *Churchill's Unexpected Guests* (2010)

King, Henry T. Jr, *The Nuremberg Context from the Eyes of the Participant* (Military Law Review 1995)

Kipling, Rudyard, *If*

Lancashire At War.co.uk

Maxwell Fyfe, Sir David, Personal correspondence to Wolfe Frank

*New York Herald Tribune* (various editions 1945–6)

*New Yorker, The* (7 September 1946)

*Oregonian, The (1970)*

Francis, Patricia (née Leonard) various biographical notes

Persico, Joseph, *Nuremberg: Infamy on Trial*, (Viking-Penguin New York 1994)

Speer, Albert, *Inside the Third Reich: Memoirs of Albert Speer*. Translated by Richard and Clara Winston, (Macmillan 1970)

Steer, Alfred G., *Interesting Times: Memoir of Service in U.S. Navy, 1941–47*

Taylor, Telford, *Anatomy of the Nuremberg Trials, The* (Alfred A. Knopf New York 1992) and *Final report to the Secretary of the Army on the Nuremberg War Crimes Trials*

*Time Magazine – Germany; The Defendants* (29 October 1945)

Tusa, Ann and John, *The Nuremberg Trial* (London, Macmillan, 1983) and *The Nuremberg Trial* (Skyhorse Publishing 2010)

U.S. Library of Congress, *War Crimes Before The Nuremberg Military Tribunals – Volume IV* (1949) and *Military Law Review, Volume 149* (summer 1995)

Washington, DC: Government Printing Office

Watson, Patrick, *Watson's Really Big WWII Almanac – Volume 2* (Xlibris 2007)

*Wikipedia* and the further links and sources it includes

*YouTube*

NEW YORK

Herald Tribune

EUROPEAN EDITION

21 RUE DE BERRI, PARIS.8e, FRANCE

Telephones,
ELYSEES   12-87
BALZAC    03-83
—         03-99
Teleg.  Address:
HERALD - PARIS

## NEW YORK HERALD TRIBUNE SYNDICATE
## SPECIAL FEATURE
### For release after November 26

### HANGOVER AFTER HITLER

*A startling series of articles on Germany. . . the Germany everyone should know. . . and watch.*

*WOLFE FRANK, 36-year-old ex-German, ex-British officer, chief interpreter at the Nuremberg Trials, returned to the country he fled 12 years ago to make an "undercover" survey of the main facets of post-war German life and viewpoints. . . to work as a German alongside Germans in factories, on the Hamburg docks, in a refugee camp and elsewhere.*

*Equipped with false papers to use if necessary, living again as a German among Germans, he sought objective answers to many questions: refugees, anti-Semitism, morality, de-Nazification, religion, dismantling, nationalism.*

*His enterprise was assisted by the New York Herald Tribune for these reasons:*

Misinformation about Germany has led to unpleasant surprises in the past.

A true picture of Germany is elusive because Germans often present different aspects to "outsiders."

A fresh appraisal of the German question could only be obtained by a German, and Mr. Frank had all the exceptional qualifications necessary.

*We believe that the result of five months' "undercover" work, told in human, factual terms, is an important contribution to one of the great key problems of the post-war world. . . and incidentally it contains some unexpected revelations and dramatic surprises.*

*Asked price for exclusive newspaper serial rights for............................*
*.......................................................... is ...................................................*
*payable ......................................................................................................*

*Please wire me*

*Proofs will be airmailed to buyers from our Paris newsroom as ready. Two specimen installments are enclosed for editorial reading only—NOT FOR PUBLICATION.*

*Memorandum from C. PATRICK THOMPSON*
*World Representative ex American Continent*
*& European Syndicate Manager*
*NEW YORK HERALD TRIBUNE SYNDICATE*
*21 Rue de Berri, Paris 8e, France.*
*Cables: HERALD-PARIS, and start message: "for Thompson Syndicate. . . . ."*

The *New York Herald Tribune* flyer announcing the '*Hangover After Hitler*' series of articles (see page 175)

# INDEX